Black Women as Cultural Readers

FILM AND CULTURE
JOHN BELTON, GENERAL EDITOR

FILM AND CULTURE
A SERIES OF COLUMBIA UNIVERSITY PRESS

EDITED BY JOHN BELTON

What Made Pistachio Nuts?: Early Sound Comedy and the Vaudeville Tradition
Henry Jenkins

Showstoppers: Busby Berkeley and the Tradition of Spectacle
Martin Rubin

Projections of War: Hollywood, American Culture, and World War II
Thomas Doherty

Laughing Screaming: Modern Hollywood Horror and Comedy
William Paul

Laughing Hysterically: American Screen Comedy of the 1950s
Ed Sikov

Primitive Passions: Visuality, Sexuality, Ethnography, and Contemporary Chinese Cinema
Rey Chow

The Cinema of Max Ophuls: Magisterial Vision and the Figure of Woman
Susan M. White

Black Women as Cultural Readers

JACQUELINE BOBO

COLUMBIA UNIVERSITY PRESS   NEW YORK

Columbia University Press
New York Chichester, West Sussex

Library of Congress Cataloging-in-Publication Data

Bobo, Jacqueline.
Black women as cultural readers / Jacqueline Bobo.
p. cm.—(Film and culture series)
Includes bibliographical references and index.
ISBN 0–231–08394–7 (cl.)
ISBN 0–231–08395–5 (pa.)
1. Afro-American women in motion pictures.
2. Afro-American women in literature.
3. American literature—Afro-American authors—
Film and video adaptations.
4. Motion pictures and literature—United States.
I. Title II. Series.
PN1995.9.N4B57 1995
791,43'652042'08996073—dc20
94–25317
CIP

Casebound editions of Columbia University Press books
are printed on permanent and durable acid-free paper.

Printed in the United States of America

c 10 9 8 7 6 5 4 3 2 1
p 10 9 8 7 6 5 4 3 2 1

Dedicated to MMHB

Contents

Acknowledgments

First, I wish to gratefully acknowledge the cooperation of the women I interviewed. They gave generously of their time and insights and are a vital part of this analysis of black women's cultural experiences.

Colleagues and friends have been essential for support and advice during the writing of the book. Among those I wish to thank are Jane Gaines, Anne Johnston, Barbara Christian, Molly Bloomfield, Manthia Diawara, Zeinabu irene Davis, Gloria Gibson-Hudson, and O.Funmilayo Makarah. Ellen Seiter, a superb scholar and teacher, provided invaluable intellectual sustenance during the conception and development of the project's core concepts.

I thank my editors at Columbia University Press–Jennifer Crewe, John Belton, Anne McCoy–and my copyeditor, Lauren Oppenheim, for their thorough understanding of and careful attention to the manuscript.

Bouquets to Stephanie and Varnette Honeywood for permission to reproduce Varnette's painting *Snuff Dippers* for the book's cover.

I owe family for being there (as usual) during the course of my research and writing, and I look forward to our celebration of the book's completion.

I acknowledge the support of the University of California President's Postdoctoral Fellowship, especially the excellent assistance of Jane Gonzalez. Support was also provided by the University of North Carolina/Chapel Hill Research Council.

Black Women as Cultural Readers

Introduction

For all the critical discussions generated by black women's texts that achieve any degree of success, little attention is paid to their significance for black female cultural consumers. When Terry McMillan's *Waiting to Exhale* (1992) landed on the *New York Times* best-seller list after only a few weeks in print, critics dismissed it as another example of black male–bashing by a black woman writer.[1]

The novel's four black women protagonists do indeed talk a great deal about their relationships with the men in their lives. The women are also preoccupied with material goods: they routinely discuss their memberships in health clubs and their purchases of expensive automobiles such as BMWs and Nissan 300ZXs. They buy brand-name clothes, perfumes, and accessories. To relieve the stress in their lives, therapy takes the form of excursions to shopping malls. The fictionalized characters' rampant materialism prompted critics to describe McMillan disparagingly as a black Judith Krantz.

Because critics misunderstand black women's experiences, they misconstrue the significance of these women's cultural work. Middle-class black women whose sexual relationships are topics of conversation with their friends and who spend money on the same consumer goods as others who can afford it appear as anomalies to mainstream reviewers, who fail to note that there are women, such as those in McMillan's novel, who are also productively involved with their families, their communities, and pressing social issues. Thus these analysts, with no clear understanding of the subtleties and nuances of black women's lives, are confident that their evaluations of these women's creative work are adequate. The opinions of those who are actually reading the works (or, in the case of films, viewing them) are never considered. As a result, any potential value the works may have for audiences is neutralized.

Recently, black women's texts have attracted much more receptive audiences. The emergence of an influential group of black women cultural consumers has proven essential to their success. Consequently, black female voices are being heard by audiences who truly want to listen to them. In this book I examine this phenomenon. Through interviews with selected groups of black women and through formal analyses of the texts I analyze black women's responses to Terry McMillan's *Waiting to Exhale* and Julie Dash's independently produced film *Daughters of the Dust* (1992). These texts have had a significant effect on American life, in large part because of their importance to a substantial number of black women.

The third text considered in this analysis is the film adaptation of Alice Walker's *The Color Purple* (1985). There are, of course, drastic differences between Walker's novel and Steven Spielberg's film version, one being the creation of a black woman writer, the other a mainstream media product constructed by a white male, perhaps the most famous director in Hollywood's history. However, during the heated and bitter exchanges following the release of the film, the two were fused together in the minds of the harshest critics, with most of their perceptions of the novel based upon their viewing of the film.

For many black women the heightened attention to the novel in the wake of the film's release directed them once again to the novel. Or they were motivated to read it for the first time after seeing the film. In their minds there was a clear separation between the two works, but the issues addressed in both were meaningful for them. Aspects of their lives and histories, missing from other well-known works, were depicted for the first time in a medium accessible to a large number of black females. Although they were very vocal in their praise of the film, fuller examination of these women's responses revealed that their seeming conflation of the film with the novel was due to a complex process of negotiation. Black women sifted through the incongruent parts of the film and reacted favorably to elements with which they could identify and that resonated with their experiences.

Black women were also less critical of the film than other commentators. Black male detractors considered the film to be racist and harmful to the image of the black family, and an especially reprehensible portrait of black men. Mainstream reviewers judged the film as lightweight, inconsequential, and a travesty of the intentions of the novel. Radical analysts, many of whom found the novel politically progressive, felt that the film version of *The Color Purple* eviscerated the novel. They thought the film ran counter to the best interests of black people, and they viewed black women's positive reactions as treacherously gullible. In their opinion, black women followed an all too familiar pattern of political culpability, which radicals found to be regressive.[2]

Ironically, the range of diverse reactions to the film served as a catalyst for black women in many socioeconomic groups. Black women critics and scholars also became involved. They offered reasoned rebuttals to the diatribes against Walker and the film presented in the media. Black women activists used the opportunity to provide much-needed background information about issues related to the film: domestic violence, social and economic inequities, and the range of black women's sexual experiences, among other topics. Moreover, themes central to Walker's novel, such as black women's historical and cultural past and their centuries-long efforts on behalf of black women's rights, were finally discussed in a public forum.[3]

Consequently, although the film was highly contentious and extremely problematic, black women made productive use of its appearance. Collectively, they carved out a space for their causes and their concerns. This was a spontaneous, unorchestrated reaction, which united a significant number of women in a fight for something that was meaningful to them.

In his book *Understanding Popular Culture* John Fiske writes of the political potential of popular culture. He notes that popular culture is integrally connected to the play of power in society even though it is produced and consumed "under conditions of social subordination." But, states Fiske, the potential of popular culture is such that it can disrupt the social surface.[4] In this way radical analysts, who study the workings of power in society and examine ways in which social groups are affected by various manifestations of power (socially, culturally, politically), underestimated black women's abilities to resist the ideological domination of the film *The Color Purple*.

Fiske explains that popular culture has a function different from that of radical art forms, which are presumed to be more progressive:

> Popular art is progressive, not revolutionary. Radical art forms that oppose or ignore the structures of domination can never be popular because they cannot offer points of pertinence to the everyday life of the people, for everyday life is a series of tactical maneuvers against the strategy of the colonizing forces. It cannot produce the conditions of its existence, but must make do with those it has, often turning them against the system that produces them. (p. 161)

The failure of some leftist academic and political theorists to acknowledge the ways in which a populace reacts to and uses popular cultural forms is in part responsible for the left's not gaining the support and following of the people for whom it attempts to speak. Fiske asserts that as leftist theorists continue to demean the consumers of popular culture, the problem will persist and schisms will remain between the left and the populace. Fiske states further that the left often fails to understand the subversive capabilities of audiences. He then points to the critical elements that the left refuses to acknowledge: "The intransigence of the people in the face of this system, their innumerable tactical evasions and resistances, their stubborn clinging to their sense of difference, their refusal of the position of the compliant subject in bourgeois ideology that is so insistently thrust upon them" (p. 162).

Fiske's analysis of cultural consumers' subversive capacity applies to black women and their engagement with *The Color Purple*. Although the film is a patriarchal text, its black viewers found ways to empower themselves through their negotiated reception of it. Using their own resources, they responded favorably in spite of Spielberg's direction.

For *Daughters of the Dust*, black women's interpretive abilities were not as strained. Dash's film overtly resists the strictures of the dominant culture. In this respect Dash aligns herself with other black women within the history of these women's creative tradition. It is an activist tradition that opposes the forces that negatively affect black women. Black female creative artists bring a different understanding of black women's lives and culture, seeking to eradicate the harmful and pervasive images haunting their history.

Novels such as *Dessa Rose* (1986) by Sherley Anne Williams, Margaret Walker's *Jubilee* (1966), and *Their Eyes Were Watching God* (1937) by Zora Neale Hurston all contest the pervasive notion that black women during slavery were sexually promiscuous. These works offer compelling evidence that the myth was perpetuated to absolve slave owners from their sexual exploitation of black women. Other works challenge the perennial depiction of black women as passive victims lacking the will to act against their oppression. Independent films by black women tell a more accurate story of their activism. Examples include Madeline Anderson's *I Am*

Somebody (1969) and the late Jacqueline Shearer's *A Minor Altercation* (1977). Anderson's film documents the successful strike for better working conditions by black female hospital workers in Charleston, South Carolina. Shearer's film is a dramatic exploration of black women's struggles during the conflicts over busing in the 1970s.

From their creative texts readers and viewers gain a clearer understanding of these women's social circumstances. The works provide a coping mechanism, enabling black women to recognize the array of forces controlling their lives. And their cultural texts, in conjunction with other factors, prompt black women to act to change the negative conditions impeding their advancement. In a sort of symbiotic relationship, black women's texts nourish and sustain their readers, while the readers are indispensable for interpreting the works appropriately.

Black women's reception of *Daughters of the Dust* is an effective illustration. The women proved to be invaluable for the film's nationwide exposure. Without their support, the film may have gone the route of other black independent media: limited distribution on the festival circuit and minimal exhibition elsewhere. Black women's wide embrace of the film served as impetus for the critical acclaim it eventually achieved. This time, however, there was no intermediary involved in the final form in which the text appeared, as was the case with Spielberg's version of Alice Walker's novel.

Daughters of the Dust was the first film created by a black woman that was released in commercial distribution. Now there is a major cinematic work equivalent to that found within the history of black women's literature. Dash's film is concerned with themes of empowerment, resistance, and collective action, which also predominate in works such as *The Color Purple*, *Dessa Rose*, Paule Marshall's *Chosen Place, Timeless People* (1969), and Toni Cade Bambara's *The Salt Eaters* (1980), among others. Set at the turn of the century on a mythical island located off the Georgia coast, *Daughters of the Dust* features four generations of black women and their attempts to reconcile their past of enslavement with their present circumstances.

These include a young wife's rape by an unseen white landowner and the return of the prodigal granddaughter accompanied by her female lover. The women also confront generational clashes revolving around members of the clan who are planning to move away from the island to what they hope will be a better life in the North. Additionally, the family is struggling to accommodate their various religious practices, from Christian fundamentalism to Islam to agnosticism, with their great-grandmother's fervent belief in the efficacy of the spiritual "other world."

The film's production and distribution background is important because it establishes the magnitude of black women's contribution. Dash began her research for the film in 1975. The film was completed in 1991 and opened at the Film Forum in New York City in January 1992. Preliminary funding came from a combination of early grants that Dash was able to secure, but the majority of the money for production was provided by the American Playhouse division of the Public Broadcast Service in the amount of $650,000. An additional $150,000 was supplied by the Corporation for Public Broadcasting. This $800,000 outlay guaranteed the television rights to *Daughters of the Dust* for broadcast on "American Playhouse." The air date was set for July 22, 1992. (Dash would later obtain an additional $300,000, which helped her complete the film, by selling limited foreign rights to German and Japanese organizations.)[5]

From January until fall 1991 Dash searched for a distributor. Potential distributors who saw the film at festivals and preview screenings expressed doubt that the film would appeal to a sufficient number of people. The fact that the first reviews of the film were sarcastic and extremely condescending did not help, either. Although later articles would describe the film in glowing and complimentary terms, the first critique, which appeared in a widely read entertainment industry publication, dismissed the subject matter as inconsequential and discredited the filmmaker, describing Dash as incompetent and self-indulgent. The writer in *Variety* objected to what he viewed as the excessive use of slow-motion cinematography and to the actresses' unconventional costumes. Their long, flowing, white dresses, coupled with the ubiquitous authentic African hairstyles worn by the women, caused this reviewer to label the film as pretentious, art-house fluff. The reviewer in *Variety* even went so far as to describe the film as a "two-hour Laura Ashley commercial."[6]

It is hard to imagine that a filmmaker with Dash's training and body of highly regarded films would incur such condemnation and have such difficulties placing her most ambitious work before the public. Dash first studied film at the Studio Museum of Harlem and later earned an MFA from the University of California at Los Angeles, one of the most prestigious film schools in the country. She went on to study at the Center for Advanced Film Studies at the American Film Institute, an elite institution of film instruction. Dash's list of films and videos was already extensive before the completion of *Daughters of the Dust* and includes *Illusions* (1983), which won numerous awards and was designated one of the best films of the decade by the Black Filmmaker Foundation. Dash is also widely recognized for her films *Four Women* (1975) and *Diary of an African Nun* (1977), an adaptation of a short story written by Alice Walker. Before its exhibition before a nationwide audience, *Daughters of the Dust* was presented with the Best Cinematography award at the 1991 Sundance Film Festival, an annual gathering that promotes the work of independent filmmakers.

Dash was finally offered a distribution contract from Kino International, a distributor of restored classics and foreign films. The film would have limited exposure, being presented market by market nationwide rather than shown simultaneously at a large number of theaters across the country. This method of exhibition can dampen theatergoers' interest because their desire to see the film must be maintained over a much longer period of time. Time was an even more important factor for *Daughters of the Dust* because the national television broadcast on PBS was scheduled within seven months of the film's first showing. Watching the film in theaters would lose its appeal for audiences after they had seen it on television.

In order to publicize *Daughters of the Dust*, Dash negotiated a deal with Kino for KJM3 Entertainment Group, a newly formed black public relations firm that was created because there were no other black organizations promoting black films.[7] For *Daughters of the Dust*, the marketing company tapped into a waiting audience that no one had ever appealed to before.

As part of its grassroots strategy, the members of KJM3—Michelle Materre, Kathryn Bowser, Mark Walton, and Marlin Adams—took their campaign to establishments within black communities that had regular contact with black people. They organized mailings to black churches and social organizations, postcards to black radio and television stations, and letters to black newspapers and magazines and even placed posters advertising the film in black bookstores and other outlets that catered to black patrons. Black women's groups, such as the Links and the National Coalition of 100 Black Women, were pivotal in spreading the word about *Daughters of the Dust*. The New York chapter of the Coalition of 100 Black Women sponsored a reception for the film's premiere in New York City, and other chapters around the country hosted events as the film opened in their cities. As a result of disseminating information to a receptive audience, *Daughters of the Dust* played to full houses across the country. Extra screenings were scheduled, and more exhibitors agreed to show it. Eventually *Daughters of the Dust* became the highest-grossing film that Kino had ever distributed.

According to published reports, 90 percent of the audience was composed of black women, who deliberately sought out the film's showings around the country.[8] In New York City, black women attended in such numbers that a writer for *New York* magazine devoted an entire piece to the topic. She noted the long lines of black women standing outside the theater waiting to see the film. One woman stated that she heard about the film from her mother and, after seeing it, found it to be a sustaining force in her life: "It's definitely a film that gives women of color a feeling of empowerment." Another commented, "It makes you feel connected to all those before that you never knew, to parents and grandparents and great-grandparents. I'm a different person now from seeing this movie. It's a rejuvenation, a catharsis."[9]

Black women evolved from showing critical approval for a film they valued, such as *The Color Purple*, into demonstrating economic leverage. Previously, they were an unacknowledged audience. Through their support of *Daughters of the Dust* they were able to express themselves in a way that enabled them to achieve empowerment.

Black Women and *Waiting to Exhale*

On a stormy treacherous winter night in 1993 I accompanied six other women of color to hear Terry McMillan read from *Waiting to Exhale*. Several of the women were members of one of the groups I had been interviewing about their reactions to Julie Dash's film *Daughters of the Dust*.

My interest in McMillan was piqued by the women's following of her work intensely. They had read all three of her novels—*Mama* (1987), *Disappearing Acts* (1989), and *Waiting to Exhale*—and had passed them around to others including their husbands, boyfriends, and former husbands and lovers. Amazingly, the women had purchased multiple copies of McMillan's works: one to keep, the others to give as birthday presents and Christmas gifts. Even more remarkable, the women bought the clothbound copies of the books, for some of the paperbacks were not yet available or were out of stock. These women avidly followed anything that was said or written about McMillan and discussed her work often among themselves. During many of the encounters I had with these women they talked about one or all of McMillan's novels. They had even bought the anthology of short stories for which McMillan was the editor, *Breaking Ice* (1990), and had passed *it* around among themselves. At the time I went to see McMillan I had read about her but had not read any of her novels. Because of my research on cultural phenomena, especially as it relates to black women, I had started a clip file on

McMillan and had shared with the women several of the articles, which they read voraciously, photocopied, and circulated among their friends. At the time of the reading I had no intention of addressing McMillan's work in this book, yet I became even more intrigued when *Waiting to Exhale* landed on the best-seller list and, even more incredibly, stayed there. My knowledge of the specifics of the novel was limited to newspaper and magazine articles, which presented a much-generalized account. The novel was encapsulated as the story of four middle-class black women who bemoan their relationship with the men in their lives. In spite of this cursory introduction, I felt intimately connected with the women in the novel because the women in my research group talked about them so much, even calling them by name as if they were part of their daily lives.

The critical reaction to the novel's prolonged success was also valuable for my research, for the story was set within the milieu of middle-class black women who had very complete lives, separate from their significance as statistical studies in sociology texts. Black women's recognition of the environment created in the novel was instructive: it severely undermined mainstream scholars' perpetual expressions of skepticism about anything having to do with average black women who did not fit expectations the scholars had formed from reading *Time* or *Newsweek* or watching television news programs and documentaries.

Underlying the surprise about articulate, economically secure black women is an unstated presumption that the only reliable information about them is that collected by white observers. This is the information that is used to corroborate prevailing ideas that reinforce oppressive government and institutional policies against black women.

On the night that I and the women from my research group saw McMillan the auditorium where she appeared was crowded. There were about five hundred people in attendance; the majority were women, and many of them were black. It was a committed crowd as the stormy weather made for a dangerous drive to the remote location of the university where she was appearing. McMillan was delayed over an hour by the weather, but the audience waited patiently and expectantly.

When she arrived, McMillan was accompanied by her nine-year-old son. At one point in the reading she became concerned that her son was within hearing. She questioned the sponsors regarding the whereabouts of her son, because the chapter from which she was reading contained bawdy sexual acts and graphically explicit language. One of the women in my research group was forced to bring her ten-year-old daughter because of a babysitter mix-up. McMillan, at certain points in her presentation, looked over at the young girl. Afterward, I asked the woman about her daughter being at the reading. She answered that she had no choice other than missing the reading herself, which she was very reluctant to do. As it happened, the young girl thoroughly enjoyed being at the reading, more because of the enthusiastic verbal displays from the audience than from understanding what she was hearing. She was eventually rewarded for her forbearance when she was able to get a picture of herself and McMillan together.

After McMillan was introduced, she thumbed through *Waiting to Exhale*, trying to decide which part of the book to read. When she announced that she would read the part about the character Robin, the audience groaned. McMillan agreed that she felt about Robin as the audience did. Robin was the kind of woman that she did not like, because she was man-hungry and gullible and never learned from her mistakes.

Robin is one of four main characters in the novel. The other three are Savannah, Bernadine, and Gloria. All the women live in Phoenix, Arizona, have college degrees, and work at professional jobs. Robin is an underwriter at an insurance company; Bernadine is a controller at a real estate firm; and Savannah is leaving her job in Denver, as a media relations specialist for the gas company, to take a position in publicity at a Phoenix television station. Gloria owns her own beauty salon. She has a degree in theater arts from a university in Northern California in addition to a certificate in cosmetology. All the women belong to an organization called Black Women on the Move, a support group for black women that also undertakes community service projects. All the women are single. Robin and Savannah have never been married although they have lived with a succession of men. Neither has children. As the novel opens, Bernadine's husband is leaving her, after eleven years of marriage, for the white bookkeeper who works in the computer software firm he co-owns. Bernadine has two children. Gloria has a sixteen-year-old son from a one-time sexual encounter while she was in college. Her son's father rarely visits him; when Gloria tries to put the move on him the last time he arrives in Phoenix to see his son, he informs her that he is now exclusively gay after having participated for many years in bisexual relationships.

All the women want a secure relationship with men but are wary of the ones they meet because of their past track records. Robin is described as a nymphomaniac (Bernadine and Gloria label her a whore) who craves sex constantly and has slept with most of the men in Phoenix. She says that all she wants is a home and a relationship that will free her from having to work, and she desperately wants to have children. At the end of the novel she gets pregnant and decides to keep the baby. During the course of the novel she is obsessed with a chronic liar named Russell who preys on women for support and lives with several women simultaneously and whom Robin allows back in her life continually.

While McMillan was reading the chapter on Robin there were loud and boisterous responses from the audience, and McMillan seemed to expect that the listeners would react this way. The audience appeared to be in full agreement with McMillan's wry expressions and cynical asides about Robin's persistent fallibilities: Robin strongly believes in astrological signs and numerology, she constantly evaluates the sexual attributes of every man in her life, and she goes on shopping and mail-order catalog sprees whenever she needs to get over her latest romance.

Much of Robin's story seemed to consist of events that many of the people in the crowd had experienced themselves. For example, there is a passage in the book where Robin is expecting the initial arrival of Michael at her apartment. Michael is a man with whom Robin works and is also someone she is using to help herself get through her latest separation from Russell. In the novel, McMillan describes in vivid detail Robin's preparation for Michael's visit: the orange outfit she first puts on because her color chart revealed orange to be a color that will lend warmth to her personality; and the Halston perfume she sprinkles on her pillowcases in anticipation of sex with Michael. What seemed to strike an especially responsive chord was that Robin was not a good cook. She had bought a complete dinner from the Price Club, a discount shopping outlet. When McMillan described the meal most of the women laughed harder and applauded louder. There was never a moment when McMillan seemed to move beyond the audience's experiences or when the crowd was not in agreement with what she said.

The comments after the reading were complimentary and respectful. Someone in the audience questioned McMillan about selling the film rights to *Disappearing Acts*, and even though there were groans when she said she had done so, there was applause when she explained why. McMillan said that to her a book is different from a film and that she was done with the book; she had lived with it long enough. She didn't care what the filmmakers did to it, she had no desire to write the screenplay or to have anything to do with the making of the film. She said: "I'll be just like you when I see it. I'll be looking to see what they've done to the book, too." There was a question about who might be selected as the director of the film, and wild cheering followed McMillan's response that they were hoping to get Julie Dash to direct it.

The women in my research group sat right in front of McMillan, front row center, directly in her line of sight. There was almost a call-and-response feel to the reading, for the women were so attuned to what McMillan was saying that many times her asides and reactions to Robin's misdeeds were directed right at them. There seemed to be no barriers separating McMillan from the women in the group. Their interaction appeared as if the women felt they had known her for a while and that she was a member of their group. McMillan ended the presentation with a statement with which the women adamantly agreed and repeated often after the evening. She said she wrote *Waiting to Exhale* to answer for herself the question of whether women expect too much from relationships. The answer she discovered, she said, was no. McMillan continued: "Human beings are put on this earth to have a companion, and no one should feel embarrassed about wanting love, affection and companionship. The eighties said that we [women] should feel okay by ourselves, but after a while it gets lonely. That's what I was saying."

There were some remarkable similarities between the women in McMillan's novel and the women in my research group that I did not attribute to coincidence. Mass market publications' descriptions of many of the black women who stated that McMillan told their stories were similar to the descriptions of the women in the research group.[10] The women had been friends for a number of years; all except one had college degrees; four had advanced degrees; three were not married but had been and were currently divorced single parents; two of the single women were involved in relationships with men; and all but one of the women went to the same hairdresser, who was also a member of the group. The women were voracious consumers and proud of it. They drove some of the same cars mentioned in the novel—BMW, Mercedes, utility vehicles, and Chrysler minivans—and shopped for solace, comfort, and a release of tension. A trip to the mall was considered mandatory on any vacation. They took cruises whenever the rest of the group could get away and, while there, bought their legal allowance of jewelry and rum. Their list of credit cards included Nordstrom's and Macy's as well as Neiman Marcus, I. Magnin, and Spiegel, one of the mail-order catalogues. Their homes were decorated with many of the brand names identified in McMillan's novel. They, like the women in the novel, fiercely believed that Martin Luther King's birthday should be a national holiday. Before it became one in their state they had taken unpaid leave from their jobs to commemorate the day each year and still went to every annual celebration.

I wasn't surprised that they liked McMillan's novels, but I did wonder about the intensity of their response and the specifics of what they found so intriguing. One of the first questions I asked was why they liked Terry McMillan's books. One of the women responded, "I'll tell you why she's selling. Because she's just like one of us sitting right here talking about all the stuff that we usually talk about. That's why we could identify. Anybody who's been single could definitely identify, because you've met some Michaels and been in some relationships with some Russells. And then she writes it just like we would say it."

There was spirited agreement from others in the group. Another replied, "Exactly. She writes it just like we would say it. And another thing—you don't want to think that you are a Robin. Remember when she started off and said she was going to do Robin and then she gave that disgusted look? You know that stuff that Robin did? I have done some of that same stuff." And another added, "And said exactly the same thing. You don't want to think you've been as dumb as Robin, but we've all been Robin at one time or another." To which another commented, "But you know, everybody in the book did something dumb at one time or another, in terms of men."

One of the women related an event that was similar to what had happened to a character in the novel: "Like that story about the woman who was on her way to Phoenix; what was her name? Savannah. Yeah, Savannah. And she took that dude to help her drive—it just reminded me of something that happened to me." She was interrupted by one of the women who was laughing about her husband finding that part of the novel so funny that he could hardly read the rest of the book because he was laughing so hard.

The women are referring to Savannah's story and her drive to Phoenix when she was moving from Denver. She was traveling with a man who was supposedly well off, owned his own home and his own business, had rental property, and so on and was driving to Phoenix simply to keep her company. On the way, Savannah discovered the man was not the prize she had taken him for. He had absolutely no money. He kept her change after filling up the gas tank. When the two had sex, he growled repeatedly and in general behaved like a madman. He also wanted to smoke marijuana while driving the car and asked her for money for his return trip to Denver. Savannah ended up giving him $200 and a fake telephone number in Phoenix so that he can't get in touch with her again and deeply regretting what she had hoped would be a romantic drive to her new job.

The woman who had had a similar experience related the following:

> Savannah's story reminded me of this guy I used to date in Los Angeles when I was single. We had gotten together and had this wonderful weekend. It was just great. But then, when it was time to go home, come to find out that he had conveniently left his wallet at home. Said he had forgotten it. And I was ready for him to go home, you hear me. And he kept pussyfooting around there and carrying on. I just got out my credit card and said, Here—anything to get this man out of my life. I said to myself, I don't care what it takes—go home. I mean, it was a great weekend, but go, go; I've had enough of you. And that's what Savannah did—she paid this man's way back and said, Go.

Another woman disagreed with the others that McMillan's books were all entertaining. She said:

> You know it's interesting—you ask, Why do we like Terry McMillan's books? If I had read *Mama* first, I probably would not have read anything else, because *Mama* was so depressing. I need a book to give me . . . I don't want it to be true to life. And there were very few highs in that book. I'm sorry. Now, I would have read another one of her books after *Disappearing Acts*, and I finished that in a couple of days. But *Mama*—there was just nothing there but sadness; there was just a sadness about the whole book.

To these comments another woman added this revelation:

> You know how sensitive you are. You probably read more into *Mama* than Mama did. You probably cried places Mama didn't cry herself. I'm just saying you're sensitive to a lot of things; you know how sensitive you are. It seemed that Mama should have been getting upset at what was happening in her life, but she just went on living her life. I loved it. I really did. I also thought it was better writing than *Disappearing Acts*. I'm not saying I wasn't depressed. I'm just saying that I liked the book. And to me her writing was better in *Mama* than it was in any of the other books.

McMillan's first novel, *Mama*, chronicles the lives of Mildred Peacock and her five children. The novel opens in 1964 in Port Haven, Michigan, where twenty-seven-year-old Mildred is being beaten once again by her drunk husband. The children listen to the by then familiar sounds of the beating and, later, to the expected noise of their father, Crook, as he has sex with Mildred. After Mildred divorces Crook, she feels that her life is better and her children are better off, even though she has to continue to work at a succession of unsteady jobs from doing day work in white people's homes to working at factories, at times even going on welfare. Before the oldest child, Freda, who is ten at the beginning of the novel, graduates from high school and leaves Michigan to live in Los Angeles, Mildred has married two more times. She has had several affairs, slept with white Canadians for money, and used her house as a gambling establishment, until she gets arrested. In the novel, Mildred feels that her children are the center of her life, and she does whatever it takes to keep them warm and fed. She also feels that her sexual needs should not be neglected, and she seeks out a succession of men to satisfy them. Freda eventually encourages everyone to move to California, where she and two of the younger girls earn college degrees and Mildred lives a different life from her former one in Michigan. Freda also, at novel's end, wins a writing fellowship and secures her dream of helping her mother to live a better life.

McMillan's second novel, *Disappearing Acts*, is a tale about the relationship between Zora Banks and Franklin Swift. At first, the two feel that they have finally found their ideal partners after suffering through many unsatisfactory matings. Zora is a junior high school teacher who is saving her money to buy a piano and rent a music studio so that she can record a demonstration tape. Franklin is a perennially unemployed construction worker who is unable to break into the white controlled construction unions that would enable him to secure a steady position. The relationship between Zora and Franklin ends violently after he vents his frustrations on her and their newborn son. Zora comes to realize that she needs to make a life for herself and her son regardless of whether she has a man in her life.

During the interview, the woman who found *Mama* too depressing to finish would not be convinced that it was an uplifting book about a black mother who was able to live life on her terms and successfully raise five children. After repeated assertions from the other women that the book was worthwhile reading that she would enjoy at the conclusion of the story, she replied: "I don't need to read it. Between *Disappearing Acts* and *Mama*, shit, I've lived it. So I really don't need to read it. I've lived it."

Another woman talked about the way that McMillan's novels were written about in newspapers and magazines. She said that if someone had not read the novels, that person would assume that McMillan wrote only about black women's problems with black men. She noted that what most critics failed to write about were portions of *Waiting to Exhale* that were about other aspects of the women's lives. She said that she was touched by Savannah's relationship with her mother and the way she took care of her so that she had enough money. The woman also said that although the critics wrote about Robin as if she were only a dingy, sex-starved woman, Robin also lived another life. She looked after her parents, because her mother was overburdened with caring for the father, who was slowly drifting away with Alzheimer's.

Another woman followed up with the comment that critics

shouldn't try to compare McMillan's novels to those of Alice Walker or Toni Morrison or Gloria Naylor: "It's like she [McMillan] said herself. She's a storyteller. I don't think she's concentrating on being heavy. So we don't compare her with the other writers. We read her differently; we relate to her books differently."

As these comments indicate, these women have a different set of expectations regarding McMillan's novels, and the works serve a specialized function in their lives. This is an important consideration, for there is the danger that *Waiting to Exhale*, because of its enormous financial achievements, could overshadow the social benefits of other cultural works produced by black women. To be sure, the novel does not have the overt political focus of other works by black women writers. But there will be attempts to translate the effects of McMillan's novels into further capital. The works will be framed in such a manner that other black female cultural producers will receive minimal backing if they do not follow McMillan's formula. This will be especially true if black women are represented outside of circumstances familiar to mainstream overseers.

For this reason, the tremendous economic influence of *Waiting to Exhale* on mainstream institutions of cultural production and cultural criticism needs to be examined. As history has taught us, those within the dominant culture will attempt to reproduce the material conditions that enabled their dominance, while seeking to contain any subversive elements. In the case of *Waiting to Exhale*, it is more than the amount of money the novel has earned, for other novels have also been very profitable—especially those of Alice Walker and Toni Morrison.

What McMillan's books underscored is a claim that black cultural producers have long made: stories about black life that were different from sanctioned representations could find a market and have widespread appeal, especially within the black community. Thus the importance of *Waiting to Exhale* is that it effectively demonstrated that black culture is not monolithic and that black readers respond to a range of stories of black life. They are attracted to more than simply those that, as one of the few black editors expressed it, present the "escape from the ghetto story."[11] Malaika Adero extends her critique of white editors who attempt to control which books by black authors will be published. She contends that white editors arrogantly presume they have the ultimate knowledge of black life: "People assume they know everything, but a lot of editors don't pay much attention to black culture. They never sit down and read *Essence* or *Ebony* [national publications directed at black readers]. They don't know about *Callaloo*, the black literary journal."[12]

White cultural gatekeepers have also drastically undervalued the social and economic impact of black women as cultural consumers. They were taken off guard by the response to *Waiting to Exhale*. As Daniel Max wrote in the *New York Times Magazine*,

> Of course, black authors have been a fixture on the literary landscape for decades, but the majority of their books have been consciously literary efforts, or novels in which ideology is as least as important as character development and plot. Readers of these books have been—or were thought to have been—whites and a small group of black intellectuals. McMillan, by contrast, writes about the lives of essentially conventional blacks, who have up to now received little attention. Her success has opened publishers' eyes to a growing black middle-class readership.[13]

Additionally, McMillan depicted, in *Waiting to Exhale*, black women who had not been presented before in a mass public forum. They are economically secure and live their lives unconcerned about the approval of white society (and in many instances are disdainful of its mores). This representation of these women destabilizes the widely perpetuated image of the hopelessly dependent black single female. And the novel's following among a large number of black women opens up a crucial space for critical intervention that should not be overlooked.

Black Women as Interpretive Community

Black women's challenge to cultural domination is part of an activist movement that works to improve the conditions of their lives. Included in the movement are black female cultural producers, critics and scholars, and cultural consumers. As a group, the women make up what I have termed an interpretive community, which is strategically placed in relation to cultural works that either are created by black women or feature them in significant ways. Working together the women utilize representations of black women that they deem valuable, in productive and politically useful ways.

An interpretive community is usually thought of as comprising academic scholars who read certain literary texts in a particular way so that definable meanings can be isolated and analyzed. Audience researcher Janice Radway discusses the evolution of the concept and points to ways in which the idea of an interpretive community can be expanded beyond the professional literary academy.[14] In this book the black women who have been interviewed about their reactions to specific works are not professional media analysts but are members of an audience who have been brought together to talk about their relationship to specific cultural texts. This study is concerned not only with the ways black women make sense of media texts but also with their battles against systematic inequities in all areas of their lives, socially as well as culturally. Thus, *Black Women as Cultural Readers* is not simply an analysis of texts and audiences. It examines how the cultural is intricately interwoven with other aspects in the lives of cultural readers.

In cultural studies there has been a move away from research on media audiences and toward an analysis exclusively of media texts. Cultural scholar Charlotte Brunsdon, writing in *Remote Control* (1989), a collection of essays about television audiences, details the origins of audience analysis within the disciplines of film and television studies.[15] Brunsdon notes the proliferation of certain kinds of textual analyses in the 1970s. These were primarily political readings of texts, what Brunsdon categorizes as "redemptive readings," for the critic was searching out the incoherences and inconsistencies within the text in order to salvage the work for a particular audience. This form of critical practice became problematic. As Brunsdon states, "The redemptive reading frequently meets with a certain skepticism, a doubt that real readers read like that" (p. 122). Scholars, at that point, became interested in finding out how nonacademic readers actually made sense of texts.

Media researcher Jane Feuer commented, then, that the media text was being replaced by the "text of audience." In this kind of analysis, the focus shifts from an examination of the workings of ideology by way of a cultural product, to merely writing about the people who view it. Brunsdon agrees with Feuer that there is a problem with an overreliance on audience responses at the expense of textual analysis, because she feels the critic can disavow any responsibility by simply suspending judgment of the text. This suspension permits the critic to ignore the ideology of the text and deal solely with what audiences get out it. Consequently, the critic runs the risk of not challenging detrimental films and television programs because of an unsubstantiated belief that creative audiences are astute enough to circumvent the harmful meanings of any text.[16] Conversely, to take Brunsdon's point another step, films that may offer socially redeeming qualities remain unexamined as audiences are considered to be perceptive enough to figure the films out for themselves. There is still a need for close readings of texts. At the same time, the responses of those who are present in the audience also need to be taken into consideration. Thus there is the potential for a more coherent blend of theoretical supposition with actual audience reactions.

In line with this reasoning, the work of film scholar Annette Kuhn offers an understanding of the theoretical construction of readers of texts and research on audience activity. Kuhn writes about media audiences and concepts about "the spectator" and makes a clear distinction between media viewers as members of a "social audience" and as "spectators." Those who compose a social audience are the actual empirical viewers who physically buy tickets to watch a film or who are seated in their homes watching television programs. A spectator is a theoretical construction used to analyze meaning construction within the text-spectator relationship.[17]

The women interviewed in this book are members of a physical audience who have viewed or read specific cultural texts. They become a theoretical construction in the process of my analysis of the texts and in the process of linking their statements to a broader framework of assessing black women in the totality of their lives, their history, and their social activism. This book, then, is a merging of theoretical concerns with information gleaned from contact with actual audience members.

Essentialist Black Women

A question constantly posed in any consideration of black women as a group—especially if the women are presented not as powerless but as active agents working against oppression—is whether the claim can be made that all black women are politically active or, further, whether black women can be collapsed within a monolithic grouping. I am aware that by categorizing black women in this manner I run the risk of appearing "essentialist" and "reductive." I know that all black women are not the same, nor can the black women I have interviewed be considered representative.

At the same time, I agree with media audience researcher Rosalind Brunt, in "Engaging with the Popular: Audiences for Mass Culture and What to Say about Them," when she challenges media audience analysts who feel compelled to make claims that those they have surveyed are representative of the majority. As Brunt states, they are not representative of the totality. To say that they are

> is to downplay precisely what is the value of this kind of ethnographic work. Whether it is researching with groups or with individuals, it is working not in the realm of "the aver-

> age" but of the typical in the sense that Lukács or Weber meant the term. "The typical" engages with often heightened circumstances, special conditions, exceptional cases, extreme positions, precisely in order to highlight tendencies that may in "normal circumstances" be merely incipient—and hence the concern in that tradition that carries on with Lucien Goldmann, not with the immediate, but with "the maximum possible consciousness of the group." And that is because something is perceived, both by the researcher and by the community researched, to be at stake.[18]

The women who have been interviewed in this book are not meant to be stand-ins for every black female reader. Brunt's proposition, just quoted, applies to those who are consciously politically committed, or who are in the process of coming to consciousness, rather than every black woman. They confront "heightened circumstances," which have the potential to draw black women into activism who may not otherwise become involved (p. 74). At stake are black women's abilities to maintain some control over their collective lives.

Historian Darlene Hine has examined the heightened circumstances for black women during enslavement. Although traditional studies have presented enslaved black women as either complicit in the system of slavery or as passive participants, Hine's research shows that numerous black women engaged in continual acts of resistance. She is adamant that these subversive acts were consciously committed, that the women were fully aware that they were undermining the system of slavery when they committed such acts as aborting their pregnancies or removing their offspring from the devastating effects of slavery.[19] These are circumstances that are rendered so poignantly by Toni Morrison in the novel *Beloved* (1987) when the protagonist, Sethe, after learning what the term *characteristics* means, declares that in killing her child she put her someplace where she would be safe. As Morrison writes: "And no one, nobody on this earth, would list her daughter's characteristics on the animal side of the paper. No. Oh no. Maybe Baby Suggs could worry about it, live with the likelihood of it; Sethe had refused—and refused still."[20]

Hine considers acts such as those re-created by Morrison in fiction, to be challenges to slavery, as if the women were "rejecting their vital economic function as breeders."[21] She submits that enslaved black women were aware that their sexual exploitation was part of the economic underpinning of the slavocracy. Thus the women shaped their acts of resistance accordingly, "consciously and with full awareness of the potential political and economic ramifications involved."[22]

The same holds true for many other black women. They have opposed cultural as well as social domination and have contested detrimental images in a specific text, either as audience members or as cultural producers who created alternative and more viable images. Lorraine Hansberry served in both capacities: she stood alone in her harsh censure of Otto Preminger's *Porgy and Bess* (1959). Later, in reaction to what she perceived as the persistently false representation of the faithful servant, epitomized in works such as *The Member of the Wedding* (1952), Hansberry wrote *The Drinking Gourd* (1960), a drama for television. In the teleplay, the black servant rebels against the slavemasters when the security of her family is threatened.

Black women were also resisting when they reacted strongly to the critical dismissal of *The Color Purple* and *Daughters of the Dust*. Although their opposition is not always so pronounced, black women are continually involved in patterns of resistance.

Sociologist Patricia Hill Collins, writing in *Black Feminist Thought* (1990), feels that black women's individual acts as well as their group actions, oriented as they are toward social change, are constant and are supported by other black women. It can thus be considered part of an ongoing resistance movement. Collins refers to the work of James Scott in *Weapons of the Weak: Everyday Forms of Peasant Resistance* (1985). Scott suggests that there are levels of political activity that can be thought of as forming such a movement, one "with no formal organization, no formal leaders, no manifestos, no dues, no name, and no banner."[23] Collins states that black women's individual acts of resistance can be seen in the context of a culture of resistance, where there is a supportive black female community. Consequently, their collective actions are part of a sustained movement.

Black women within an interpretive community are also part of this movement. As cultural producers, critics, and members of an audience the women are positioned to intervene strategically in the imaginative construction, critical interpretation, and social condition of black women.

The first chapter, "Black Women as Interpretive Community," begins with an overview of black women's representation in mainstream media. I then analyze why effective counters to those demeaning images are the presentation of works by black women themselves. Rather than a continual protest against the actions of others, black women have created views of themselves for themselves as audience. The narratives written during enslavement were a few of the first efforts to erase the mythology surrounding black women's sexuality, to contest the implication that they were uncontrollable vixens whose sexual appetite was unlimited.

Black women's creative efforts to eradicate these images were aligned with their fight against slavery itself. The research of Angela Davis documents black women's history of resistance to inequality. Davis demonstrates how this resistance was forged during the slavocracy as the women continually battled for freedom. With this information as a base, *Black Women as Cultural Readers* illuminates how black women's history of resistance to social domination forms the essence of their resistance to cultural domination. Black women are well aware of their heritage of reprehensible treatment in cultural works, and they bring an oppositional stance to their interaction with mainstream media. They have not simply reacted but also worked to counteract the effects of the images. From the nineteenth century onward black women have written books, political pamphlets, and social documents urging other black women to activism. *Black Women as Cultural Readers* documents the ways that they have responded in numerous instances. These were successful resistance battles that merit public acknowledgment. Even though some were incremental victories won through an accumulation of years of efforts, the spoils of victory are evident in improved social conditions for many black women. The fight is not over, but chronicles of past victories lay the groundwork for future struggles. *Black Women as Cultural Readers* is such a chronicle.

The second chapter, "Text and Subtext: *The Color Purple*," compares Steven Spielberg's film adaptation with Alice Walker's novel. I contend that the novel was deliberately structured as a part of a continuum of cultural works written by black women that sought to present a different version of their social and cultural history. Walker's novel, along with earlier black women's literature, repudiates long-standing negative ideologies and establishes a new way of thinking about black women. As such, these writings are critical components of a cultural transformation for black women.

The film version of *The Color Purple* works against this transformation. Through its overt ideology and formal structure the film seeks to displace black women as the center of the story and to reinsert traditional demeaning images of them. The three central female characters in the novel—Celie, Sofia, and Shug—in the hands of Spielberg become throwbacks to an earlier age of cultural representation. Celie becomes an isolated character bewildered by forces she not only doesn't understand but is powerless to control. Her eventual resurrection in the film version seems more a quirk of fate than a tremendous effort by an oppressed black woman, through the emotional and physical support of other black women, to throw off the mechanisms of her oppression. Celie's success is thus not presented as an example that other black women can follow, as it is in the novel, but requires the intervention of outside forces. Sofia in the film is re-created as the traditional overbearing matriarch, the large, emasculating black female who is a staple of dominant media. In contrast, the Sofia of the novel is someone who rejects society's definition of how a black woman should be treated. In the book Sofia stops her husband, Harpo, from beating her and stands up to the mayor and his wife when they ask her to work for them as their maid. In the film, however, Sofia is presented as a bossy woman who lashes out indiscriminately while totally destroying her husband's manhood.

The Spielberg version of Shug undercuts her strength as presented in the novel. The character in Walker's story is a powerful reconstruction of the black woman of mainstream mythology who is driven solely by carnal desires. Walker's Shug is not simply an independent woman but someone who exercises the same privileges formerly considered exclusively male. In the novel she has the economic means to do so and is not defeated by the choices she makes. In the film the invention of a father who is a preacher further calls into question her autonomy and empowerment. Spielberg's Shug doubts herself and is on a continual quest for absolution from her father.

That the film version of Walker's novel was a reversion to past racist works brought to light the ways in which audiences negotiate their interactions with mainstream media. Were it not for black women's overwhelming endorsement of the film in the face of an outpouring of critical condemnation there would not be an understanding that the power of mainstream media to influence audience reception is not as total as had been previously thought. Particular audiences have the power to control their reception of certain cultural works and to employ them toward a different end. Many black female viewers of *The Color Purple* reconstructed the film by filtering out that which was seen as the standard negative images and by recreating a more satisfactory story. The next chapter examines the process of black women's reconstruction of the film *The Color Purple*.

Chapter 3, "Watching *The Color Purple*: Two Interviews," presents the results of two separate interviews conducted with black women who had seen the film. The chapter is not an examination of the ways in which a social group uses media in its daily lives but a means of understanding what had formerly been only theorized. It is an examination of the process a particular social group undergoes in its negotiation of a cultural product. It is presented in the words of the people who are the subjects of the investigation. Rather than make a supposition of the thoughts, feelings, and experiences of black women, I let them speak in their own words about their lives.

Chapter 4 is an analysis of *Daughters of the Dust*. The film is deliberately structured to honor the history, culture, and traditions of black people. Through cinematic techniques that are an *hommage* to past black filmmakers and creative artists, director Julie Dash serves notice that black people can be presented in film in ways that are a celebration rather than a caricature. It is a film that is intended for black women as its primary audience and shows aspects of black women's history that have gone unheralded. Dash makes a valuable contribution to the reconstruction of black women's history in this country.

Chapter 5, "Black Women Reading *Daughters of the Dust*," is the result of three separate interviews with three groups of black women who had seen the film. The first interviews were conducted during the first part of the film's commercial release in early 1992, and the last was conducted in June 1992 after the deluge of nationwide publicity about the film. Because *Daughters of the Dust* was distributed in a staggered fashion among a limited number of selected theaters across the country, many people who heard about the film were not able to see it in the theaters. Much later than its theatrical run the film was broadcast on PBS's "American Playhouse" series and became available on videocassette. That *Daughters of the Dust* maintains its impact in a variety of formats is a testament to the power of the film and to the filmmaker's vision. It substantiates the power of black women as cultural consumers in that their widespread commendation of the film resulted in its remaining in commercial distribution long enough for its impact to be felt beyond the limited sphere of the art cinema circuit and film festival route. My interviews with black women about their reactions to *Daughters of the Dust* illuminate the ways black women respond to a film created by a black woman that features black women at the center of the story. The sixth chapter identifies the current insurgency of black women filmmakers and critics as a part of the tradition of black women's reclamation of social, political, and cultural texts. As black women have established that there is indeed a heritage of black feminist literary and political activism, black female film scholars are excavating these women's cinema history as part of the continuing movement for black female empowerment. Within this movement black women as cultural readers are a critical component. The women interviewed in this book provide substantial evidence that black women are constantly engaged in interacting forcefully with the various structures of power. As they transform their lives in the face of oppressive circumstances, so too can their responses be used to effect a transformation of the perception and condition of other black women. When their statements are analyzed in conjunction with a presentation of black women's cultural, social, and political history, the women's words resonate beyond a simple analysis of the effects of the text.

CHAPTER ONE

Black Women as Interpretive Community

Representations of black women in mainstream media constitute a venerable tradition of distorted and limited imagery. Dating back to the earliest years of the cinema, with the films *The Wooing and Wedding of a Coon (1905)* and *The Masher (1907)*, the trend has continued full force. In *The Masher* the filmmakers attempt a radical rewriting of history when they present a white male character who has previously made sexual overtures to every white woman he meets, reacting with horror and contempt when he learns that a veiled woman who accepts his advances is black.[1] A more accurate representation would have shown black women as they had been treated for centuries, as, in the words of Lorraine Hansberry, the "special victim[s] of the lust of brutes."[2] Since these early films black women have been presented as sexually deviant, as the dominating matriarchal figure, as strident, eternally ill-tempered wenches, and as wretched victims.[3] This last characterization is seen in the ubiquitous depictions of black women as domestic servants and in the latter-day representations of "welfare" mothers.

The sexual siren has proven to be an especially resilient representation. Nina Mae McKinney epitomized this part in *Hallelujah* (1929), whereas Dorothy Dandridge was virtually confined to such roles, the most notable being in *Carmen Jones* (1954) and *Porgy and Bess*.[4] Even contemporary black male directors have paid homage to this construction in their films. Felly Nkweto Simmonds, writing about the characterization of Nola Darling in Spike Lee's film *She's Gotta Have It* (1986), finds the film's author culpable for his perpetuation of one of the most damaging assumptions about black women: that they are hot-blooded sexual creatures who've got to have "it" constantly. Simmonds contends that "Spike Lee, as a black director, is treading dangerous ground by using his first film to be the teller of this 'truth' about black women's sexuality. He has joined the ranks of men, themselves products of white racist views of a black woman's sexuality, who have contributed to this myth about black women."[5] Simmonds also feels that Lee's presentation of Nola Darling was not accidental. As she states, "Spike Lee could not have been unaware of the attraction a black woman on the screen, presented as an erotic being, would have for an American audience. This is why he makes Nola the central figure. It is around Nola, not around male sexuality, and certainly not around black women's views on sexually promiscuous young men, that the film revolves."[6]

Jacquie Jones, in "The New Ghetto Aesthetic," takes Simmonds's point further when she compares the two roles of actress Tracy Camilia Johns in *She's Gotta Have It* and in Mario Van Peebles's *New Jack City* (1991). Johns plays Nola Darling in Lee's film and the girlfriend of the central character in *New Jack City*. Jacquie Jones writes that the two roles may be emblematic of our time:

> It is ironic that Nola Darling should be the mother of black female characters in contemporary mainstream black film—and it is eerie to watch Tracy Camilia Johns stripping down to red satin lingerie in Mario Van Peebles's *New Jack City*. The significance of Johns' two major roles to date is profound because, unfortunately, they express the entire range of female representation in commercial films made by black men. Black

> women are allowed to occupy two narrow categories in this cinema: that of the bitch and that of the ho.[7]

Jones defines the "bitch" as strong-willed and susceptible to destruction, while the "ho" is sexually insatiable.[8]

Fiction films have also helped to establish other images of black women firmly. The overpowering matriarch may have been given a name in the 1960s' *Moynihan Report*, but American cinema established the character much earlier in films such as *Judge Priest* (1934) and *Gone with the Wind* (1939), both featuring Hattie McDaniel. The image was given new life in 1970s' television situation comedies such as "That's My Mama" and "Good Times." The representation of the black woman as a hard-hearted castrating "Sapphire" was developed in the television program "Amos 'n' Andy," which aired on CBS in the early 1950s. Films that featured black women as domestic servants are ubiquitous in cinema history, including both versions of the Fannie Hurst novel *Imitation of Life* (1934, 1959), and the less-studied *To Kill a Mockingbird* (1962).

An example of the depiction of the welfare mother is shown in *Claudine* (1974), featuring Diahann Carroll and James Earl Jones as her working-class lover, but this characterization of black women has become a staple of television news and documentary programs. One of the most damaging portraits is given in the 1985 network television documentary "The Vanishing Family: Crisis in Black America," hosted by Bill Moyers. The CBS documentary shows young, black, unwed mothers who are living on government assistance. The program indicts them for what it presents as their perpetuating a cycle of poverty and government dependence.

Although it is patently evident that representations of black women in mainstream media have been persistently negative, scholarship by black women should not limit itself to a hunt for negative imagery. This can be self-defeating in that it diminishes any hope for change. As a critical practice the hunt for and dissection of negative imagery also centers and makes concrete the thought of black women as being something other than human. Paradoxically, in designating black women as "mammy," "Aunt Jemima," "slut," and "whore," such labels become the reality, and other (white) scholars become comfortable referring to black women in this manner. Thus those so named become cardboard characters rather than multidimensional people with actual lives, with little separation between the representation and the actual persons.

Furthermore, these fictionalized creations of black women are not innocent; they do not lack the effect of ideological force in the lives of those represented in that black women are rendered as objects and useful commodities in a very serious power struggle. By centering these images of black women in public perceptions the women seem powerless, lacking the initiative to change their social conditions. No recognition is given that black women are and have been powerful agents conscious of their historical circumstances and deliberately working toward bettering their lives.

Within the last several decades black women have effectively written themselves back into history; they have retrieved their collective past for sustenance and encouragement for present-day protest movements. The research studies documenting black women's literature, scholarship, and social activism bear witness to a history of black women taking collective action in the face of continual victimization.[9] The women lay claim to an inheritance derived from enslavement on through the postbellum period, during the civil rights struggles, up to the current moment. This legacy of resistance forms a foundation for the oppositional stance that a number of black women take to much of the forms of repression in many areas of their lives: political, social, institutional, and cultural.

Black women are also knowledgeable recorders of their history and experiences and have a stake in faithfully telling their own stories. As the "ruthless" system of slavery spawned generations of rebellious black women,[10] so too has their cultural past bred a history of fighting back. Even as the image of docile, obsequious black women remains a popular construction for mainstream cultural producers, the history of black women's activism shows that black women are not the acquiescent martyrs of popular imagination but women who effectively meet the repressive challenges of mainstream society.

A graphic example is presented in Madeline Anderson's documentary about black women hospital workers who waged a successful 113-day strike against two hospitals in Charleston, South Carolina, in 1968. Anderson's film, *I Am Somebody* (1969), details the dehumanizing conditions within which the women worked. The strikers labored as nurses, nurse's aides, kitchen helpers, laundry workers, and orderlies for a wage of $1.30 an hour. They were asking for an increase in wages to $1.60 an hour, union recognition, and, at the very least, the establishment of a grievance procedure. The strike began when twelve workers who were union members were fired for leaving their positions without permission after they tried to arrange a meeting with the director of the hospital. During the height of the strike this same hospital administrator felt free to express to a national publication that he would never relinquish the administration of "a $5 million hospital to people who never had a grammar school education."[11] Earlier, when the women had faced this same administrator to ask for a redress of past discriminations, he contemptuously offered them an extra vacation day to celebrate the birthday of Robert E. Lee, the Confederate general who lost the Civil War.[12]

All the approximately five hundred Charleston strikers were black, and all but twelve were women. They remained steadfast in their strike even when confronted by twelve hundred armed state troopers and the South Carolina National Guard, the arrests of a thousand strikers and community supporters, and the organized retaliation strategies of the Charleston power brokers, led by the owner of one of Charleston's major industries. This textile magnate sent his top antilabor lawyer to design a way of blocking the strikers from carrying out their protest marches, meetings, and boycott plans.

Because the women refused to back down, the hospital administrators eventually compromised to settle the strike. Although the women were not given union recognition, the fired workers were reinstated, and there was an increase in all the hospital workers' wages along with the establishment of a credit union from which union dues were deducted. During a press conference at the end of the strike one of the women was questioned by a white reporter who appeared puzzled that the gains won were so small in comparison to the enormity of the battle waged. The woman replied with dignity about what she felt the strike had accomplished: "We won recognition as human beings, for one. We won recognition as human beings."[13]

As one of the first black female filmmakers Anderson presented a compassionate, empathetic chronicle of black women who were forced to take on the city's power structure and in the process learned that they had the resources to carry out their plans successfully. Anderson's documentary remains visible evidence of black women's ability to resist inhumane treatment and, more important, shows how the women began to recognize that they were valuable even as others were aligned in a concerted effort to prove that they were not. One of the women who had gone out on strike later commented that the women's efforts to secure equitable treatment altered her perceptions of herself. She stated: "It helped me to realize how important I am as a person, which I'm afraid I didn't quite realize before. I further realized that the power structure isn't all powerful, but that they are there to do the bidding of the people, and the people can make them do it."[14]

Cultural and Ideological Transformation

British cultural studies scholar Stuart Hall writes of the process of cultural transformations through the disruption of prior oppressive ideologies. He notes that specific ideologies have long been inserted into certain cultures in a particular way.[15] Examples are present in standard depictions of black women in traditional texts such as *Gone with the Wind*, *To Kill a Mockingbird*, and *The Member of the Wedding*, which feature the standard characterization of the self-sacrificing black servant. The ideologies that are the foundation for these works, because of their use over time, have what Hall labels "lines of tendency" that are difficult to disrupt. When they are disrupted a cultural transformation can be accomplished. The transformation is not something totally new, nor does it have an unbroken line of continuity from the past. It is always in a process of becoming. Hall suggests that the transformation occurs through the reorganization of the elements of a cultural practice. These elements do not in themselves have any necessary political or ideological connotations. It is not the individual elements of a discourse that are significant but "the ways these elements are organized together in a new discursive formation."[16]

Hall states that the ideology that emanates from the reformation of ideologies in a discourse "transforms a people's consciousness and awareness of themselves and their historical situation." Although this explodes culturally, "it does not constitute itself *directly* as a social or political force." When it becomes connected to a social movement or, as Hall states, a movement that is in the process of formation, then it has the potential to be a social force. The potential becomes a reality when the group presents itself as "collective subjects within a unifying ideology." Then the group becomes a unified social force.[17]

Black women have long responded to the need to transform their social situations, as the women in *I Am Somebody* demonstrated, and to reconstruct the ways in which they are represented, as Anderson's film illustrates. An earlier cultural activist also responded to the need for cultural change. As part of a panel discussion entitled "The Negro in American Culture," Lorraine Hansberry spoke out against white writers' depictions of black people as loyal servants. She explained that what white artists think is true about black people and black culture is not accurate. As she states to a white member of the panel:

> You mentioned Carson McCullers. There's a scene in *Member of the Wedding*, when the young Negro nephew of Bernice is being chased by a lynch mob, and she takes the young white

> boy whom she has nursed all his life—he's about to die, I think, because of some constitutional weakness—and this woman's preoccupation is with this child. I happen to think that it was a lovely play and I believe Bernice's character, but we are talking about these extra nuances, and my point is that the intimacy of knowledge which the Negro may have of white Americans does not exist in the reverse. . . . William Faulkner has never in his life sat in on a discussion in a Negro home where there were all Negroes. It is physically impossible. He has never heard the nuances of hatred, of total contempt from his most devoted servant and his most beloved friend, although she means every word when she's talking to him, and will tell him profoundly intimate things. But he has never heard the truth of it. For you, this is a fulfilling image, because you haven't either.[18]

In her teleplay *The Drinking Gourd*, which examines the lives of those who were enslaved as well as the lives of the plantation owners, Hansberry presents a character, Rissa, who appears to be the prototypical devoted servant. After her son's eyes were gouged out as punishment for attempting to learn to read—a cardinal sin under the rules of the slavocracy—the owner of the plantation comes to Rissa's cabin to explain that it was not his doing, that his overzealous son was responsible. As the owner, Hiram Sweet, leaves Rissa's cabin to return to the manor house, he has a heart attack and cries out for help as he collapses to the ground. In a profound reversal to what is presented in mainstream stories, black people in the surrounding cabins do not rush to Sweet's aid even though they hear his cry for help. Rissa, hearing that Sweet is in trouble, ignores him and continues ministering to her blinded son. As the teleplay comes to a close, Rissa takes a gun from the manor house and gives it to her son to aid him and other members of her family in their flight toward freedom.

What Anderson presented in her documentary and what Hansberry rendered in fiction—that black women have worked strenuously to resist systems of oppression and are adept at transforming the nuances of the mechanisms of their oppression—has a basis in their political writings and is omnipresent throughout their history. To cite several among a bounty of available examples: more than forty years ago 132 black women converged on Washington, D.C. The 1951 march on Washington was called "the Sojourn for Truth and Justice" and had been organized for a redress of grievances against black people, especially black men. The women were supported emotionally and financially by numerous other black women around the country who either could not make it to the demonstration in time or were otherwise detained as political prisoners in the South.

A report of the march was presented in the socialist newspaper *Freedom*, a publication started by the legendary actor and singer Paul Robeson, with the well-respected journalist Louis Burnham as the editor. As chronicled by Hansberry, among the protests were those presented by a black woman whose son had just returned from "the senseless war in Korea" and whose nephew had also returned, but "in a box." This same woman had her passport taken away by the United States government because she had attended a peace meet in Poland. There was another woman in attendance whose son had been shot by a policeman while he lay on the operating table in the emergency room as doctors were attempting to treat him. Another was there because her husband and six other black men had been, as she put it, "legally lynched" in Virginia.

As the women were meeting prior to their planned visits with government officials, the chair of the meeting addressed the women with these words: "Negro women, dry your tears and speak your mind. We have a job to do!" And for three days 132 Negro women set about accomplishing their task.[19]

Forty years later a similar action was taken by black women to redress another injustice. The latter-day protest action was occasioned by the televised testimony of law professor Anita Hill in October 1991 before the United States Senate Judiciary Committee. Hill gave evidence against the confirmation of Clarence Thomas to the United States Supreme Court and charged that Thomas had continually sexually harassed her while she worked with him at the Department of Education and also at the Equal Employment Opportunity Commission. During the course of Hill's testimony the phrase "credible witness" was continually used in reference to her (and others giving evidence). The issue subsequently became the character and credibility of Anita Hill herself: not so much whether what she was relating actually occurred but whether she would be believed in the much larger court of public opinion.

Close on the heels on Hill's testimony and the subsequent confirmation of Thomas as associate justice of the Supreme Court,[20] another event occurred. This one was much less publicized but profoundly significant. The event was an advertisement in the Sunday *New York Times* dated November 17, 1991. It was paid for by a coalition of black women (and others) to proclaim that the group, African-American Women in Defense of Ourselves, did indeed believe Anita Hill and was mobilizing nationwide in support of her right to testify about a wrong that had been committed against her. The advertisement contained the names of 1,603 black women and noted that historically black women had never been believed when they spoke out against abuse or about any matters relating to their ability to resist oppression. Specifically the women noted the nation's history of profound mistreatment of black women:

> This country, which has a long legacy of racism and sexism, has never taken the sexual abuse of black women seriously. Throughout U.S. history black women have been sexually stereotyped as immoral, insatiable, perverse; the initiators in all sexual contacts—abusive or otherwise. The common assumption in legal proceedings as well as in the larger society has been that black women cannot be raped or otherwise sexually abused. As Anita Hill's experience demonstrates, black women who speak of these matters are not likely to be believed.[21]

The women proclaimed in the face of this attack upon the "collective character" of black women that they would meet it with protest, outrage, and resistance. They further declared that no one would speak for them but themselves and that they would not be silenced.

As the examples demonstrate, black women have successfully struggled against injustices: the hospital workers striking for equitable pay and working conditions; the march on Washington, D.C., by over a hundred black women in the early 1950s; and the show of solidarity by hundreds of black women around the country who rallied to the defense not only of Anita Hill but against the assault on the collective image of themselves.

In each of these instances the initiative was taken by "ordinary" black women who pushed forward alone or with a handful of others. As more black women learned of the struggles, they entered into coordinated efforts on many fronts with the initial participants. The struggle continued beyond the initial participants' actions as cultural workers documented the women's efforts: Anderson's pathbreaking film will forever preserve the hospital workers' victory. Hansberry's *Freedom* article remains as a historical record of the 1950s march. And the organization, African-American Women in Defense of Ourselves, seized the momentum generated by black women's outrage over the treatment of Anita Hill to put their issues on the public agenda in a variety of formats.

The organization sponsored the creation of posters of the *New York Times* advertisement with all the women's names. The women involved in the organization held conferences, wrote books and pamphlets, and mailed out questionnaires and other information. All these activities were designed for a redress of a multitude of other inequities. Black women have thus underscored their existence as "collective subjects" who reaffirmed that they would take whatever measures were necessary to protect their rights and defend their cultural image.

Taking on one of the more damaging assaults against black women, Angela Davis provides a much-needed explication of the struggle needed to challenge the prevailing justification that black women can be raped, either symbolically or literally, with impunity. Davis writes about an earlier publicized case involving the rape of a black woman who subsequently killed her attacker in defense of her life. The murder trial of JoAnne Little in 1975 in Raleigh, North Carolina, mobilized a large number of activist groups in a sustained and ultimately victorious fight to free her.[22]

Davis reiterates her charge (written over twenty years ago) that the rape of black women was institutionalized during the slavocracy as she emphasizes that the "vestiges" are ever present today. As she states: "How many black women working in the homes of white people have not had to confront the 'man of the house' as an actual or potential rapist?" Davis goes on to explain how the rape of black women cannot be divorced from the context of its social function as an "arsenal of racism."[23] The campaign against rape must therefore be explicitly antiracist. As Davis explains, "And, as incorrect as it would be to fail to attack racism, it would be equally incorrect to make light of the antisexist content of the movement. Racism and male supremacy have to be projected in their dialectical unity. In the case of the raped black woman, they are mutually reinforcive."[24]

Davis's comments were made about the rape of a black woman by a white prison guard, a person authorized by the state to protect its citizens rather than harm them. Ironically, in Davis's chronicle she is tying the rape of black women to its corollary, which is the persistent depiction of the black man as rapist, thus justifying his continual brutalization through the time-honored tradition of lynching. That Clarence Thomas should perversely use this symbol of the lynched black man to secure his seat on the Supreme Court (the ultimate arbiter of state authority) is further substantiation of the prescience of Davis's 1975 arguments that black women's struggles against inequities need to be ever vigilant against the ravages of racism *and* sexism.

Cultural scholar Hazel Carby makes an appropriate point about the effects of historical symbols on the status of black women and the value of the work of image reconstruction by black women cultural workers. The early narratives *Our Nig* (1859) and *Incidents in the Life of a Slave Girl* (1861) and the later *Jubilee* (1966) all demonstrate that black women were not willing partners in the exploitation of their bodies. The authors of the works created an alternative vision of black women as a response to the consistent portrayal of the sexually compliant black woman. This was a political necessity because of its long-term effects. As Carby explains, "The institutionalized rape of black women has never been as powerful a symbol of black oppression as the spectacle of lynching. Rape has always involved patriarchal notions of women being, at best, not entirely unwilling accomplices, if not outwardly inviting sexual attack."[25] In *The Color Purple* Alice Walker uses the rape of Squeak and the beating of Sofia as symbolic lynchings to show that black women had also been victims of the "deformed equality of equal oppression."[26] Although black women had been equal in oppression they were not equal in representation. Ideologically constructed as objects to be used at will, as sexual fleshpots devoid of human feelings and as accomplices to an oppressive system, black women were in need of relief.

Black Female Cultural Producers

As cultural producers black women have taken on the task of creating images of themselves different from those continually reproduced in traditional works. James Snead, in "Recoding Blackness: The Visual Rhetoric of Black Independent Film," submits that black film- and video makers have undertaken a process of revision regarding the visual codes traditionally associated with the representation of black people. Snead feels that stereotyped images mask real "paradoxes, contradictions, and inequities in society underneath the unthinking pleasure of filmic recognition." By continuous association and repetition false codes about black people have come to be validated as correct. Black independent filmmakers "recode" these visual associations and use "unconventional associations" for black people while utilizing traditional film and media language.[27]

Snead's work is important for insights into the work of black women as cultural producers because it permits a greater understanding of the process of revision or reconstruction, as the term has been used within black feminist scholarship. Rather than simply say a representation is negative or positive, the historical and cultural impetus that gives rise to the images needs to be analyzed along with the presentation of the ways in which black women creators politicize the images.

Daughters of the Dust, for example, presents images that evoke memories associated with traditional Hollywood films that feature black women, such as the two productions of *Imitation of Life*. In both the earlier film and the later revised version the black servants are shown massaging the feet of the white employers. This is a powerful visual presentation of black women, who are shown in a subservient physical position, sitting at the feet of white women. The scene is visually coded such that this appears to be the "normal" and "correct" position for black women in society.

In a revealing scene in the first version of *Imitation of Life*, Delilah, played by Louise Beavers, exhibits more concern for the welfare of her employer, Bea Pullman, played by Claudette Colbert, than she does for herself. Both women are shown at the end of a long workday: Delilah labors as Bea's maid, housekeeper, and childcare provider, while Bea goes door-to-door selling pancake syrup. Bea, however, will eventually become rich from selling a profitable secret pancake mixture that Delilah has created.

This particular scene shows Bea leaning wearily against a wall removing one of her high-heeled shoes while exclaiming that her feet hurt. Delilah solicitously takes Bea by the arm, telling her to sit down while she rubs her feet. The women appear to be following a familiar pattern as they walk over to a chair in front of which is a footstool, where Bea collapses in the chair while Delilah sits at her feet massaging them. Bea, in a deliberate imitation of Delilah's speech pattern, declares that the massage "rests me all over," as Delilah laments that it doesn't seem right for Bea "to be carrying

Louise Beavers in her role as a servant, massaging the feet of employer Claudette Colbert

A 1959 reenactment of a scene from the earlier *Imitation of Life*, this time featuring Juanita Moore rubbing the feet of employer Lana Turner.

around them old heavy cans of syrup, peddling." As the scene is played out Delilah shows no concern about what doesn't seem right about her circumstances, either emotionally or socially.

The later version of *Imitation of Life* features a similar scene in which the black character Annie Johnson, played by Juanita Moore, again takes a position at the feet of her employer, played by Lana Turner. This scene is even more revealing than the first. Annie has demonstrated both visually and verbally that she is the one who is tired and emotionally drained from the continual contretemps with her daughter Sarah Jane, who refuses the social status assigned to her as a black woman.

Throughout the course of the film the two lead characters are shown as being on the parallel course of two single mothers struggling to raise their children. Out of this effort they have forged a mutual bond of respect and affection even as their fortunes take a turn for the better when Lora Meredith, the Lana Turner character, becomes a well-paid actress. However, Lora's ability to survive the rigors required of success in the theater rests on Annie as the keeper of their joint household and on Annie's skills at juggling their finances and resources. Examples are presented in scenes where Annie works out a barter arrangement with the milkman and where she does the for-pay piecework of addressing the business mailings that Lora has been consigned but has neglected.

In contrast, the women's relationship in the film is based on one serving and the other being served, for even though the Lana Turner character recognizes that Annie is obviously not well, she offers her money rather than a reciprocal foot massage. In this way she reinforces their cinematically constructed social positions—that Annie is the one who kneels and serves, whereas she is the one who has the resources to offer a handout.

That this specific image of the women is retained in the later version naturalizes both versions and makes it appear as if this is the proper social arrangement for black women. The two scenes gain additional authority in that many of the elements of the original version that were seen as obviously derogatory were minimized or eliminated in the later film. Elements changed include the inarticulate dialect spoken by the black character and the fact that the actress selected for the role is physically different. Moore is thinner and less bosomy than black actresses traditionally cast in the role of domestic servants, such as Louise Beavers, Hattie McDaniel, and Ethel Waters.[28]

In stark contrast to these two mainstream representations is the scene in *Daughters of the Dust* where the women lovingly wash the feet of Nana Peazant. The family is preparing to leave the island and their grandmother. The women and children are gathered around a regal cane chair in which the grandmother, Nana Peazant, sits, preparing a sacred ornament that will be used as a charm to protect her family on their journey northward.

Nana explains the significance of each item that the charm contains. One is a lock of her mother's hair that was given to her before her mother was sold away. To this Nana adds a lock of her own hair to reinforce the connection, the bond between the family's future in

The Peazant women gather around Nana Peazant, engaged in ritual washing of the feet, a gesture of their respect for an elder member of the family.

the North and their past on the island. As the women pour the water and gently wash Nana's feet, she instructs them about the necessity of preserving their past through honoring their history and traditions. She says: "We are two people in one body. The last of the old and the first of the new. We will always live this double life, you know, 'cause we from the sea. We came here in chains. And we must survive; we must survive. The salt water, she in we blood."

The scene is carefully and deliberately designed by director Julie Dash to countermand previous derogatory depictions of black women in film. Dash reveals that the scene was a conscious reference to the manner in which respect is shown to black elders when members of the family are traveling away from them or when the family has been apart for a long period of time. It is a ritual that Dash feels is important to recognize as a way of maintaining the value of certain traditions among black people.[29] The force of the cinematic depiction of the ritual of washing of the feet, coupled with the image of the women gathered at the feet of their grandmother, comes from the novelty of seeing black women represented in ways not seen before. For those familiar with the ways Hollywood has traditionally characterized black women, Dash's scene of black women respectfully caring for an esteemed member of their family is a powerful recoding of a visual image.

In this recoding importance is not placed on whether images are positive or negative but centers on a redress of the imbalance of who is allowed to present the image. Those who have been formerly silenced—black female cultural producers—are now creating with a vengeance. As the black British filmmakers Maureen Blackwood and Martina Attille reveal, this becomes one of the primary issues—that of control over the image.[30] Blackwood's and Attille's views are supported by the work of Kobena Mercer, who analyzes the "reality effect" or "window on the world" factors in framing black versions of reality. By using the techniques usually relied on by dominant media, black filmmakers are able to disrupt the authority of traditional representations. In doing so, Mercer suggests that the works of black filmmakers provide a critical intervention by making "present that which is made absent in the dominant discourses."[31] Black audiences therefore are given a different look at themselves and the ways they are represented.

The Role of the Critic

The task of the critic within the interpretive community is to give voice to those who are usually never considered in any analysis of cultural works. Barbara Christian, a literary scholar—one of the first to suggest that there was a tradition of black women writers dating back to the nineteenth century—writes about her efforts to construct a method of analyzing the literature of black women writers. Christian notes that being a black feminist critic involves an activism that works toward the goal of substantively changing black women's lives. She feels that the critic needs to dispense with a distanced and false stance of objectivity because, for her, a black feminist critic is a participant "in an on-going dialogue between the writer and those who [are] reading the writer, most of whom [are] not academics and for whom that writing was life-sustaining [and] life-saving."[32]

It is as a participant, not a detached observer, that the work of the critic becomes vitally important within the interpretive community. Media audience researcher Ien Ang feels that the work of the critic in audience studies is not neutral, that working within a cultural studies framework, the researcher is advancing an understanding of audience activity within "social and political structures and processes." The goal of the researcher is to develop "strategic interpretations" of audience activity, for according to Ang, "what is at stake is a *politics of interpretation*."[33]

This was never more evident than in the heated public exchanges concerning Spielberg's film version of *The Color Purple*. The widely held view that the film was a racist product directed by a racist director became complicated when black women's increasingly tangible support underscored the importance of the historical moment for cultural analysis and for an understanding of specific audiences.

Black women viewers reclaimed the film beyond its critical reception, as they later would with *Daughters of the Dust*.

The Color Purple, both novel and film, had been positioned as negative by mainstream media critics and by the continuing coverage of the protests from some black men. This in turn led to its designation as "controversial." According to film scholar Annette Kuhn, positioning a cultural form as controversial "fixes" a predominant reading of it and governs how it will be initially received by an audience.[34] Referring to the novel and film *The Color Purple* and, by extension, to Alice Walker as controversial implied that the content of the works was incendiary rather than that a particular reaction to them was negative. *The Color Purple*, both novel and film, became inflammatory subject matter because there was a vocal minority allowed to express publicly their negative reaction to them. The content of the works was not offensive to everyone in the audience. As presented in mainstream media, the predominant reading, or meaning construction, of *The Color Purple* was that the works negatively depicted black people, especially black men.

Kuhn submits, in her analysis of the way in which censorship constructed a 1920s British film as controversial, that it was entangled in "power relations" between several discourses at a particular historical moment "over the conditions under which the film was to enter the public domain." She concluded that the film "constituted a strategic intervention in a broader debate as much because of the discourses surrounding the film as the content of the film itself."[35] The same can be said of *The Color Purple*—that there were privileged discourses that were allowed to determine the significance of the film because of its influence on power relations in conflict.

The privileged discourses surrounding *The Color Purple* were those of mainstream media and black men. Black women's feelings about the film had seldom been acknowledged. The broader debate over *The Color Purple* was about the authority of black female creative artists to set the agenda for image making in fiction and film. It is this aspect of the controversy that constituted *The Color Purple*'s "strategic intervention." The power struggles that were and still are being waged over *The Color Purple* are the dominant forces in society and among black people. The media coverage of the protests from black men obscured this by framing the conflict as an in-house fight between black women and black men. Although this may have been one facet of it, the larger issue concerned black women viewers' favorable response to the film and its implications for the future course of black people's political activism. Because black women had always been a "silenced" component of black history, their vocal and visible support of the novel and film served notice of their place in black culture.

The critical climate surrounding *Daughters of the Dust* was more subtle than that which greeted *The Color Purple*. Dash's film was at first ignored by the critics, then disparaged with caustic assessments about the filmmaker's competence. Even after the film went into distribution many of the comments from mainstream reviewers were tepid and patronizing.[36] However, the exuberant reactions of audiences wherever the film played called into question the critical authority of mainstream reviewers. Also challenged was the judgment of an influential critic from a black newspaper in New York.[37]

This review by Armond White is curious because he was one of the staunchest defenders of black women's reception of the film *The Color Purple*. As he stated about the Spielberg film: "It's not simply a movie of black social history. It is particularly a history of black women."[38] In his review of *Daughters of the Dust*, however, the tone of the review is noticeably vitriolic. White seems angry that Dash made a film about black women that was set at the beginning of this century rather than depicting a contemporary story. It is less of a review than a condemnation of the filmmaker.

Again, the shots of the women in long white dresses is cause for condemnation, as is what White sees as Dash's "utter ineptitude at staging and blocking scenes." A memorable sequence featuring shots of three women playing with a discarded parasol on the beach was described by White as "nothing but a dreadful black bourgeois fantasy of refined cinema."

As a rationale for the heatedness of his review White stated:

> If my tone sounds a bit uncharitable, it's because for years now a lot of hope has been invested in Dash's project. But this isn't simple disappointment; it's despair—anger—at the sorry spectacle of serious, intelligent film people like Dash and her cinematographer, Arthur Jaffa [*sic*], making pretentious Art that is both remote from viewers' sensibilities and drably executed. *Daughters* is full of verbal and visual dissociations and symbolic imagery that never gather force simply because the ideas behind these tropes have not been transformed in a way that delights or intrigues the senses. You can pass time counting the slow-motion promenades or the impenetrable shots of a half-sunken statue.[39]

Again, as with *The Color Purple*, certain critics have a different agenda, which presents a story separate from the one that particular audiences perceive. The work of black feminist critics is to acknowledge these different voices, to explicate the responses, thus ensuring that they are also heard. In this way feminist critics can intervene strategically in the politics of interpretation. Cultural scholars are also presented with the opportunity to seize the moment of heightened awareness produced by black women's viewing of a specific story to take advantage of the potential to build upon their comments and experiences to further the movement toward social and political activism.

Black Women as Audience

In contrast to the assessments of some critics, black women's statements about *Daughters of the Dust* lend weight to its significance as a profound cultural, social, and historical event. The black women I interviewed see it as an important film for black people and feel that the film's focus on black women is long overdue. Although some of the women felt *The Color Purple* was also important in their lives, the women in another group made a clear distinction between *Daughters of the Dust* and *The Color Purple*. One of the first comments from the women was an observation about the look of *Daughters of the Dust*. One woman thought it was visually very beautiful: "And I get a big kick out of seeing all those black women in all those different shades and styles. And all those pretty white dresses." Another woman in the group responded that she had never seen so many dark-skinned people, "in real life or on the camera. I mean, dark-skinned black people are hidden in our society." Someone else in the group noted the number of dark-skinned black people in the film *The Color Purple*. Two other women made provocative distinctions between the films:

> Woman no. 1: The difference in *The Color Purple* was that those dark-skinned people were well-known people—Whoopi Goldberg and Oprah Winfrey, and all them.[40] The thing that struck me about *Daughters of the Dust* was that there were different-looking black women—different hairstyles, different shapes; the difference within blackness was just really striking to me and nice because they were all very beautiful in their own way. So there wasn't just a sort of monolithic black woman running across the screen all the time.

Another woman added this comment:

> Woman no. 2: I think the thing that really holds you throughout the film is the sheer beauty of the photography and the delight you take in the fact that here are all these—and we are so unused to seeing ourselves on the screen—dark-skinned women photographed in loving ways. Remember how the camera kind of lingers on Celie in *The Color Purple*? And it doesn't on the character who plays Nettie, even though she's just as dark—the camera never takes the time to really look at her features and say, Here is a beautiful woman. In *Daughters of the Dust*, the configuration of all of these women together is extremely seductive. In a way it doesn't matter what story she is telling—just the idea that

somebody thought this much of black women was really seductive. That's what kept me in my seat for almost two hours.

Dash says of the film that it is about the "scraps of memory" that sustain black women, the pieces of the past that they carry with them or that are recalled, recollected, or remembered.[41] In another group of black women that I interviewed, the film's evocation of memories from their past was mentioned. One of the women said:

Woman no. 1: I was thinking that the time that I was born was a wonderful time because we have a part of that [what was shown in the film]—it's still within us. And then we have the new, so you get that mixture, and it's a shame that my kids don't know about this. I think it's such an important movie for them to see—you can see where so many things come from and how much carries through. So much of their history is lost, so that makes it an important movie to me. When I went to college—I went to college in North Carolina—it was like, "Those were those Geechees"—and everybody thought they were backward because they were from these islands. And to see this rich culture that I didn't appreciate then, when I was in college, that I really do now, and that I want my son to know about. So I was thinking about that as I was watching the film, and that I would like to go to see the islands before they are completely lost to us, before some big corporation takes them over.

Her comment prompted another black woman in the group to talk about memories from her childhood:

Woman no. 2: When you, or anyone else, were eighteen or so, I don't think we had an appreciation of even our own background, not just the Geechee people, we didn't have an idea of our own heritage. I remember singing in church, and people used to line out those hymns,[42] and I would say, "Oh, my goodness, not again." And now, when I hear somebody line out one, it reminds me of a child growing up, and I think—this is something that is lost almost. They just don't do it in some places at all. At our church now, on the first Sunday, in between communion, someone will line out a hymn—

Woman no. 3: —and the people will follow—

Woman no. 2: —and it's just so spiritual to me. And I used to just hate it. I used to just cringe as a kid when they'd start doing that. And that goes back as far as we go—

Woman no. 4: —it's call and response—

Woman no. 2: —and it goes back as far as we go.

Woman no. 3: And unfortunately, if somebody doesn't keep it going—

Woman no. 2: —yeah, that's right. It'll be dead. It's just a simple "remember me."

Dash relates that during the construction of the finished film she had a master drummer playing throughout on the sound track sounding out these words in Yoruba: "Remember me, remember my name, take me with you, take me where you go." Dash says that it was very subtle, and possibly no one was conscious of the message.[43] But, it seems clear there was an effect on some who watched the film.

The women in another group talked about the film's focus on women and how that made them feel as black women. One responded: "That's all right, as far as I'm concerned. It's all right because this woman was wonderful, the matriarch, because this was her story to tell. So if it's focusing on the females, I think it's okay." Another responded that it appeared to be a balanced story because Nana Peazant did continually refer to the men: "She told about where the men were at the time [of slavery]. She gave a reason that many of the men were dead and the rest were taken away."

The women talked about the relationship between Nana Peazant and her great-grandson, Eli, whose wife has been raped. One woman spoke about how the great-grandmother talked to Eli. She said: "I loved it. I mean, she endeared herself to me in the first scene when she told Eli, 'You don't own her.' From then on I thought, This woman is before her time." Another woman reacted, "Yeah, that's right. Just because you married her does not mean you own her." These statements generated spirited comments from the other women:

Woman no. 1: And I didn't care that they said she [the great-grandmother] didn't have any schooling or anything. I thought she was wise, very wise.

Woman no. 2: But, I wonder, what could make her say that? How could she come up with that conclusion, given the time?

Woman no. 3: Mother wit.

Woman no. 2: Because I could say that real easily today and feel good about it, but given the time in which she lived and everything, how could she come up with that—"You don't own her"—when people *were* owning people?

Woman no. 3: But that's why. Because she had lived through slavery; that's how she could say that, I think.

Woman no. 4: I guess it's a bad time for me to see this film in light of all those things we've been discussing, Mike Tyson [charged with raping a contestant in the Miss Black America pageant] and all that. Because, again, it just reaffirms how insensitive men can be. Instead of him concentrating on "My wife has been raped; what can I do to help her get her self-respect, her self-esteem, back" he's concentrating on how he's feeling. And that's just typical with men. You know, it's just me, me, me.

These women's comments go a long way toward rebutting criticisms of *Daughters of the Dust* and helping to establish its importance within this historical and cultural moment.

Intimate Revelations

Toni Morrison writes of a bond of shared knowledge among black women. When she uses the phrase "quiet as it's kept" to begin her first novel *The Bluest Eye* (1970) she sees these as coded words used within a language she associates with black women conversing with one another about matters that are usually kept within their circle. The act of writing the book was to expose this private confidence. There was a shared familiarity Morrison was aiming at, an "instant intimacy" between the reader and the novel through a secret that is about to be shared. The reader knows that the one who is imparting the information is speaking from the inside and knows something that others don't; the reader also knows that the one who is speaking is being generous with privileged information.[44]

It is the public exposure of privileged information and the assumption of shared understanding between the "speaker" and the "reader" that is addressed in this analysis of black women and their relationship to cultural forms. The "instant intimacy" that I am concerned with is between black women as they intersect within an interpretive framework as cultural producers, critics, and audience members.

Black women have demonstrated their bond of collective concerns through their tangible reception of *The Color Purple* and *Daughters of the Dust*. Although their embrace of *Daughters of the Dust* is more understandable in that it is a work of a black female filmmaker rather than an adaptation by a white male director, there is a corollary in black women's negotiated reception of *The Color Purple*. The responses transcend the text and align themselves with a broader framework of the women's collective past. As I was interviewing a group of black women about their reactions to *The Color Purple* one of the women spoke about her emotions upon being in the company of other black women watching the film:

> It's a good feeling to get everybody's reactions to this film. It's interesting listening to each person, how she feels about different scenes, and whether or not we have any similarities or differences or if we see different things when we're watching the same thing. [I feel] some kind of closeness, I guess, with the people in this room because regardless of our backgrounds those situations are part of all of us. We've gone through something in there or felt *something* because of that.

As cultural producers, as critics, and as audience members, black women constitute a dynamic entity, each component of which has an impact on the others at key junctures. It is important, therefore, that each segment is acknowledged rather than examined in isolation. As black women create works that reconstruct significant elements of their experiences, and as scholars explicate those works within an appropriate theoretical framework, the influence of these women as readers provides a solid foundation for continued cultural production.

Beyond this function, though, of black women as an interpretive community, there is the greater goal of establishing stronger bonds of commonality that can help form progressive and effective coalitions. Even though it is sometimes interpreted as an act of political treason to consider the manner in which members within a social group coalesce, for black women it can be an act of survival as barriers imposed from outside forces work to impede their advancement. Also, recognizing that members of an audience can provide cogent insights into their social circumstances minimizes the distinction between those within the social group who are in different socioeconomic locations.

Although it would be a mistake to assume that black women will always communicate across lines of sexuality, class, economic status, geographic location, and so on, there is still a need to examine the ways in which they do. By considering the specific nature of black women's lives, through interviews such as those presented here, through oral histories, through examinations of cultural documents, the ways in which their experiences converge can be revealed. This has the potential to create an environment that will enable the transformation of many black women's consciousness and awareness of their historical situation to further the movement toward their unification as a social force.

CHAPTER TWO

Text and Subtext: *The Color Purple*

The Color Purple has attained a secure place in cultural history since it first entered the national consciousness. Both the novel and the film have been enormously successful. The novel sold sixty thousand copies in hardcover and stayed on the *New York Times* best-seller list for twenty-five weeks. By the time Alice Walker won the American Book Award and the Pulitzer Prize in 1983 the novel had already sold forty thousand copies. After the award of the literature prizes and the subsequent sale of the film rights, the paperback edition sold over four million copies.[1]

The film version of *The Color Purple* earned $95 million dollars in the first year of its release—a noteworthy accomplishment, for the production expenses were only $15 million.[2] A film is considered successful if it grosses two and a half times its production costs. Despite the extended and vociferous criticisms of the film, which were still being broadcast and published throughout its exhibition cycle, there was never a drop in audience consumption. Four years after the film was first released, then rereleased a year later, shown on cable television, and made available on videocassette, the prime-time network television broadcast of *The Color Purple* drew approximately thirty-four million viewers with a 17.1 rating and a 27 share, and was the eighteenth-rated program for the week in which it aired.[3] Seven years after the first release of the film, it still heads the list of black-themed video rentals.[4]

In spite of the work's financial success, the film's complex critical reception has blunted scholarly critiques and analyses. Radical critics as well as mainstream reviewers were incensed at Steven Spielberg. In their opinion, his previous films were escapist fare, and *The Color Purple* was beyond his sensibilities. For these critics it was simpler to cast the film aside as falling within the pantheon of films that have represented black people in a derogatory manner. Certainly, its production history and style are reminiscent of early films such as *Hallelujah* (1929) and *Cabin in the Sky* (1943), which employed well-known white directors overseeing a cast of black actors and actresses who offered up derogatory portraits of black people.

But the lack of consensus regarding the effect of the film makes it less easy to dismiss it altogether. The heated discussions that took place between some black men and the rejoinders by black women critics raised pertinent issues for cultural scholars. Issues considered were those that were assumed to be part of an unspoken agreement to let matters that are talked about "within the veil"[5] in black communities remain private and not air them in public forums. These topics included the mistreatment of black women, family abuse, the scope of black female sexuality, and so on. The subject became even more complicated because of many black women's favorable reactions not just to *The Color Purple* but to other film and television programs such as *The Women of Brewster Place* (1989) and *Daughters of the Dust*. Even though the heat of these debates has faded from public discussion the significance of black women's responses to these works has not.

The Novel

The Color Purple was a small, quiet book when it entered the literary scene in 1982. The subject of the book is a young, abused, uneducated black girl who evolves into womanhood and a sense of her worth, which she gains by bonding with the women around her. It is a chronicle of her life as she grows up in rural Georgia during the first four decades of this century.

Celie, the protagonist, is raped repeatedly by the man she thinks is her father and impregnated twice by him. He subsequently gives away her two children. Celie is then married off in a loveless union to a man she merely calls Mister. Mister physically and psychologically abuses her, lusts after her sister, Nettie, and is in love with a blues singer named Shug Avery. Mister and Shug have had an ongoing sexual relationship for many years, even during Mister's marriage to his first wife, Annie Julia. In the novel Annie Julia is killed by her lover, and Mister marries Celie to have someone to take care of his children.

Because of the threat of sexual abuse from their stepfather, Nettie comes to live with Celie and Mister but is forced to leave because of Mister's continual sexual pursuit. Nettie eventually travels to Africa with a black couple who are missionaries. They have, unknown to Celie and Nettie, adopted Celie's children. Nettie promises Celie that she will write to her, but when she does so, Mister hides the letters from Celie.

Mister's son, Harpo, is forced by his father to emulate him and his grandfather, Old Mister, in his relationship with his wife, Sofia. Harpo tries to dominate her in the same way that he sees Mister dominate Celie. Sofia, however, is a strong and feisty woman who resists anyone's attempt to control her. She is eventually imprisoned because she hits the mayor after he tries to bully her when his wife asks her to be her maid. Through Sofia's exhibition of strength she becomes one of the models of resistance for Celie.

Celie's other example of a strong black woman is Shug. After Nettie leaves, Celie is engulfed in loneliness until Mister brings Shug home with him. Shug is ill and is ostracized by the community because of her sexually liberated lifestyle. Celie and Shug become lovers. Through Shug's care and comfort and Sofia's example, Celie eventually learns to value herself. She finds the letters from Nettie that Mister has hidden, and her anger combined with her newly found confidence, enables her to overthrow Mister's domination. At the end of the story, Mister finally learns to treat those he cares for with respect, and Celie and Nettie are reunited when she and Celie's children return from Africa.

When *The Color Purple* is considered within the continuum of black female creativity and activism its subversive form and content become apparent. Black female writers have consistently used and modified standard literary themes and forms for political purposes. Their goal was to show a different side of the black woman's story. That the beginning of *The Color Purple* recalls earlier works is an acknowledgment of its literary heritage. Consider the following: Celie is raped by the man she thinks is her father, her children are taken away from her, she is the object of her mother's jealousy, and she is worked and treated like a mule. In Margaret Walker's fictional narrative, *Jubilee* (1966), Sis Hetta was the unwilling concubine of the plantation owner John Morris Dutton. Her child, Vyry, is taken from her, then tortured by Dutton's wife because her child and Vyry look as much alike as identical twins. In *Their Eyes Were Watching God* (1937) by Zora Neale Hurston, Janie Crawford's grandmother is beaten by her owner's wife after the birth of Janie's mother because the infant was white with gray eyes.

Celie is similar to Frado in Harriet Wilson's *Our Nig* (1859) through her status as an object as she is literally given to Mister by her stepfather. The way she is called out for Mister's inspection recalls the image of Harriet Jacobs's [Linda Brent] grandmother on the auction block in *Incidents in the Life of a Slave Girl* (1861). After Mister sees that Celie is good stock he inquires of Fonso if the cow is still part of the bargain. "Her cow," Fonso replies and goes back to reading his paper.[6] This scene is carefully constructed so that the reader knows that Fonso considers both Celie and the cow to be of no further use to him—livestock with which he can now dispense. The scene becomes a tableau where the story of Sis Hetta and John Morris Dutton is re-created. In writing her novel Margaret Walker includes a compelling sentence that reverberates throughout the history of black female writing: "He had wanted Hetta, so his father gave her to him, and he had satisfied his lust with her."[7]

Black women writers and social activists have long been concerned about the prevailing image of the sexually immoral black woman. This concern was the basis for the beginnings of the black women's club movement at the turn of the century,[8] a movement devoted to "uplift" programs for the betterment of black people and to countering entrenched and harmful images of black women. In the black female literature at the time, the negative imagery was constantly under revision. Frances Harper and Pauline Hopkins presented what they felt were positive black women characters, although later critics would dismiss their heroines because they were refined fair-skinned mulattoes. Both narratives that reconstructed the actual lives of black women during the slavocracy, *Incidents in the Life of a Slave Girl* and *Jubilee*, were designed to demonstrate that black women were forced into sexual liaisons with the slaveowners.

In *The Color Purple* Alice Walker continues the task of revising images of black women by taking the familiar and negatively constructed sexual images and imbuing them with power. One of the ways she does so is through the characterization of Sofia. With Sofia's story Alice Walker is able to attack two aspects of the nineteenth-century ideology of the cult of true womanhood: that black women were not the ideal, being neither fair nor frail, and that their sexual desires were uncontrollable.

In a revealing section of the novel, Harpo continues to have sex with Sofia even though she has lost her desire because of his unremitting quest to bend her to his domination. Sofia tells Celie that sex with Harpo was once fun, that she would get hot and bothered just watching him, but because of his attempt to master her, she has lost interest. Sofia tells Celie that the worst part is that Harpo does not even notice: "He git up there and enjoy himself just the same. No matter what I'm thinking. No matter what I feel. It just him. Heartfeeling don't even seem to enter into it. She snort. The fact he can do it like that make me want to kill him."[9] The dilemma in confronting the second part of the ideology of the true woman was to create a strong black woman who was not a perpetuation of the negatively perceived fire-breathing Amazon. The earliest black female novelists presented the refined mulatto as a rebuttal. Alice Walker constructed Sofia: a large, strong-willed, brown-skinned woman. Much is made of Sofia's color in the novel. Harpo thinks she is "bright," but Celie informs us that "Harpo so black he think she bright, but she ain't that bright. Clear medium brown skin, gleam on it like good furniture" (p. 32). Sofia is also fond of manual labor rather than the traditional "woman's work" of housekeeping. Although Sofia is capable of hard work and prefers it, she is still considered attractive and appealing to the men in her life—Harpo and the prizefighter Buster Broadnax.

Sofia is a familiar character to many black women who do not consider her traits negative. Because of this familiarity, Alice Walker is able to accomplish a reversal of earlier portraits of black women not so much by changing the imagery as by altering the way she is perceived in the novel. Consequently Sofia becomes a forceful presence whose intolerance for any form of domination is seen in a favorable light. She is a strong woman who fights back with her fists if necessary. Writing in the 1980s Alice Walker constructs an appropriate contemporary character. The fair, feminine ideal was no longer a plausible example of a black heroine, because this creation implied that black women who were not were less than ideal. Thus although Sofia's physical presence and manner of rebellion are much more omnipresent and overt, her story brings to mind battles by earlier black women. Just as these women resisted, so too does Celie, whose model is Sofia, a recognizable figure in black female history. Sofia is reminiscent of those black women who fought in the front lines of many struggles. It is thus appropriate that she becomes a model for Celie's will to resistance.

That earlier writers presented the protagonists they did, however unsuccessfully received at the time of publication, enabled later black women writers and creative artists to present the full sexual scope of black women's lives. Nella Larsen introduced the idea of sexual feelings between women friends in *Passing*; Toni Morrison took up the notion of friendship between women being a stronger bond than relationships with male partners in *Sula*. These elements are enhanced and extended in *The Color Purple*, for Shug Avery is probably one of the most sexually developed characters in literature. In the face of the persistently negative characterizations of black women, Shug is a refreshing antidote in that her sexual expressions are not tempered by others' opinions of her actions. Shug is also free to do as she wants because she has the economic means to do so.

Barbara Christian notes that contemporary black female writers explore the full range of black women's sexuality as a route to empowerment.[10] She develops her thesis through the use of Audre Lorde's reflections in the essay "The Uses of the Erotic: The Erotic as Power."[11] Christian states that although the erotic contains the sexual, it should not be confused with sex, for this is only one intense dimension of it. The erotic is the source of energy that integrates all aspects of a woman's life. Christian explains that once it is experienced a woman refuses to accept any oppression imposed upon her and resists anything that would destroy life.[12] Lorde identifies the erotic as a "resource within each of us that lies in a deeply female and spiritual plane." It provides "a well of replenishing and provocative force to the woman who does not fear its revelation, nor succumb to the belief that sensation is enough."[13] Lorde refers to the etymology of the word *erotic* from *eros*,

> the personification of love in all its aspects—born of Chaos, and personifying creative power and harmony. When I speak of the erotic, then, I speak of it as an assertion of the life force of women; of that creative energy empowered, the knowledge and use of which we are now reclaiming in our language, our history, our dancing, our loving, our work, our lives. (p. 55)

That life force is evident in *The Color Purple*. Shug, Celie, Sofia, and Squeak (also known as Mary Agnes) forge a bond to help one another through adversity. *The Color Purple* goes a step further in liberating the black heroine in that Alice Walker presents a means to harmony rather than devastation. When Celie learns that Mister has been hiding Nettie's letters, she is transformed from a meek, submissive creature into someone who wants to kill. Shug counsels her to do something to take her mind off the urge to destroy. Toni Morrison wrote of her character Sula that had she had paints or clay or another outlet to engage her creativity, she would not have been dangerous. The challenge of self-sustaining activity is taken up in *The Color Purple* with Shug's singing and Celie's "Folkspants Unlimited" business. Instead of being dependent on men for emotional or economic support, the female characters in *The Color Purple* are aided by other women.

The Film

The film version of *The Color Purple*, as directed by Steven Spielberg, presents a view of black women that is in direct opposition to these earlier works. The stories told in black women's novels were a product of a conscious effort to portray multidimensional characters who attempted to attain some measure of control over their lives. In the film, the strong black women are replaced by the standard negative images. Sofia, a model of strength and resistance, becomes the overbearing matriarchal figure. Instead of resisting the domination of her husband Harpo, Sofia seems to have him henpecked.

The Shug Avery of the film is presented as a victim of her insatiable sexual appetite rather than as a woman who exercises the same privileges as men, including acting out her desire to sleep with whomever she chooses. As a corollary, Shug is disempowered as she longs for her preacher father's approval. The introduction of Shug's father, a preacher, was fabricated for the film. He does not exist in the novel. In the film Shug is seen as someone who regrets the life she has lived and who assents to others' perception of her as a loose woman. Her constant quest for absolution from her preacher father takes away her central source of power in the novel—that she does what she wants and has the economic means to do so.

The depictions of Celie in the film are intended to show her as an unloved waif. What the film neglects to offer, however, is a clear picture of why she is this way. In the film Celie's dismal condition is a quirk of fate, but this is the extent of her oppression. Celie does not represent the black women who share her repressed state but is instead presented as an individual who suffers hardships but eventually ascends to fortune's favor. The Celie of the novel is a victim of racism, sexism, and patriarchal privilege. Her tremendous effort to realize her worth as a human being allows her to throw off the mechanisms of her oppression—her negative image of herself and Mister's omnipresent abuse. At the same time, Celie achieves a route to power as she becomes self-supporting with her Folkspants Unlimited business. This is a critical factor in the novel: that the women were or became economically independent. They also forged a supportive network with the other women.

In the Steven Spielberg production, the black female characters are not simply diminished; they are displaced as the center of the story. The film is a chronicle of an abusive black man's journey toward self-understanding. The film changes him from an evil person into one who is perplexed and confused. The film grants the male protagonist salvation because he has arranged for a happy ending for the woman he misused throughout the film. This is the antithesis of the ending of the novel, which revolves around an abused black woman beginning to appreciate herself and becoming economically independent.

Celie and Shug represent the extremes of hopelessness and strength in the novel, and in the following section I examine how their impact is diminished in the film.

Shug

The film character Shug values her preacher father's opinion of her more than she needs her "hedonistic" lifestyle. Instead of a secure black woman who lives her life according to the dictates of her value system (as she is presented in the novel) the film version of Shug is obsessed with winning her father's approval. In the novel, as Celie is bathing Shug during her recovery from her illness, Celie asks her if she misses her children. Shug replies that she doesn't miss anything.

In the film, as Celie bathes Shug, she asks her if she has any kids. Shug is lying in the tub, and the scene is shot so that what we see is the back of Shug's head and her hands waving a bottle of liquor and a cigarette around. We see Celie straight on. Shug answers that her children are with her ma and pa. There is a cut to Shug, who looks wretched and sad, lying in the tub. She says, "Never knowed a child to come out right unless there's a man around." There is a cut to a reaction shot of Celie, who is busy mixing the bath oils to pour in the tub. Celie looks at Shug innocently, and as we cut back to her Shug moans, "Children gots to have a pa." Shug then sits up in the tub and asks Celie, "Yo pa love you? My pa love me." She states this proudly. "My pa still love me," she says, then starts crying. "He still love me. 'Cept he don't know it. He don't know it." At this point she is overcome and cries harder.

"My pa still love me," Shug says, in spite of the fact that she has not been living up to his moral standards, as the film implies. To drive home the point, later in the film Old Mister comes to visit while Shug is recuperating from her illness. Old Mister walks up to the house, and we see him in a long shot from the rear as Albert (Mister) emerges from the house. They stare at each other and walk around each other in a circle in front of the porch swing. There is a cut to a medium shot of Albert at one end of the swing and Old Mister at the other. They exchange positions. Old Mister leans back on his heels, and Albert looks at his father apprehensively. They say nothing. Albert smiles at his father and sits down in the swing. There is a cut to a close-up of Old Mister's foot between Albert's legs. We see Albert over Old Mister's shoulder as Old Mister leans down to talk to him. Old Mister says that Albert couldn't rest until he got Shug in his house. There is a cut back to Old Mister's foot between Albert's legs; Old Mister pushes the swing with his foot. Old Mister asks Albert: "What is it with this Shug Avery? She black as tar. Nappy-headed. Got legs like baseball bats." Celie is in the house getting Old Mister a glass of water. She watches the two of them through the window. In a voice-over Celie says: "Old Mister talking trash about Shug. Folks don't like nobody being too proud or too free."

Old Mister continues talking under the voice-over. He says that Shug is a juke-joint jezebel and that she isn't even clean: "I hear she's got that nasty women's disease." At this point Celie spits in Old Mister's glass of water. There is a cut to Albert as he tells Old Mister that he hasn't got it in him to understand why he loves Shug. Albert says that he has always loved her and always will: "I should have married her when I had the chance." Old Mister replies that Albert would have thrown his life away along, with a good portion of Old Mister's money, and that all Shug's children have different daddies. Albert replies that he can vouch for Shug's kids all having the same father. Old Mister counters, in an passage different from the novel, "You can vouch for nothing. Shug Avery done set the population of Hotwell County a new high. You just one of the rusters, boy." Albert says nothing; he looks as if he wants to say something but is afraid to do so. When Celie comes out on the porch with the glass of water, Old Mister tells her: "Celie, you has my sympathy. Ain't many womens 'low they husbands who' to lay up in they house."

In the film Shug is presented not as someone with a normal sexual lifestyle but as a lascivious and hot-blooded woman. The dialogue that was added to the story when Old Mister says that Shug is a "juke-joint jezebel" and someone who sleeps with many of the men in the town exemplifies this. Another example is when Shug comes to visit Mister and Celie after her marriage to Grady. The two men are discussing Shug while we see her listening in another room. Mister tells Grady that they both had her in their own way, "but we had her." Shug is listening to this conversation with a pleased smile on her face as if she does not mind being talked about as someone who has been passed from one man to another.

In the novel Shug has a carefully thought-out system of values. She lives her life according to her standards and is free to do so because she is not dependent on anyone emotionally or economically. In the film she is controlled by all the men connected to her: Mister, her father, Grady. She is not the self-possessed woman of the novel but someone who is pulled by the strings of her sexuality and her insecurity about the way she lives her life. The film casts a moral judgment on Shug, and the result implies that those who follow Shug's example may not be as lucky as she. In the film, when Shug goes to her father's church singing a song of repentance, he finally accepts her. She says to him, "See, Daddy, sinners have soul, too," and he embraces her in an act of absolution.

Because the film character Shug is not a powerful presence, her relationship with Celie disintegrates into typical female pettiness. Her treatment of Celie, seen at first in the comment "You sho is ugly" and in the way she orders her around by telling Albert, "Git that thang to fix me something to eat," become harsher and meaner than they were in the novel. Her insipid demeanor in the bathtub as Celie bathes her are incongruent with what she represents to both Mister and Celie. Because Shug is presented as a weak woman with questionable morals the significance of Celie's struggle to value herself is undermined. In the novel, Celie represents those who are never acknowledged as important. They are insignificant, poor, dark-skinned black girls. Because Shug is powerful in the novel, Celie becomes powerful. Because Shug is presented as a petty jealous woman in the film, Celie is seen as the unloved, ugly duckling stepsister. She is a specific individual with a specific problem rather than the symbol of many black women who toil under similar circumstances.

Celie

In two of the least realized depictions of the subjugation of women in the film we see the young Celie used as a packhorse: first, when the stepfather gives her to Mister and the two of them travel to Mister's farm. Mister is riding the horse, and Celie is trudging along behind. She is loaded down with her belongings, ostensibly symbolizing a mule, in the sense that Zora Neale Hurston wrote of the status of black women. This same portrait of

Celie the packhorse is given when Shug leaves to go touring with her band. Mister and Shug are shown walking with their arms around each other toward the band members waiting in the car. Celie is walking behind them, again lugging everything that no one else wants to carry.

The symbol of black women as mules not only means that they were beasts of burden; it also means that they were without exercizable options in life. They were given as little thought and consideration as dumb animals. That the same scene is reenacted with Shug as the perpetrator neutralizes the first instance, because Celie is seen as a helpless victim of life's unfair circumstances rather than as someone who does not see a way out from under Mister's domination.

Steven Spielberg's inability to understand the historical conditions that shaped Alice Walker's themes and characters produced an exploration of a black woman's life that not only is simplistic but in fact overlooks the efforts of previous black women writers. The film bypasses the process that began with the slave narratives and their chronicle of the lives of black women used as breeders, chattel, and sexual repositories. It ignores the period when the black woman's perceived sexuality was redefined. The film overlooks the transitional moment when the average black girl was given a place of importance. The writers within the black female writing tradition reconstructed the perception of the black woman as a figure in culture and in history. Their efforts are sabotaged in the film version of *The Color Purple*. As constructed by Steven Spielberg, the film resurrects previous characters from mainstream media and gives them a modern-day gloss. Shug becomes the licentious cabaret singer, Sofia the castrating Amazon, and Celie an Orphan Annie.

Formal Structure

Steven Spielberg is the most successful director in Hollywood's history. His three biggest films before *The Color Purple—Jaws* (1975), *E.T.: The Extra-Terrestial* (1982), and *Indiana Jones and the Temple of Doom* (1984)—combined to gross almost a billion dollars.

Spielberg has been nominated three times for an Academy Award: in 1977 for *Close Encounters of the Third Kind*, in 1981 for *Raiders of the Lost Ark*, and in 1982 for *E.T.* His film *The Color Purple* was nominated for eleven Academy Awards and did not win any. Spielberg was not nominated as the director of the film.

The critical reaction to the film was unfavorable. The film journal *Jump Cut* labeled Spielberg "the dominant ideologue of affluent middle-class America."[14] Marti Wilson wrote in *Black Film Review* that Spielberg "should be knighted as Hollywood's most intrepid foreign film director of the year."[15] In the wake of the widespread negative reaction to the film, Spielberg was asked why he decided to direct a work that was outside his usual subject areas. Spielberg said he directed *The Color Purple* because he had long wanted to do a different kind of film, one that was not "stereotypically a Spielberg movie." He wanted to do a film that involved character rather than one that relied heavily on special effects: "I wanted to work in the same arena as directors like Sidney Lumet and Sydney Pollack—and Paddy Chayefsky, in terms of what he had done as a playwright and writer."[16] He agreed with those who said that his track record of being a successful director helped get the financial backing to make the film.

> I don't think I could have made this film ten years ago because I wouldn't have been in a position of strength to have a studio allow me to make this picture. I think only because of who I am today with my past successes added up, that the studio would say yes, do whatever you like. Do the telephone book if you'd like. Unfortunately, it took me about twelve years to get to that position in my career, but the way things are in America today all you need is one success and they ask you to direct the telephone book day after tomorrow.[17]

Spielberg felt that the readers of the novel were mostly white women. He said he wanted to make the story available to a wider audience and make the issues that the novel dealt with accessible to people: "I wanted white people to see this movie with an all-black repertoire. And I wanted a black audience for this film. I wanted the film to have older people and younger people in attendance because I think some of what it says is very important."[18] Regardless of Spielberg's intent, his comments reveal much about the status of women and black people in this society. The issues that are significant to these two groups are not important enough in themselves to be represented in mainstream media. If the story does not appeal to a broader audience that includes white males, then the subject is not considered a vital one in the culture. It is more than a need to recover the costs of the film. Spielberg's statements reflect the larger society's attitude that only a white male is able to define what is important in society. This being the case, Spielberg felt comfortable as the director of the film because he felt that the novel was not about race exclusively: "This is a human story, and the movie is about human beings. It's about men and women. This is a movie about the triumph of the spirit—and spirit and soul never had any racial boundaries." In an earlier interview Spielberg talked about aspects of his background that gave him an understanding of the novel, an emotional connection to it: "It's because *people* are not radically different. All of us are part of some minority. I was Jewish and wimpy when I grew up. That was a major minority. In Arizona, too, where few are Jewish and not too many are wimpy. So I made a lot of connections. I never looked at *Color Purple* as just a black movie. I looked at it as a story for everybody."[19] Spielberg said that the novel *The Color Purple* affected him very deeply and kept "gnawing" at him long after he read it. He came away from reading it "very much in love with Celie" and "obsessed with Mister." He questioned how such a book could have this effect on him when it was written about a culture "that I thought I didn't know much about." Spielberg assesses his relationship to the book as one in which his sensibilities about people and character matched the residue of feeling he had after reading it:

> I realized that I knew a lot about people. And the book is about people. It leaps over stereotypes and over any sort of racial questions. I felt that if it was a racial question, if the book had

> dealt very heavily in black and white issues, one perhaps against the other, in conflict with the other, then I wouldn't have been the right director for the project and I would not have done the movie.[20]

The film *The Color Purple* has been manufactured in line with Steven Spielberg's experiences, cultural background, and social and political worldview. His sensibilities have been shaped by forces different from those that produced the novel. As an example, Spielberg reveals that he was amazed at the number of black actors and actresses who came to audition for him. He said:

> I sort of missed black repertory in America. There just hasn't been a lot of it. There hasn't been enough of it. When I saw the wealth of talent out there when I began casting this film with Reuben Cannon, I couldn't believe it. It shocked me to see so many good black actors. . . . I kept thinking, Where have they been, and where is the outlet to work? I mean, if you don't have the subject matter, there's no work for these talented people.[21]

Black repertory has been around for decades, and black actresses and actors have long been agitating to be cast in roles that were not specifically identified as black. That Spielberg could be isolated from these issues stems from an environment of privilege that has resulted in a racist arrogance. His statement reflects a narrow-minded attitude that if he was not aware of a black repertory then one must not exist. Until a successful white director needs them, the group does not find work. And the issues that are dealt with by a group of black actresses and actors are overlooked until they become important to someone like Spielberg. With his body of films and his tenure in Hollywood, Spielberg's lack of knowledge about these issues is inconceivable—and also the primary reason he made the film as he did. He tapped into his consciousness and experiences and produced a work that was in keeping with his philosophy and knowledge of Hollywood films about black people.

Spielberg's impression that race was not the novel's predominant feature raises the question of how he envisioned it. He saw the story as that of a young girl who is unloved and alone; for him, the novel was "Dickensian."[22] This is an important consideration because it reveals much about the film's structure, subtle racist overtones, and overall mood. Spielberg's reference to Charles Dickens (and Hollywood versions of his novels) shows why the film was made within the genre of melodrama, as were Dickens's novels, why the center of the story shifted from a female perspective to that of a male subjectivity, and why many of the characters' actions were acted out in a stereotypically racist manner.

A melodramatic technique allows an artist to establish a connection with an audience by following a familiar pattern and establishing a recognizable code for interpretation. It emphasizes drastic shifts in mood, vastly different tempos, and a mixture of styles. According to Thomas Elsaesser in "Tales of Sound and Fury: Observations on the Family Melodrama," the novels of Charles Dickens in the nineteenth century featured discontinuity and sudden switches from horror to bliss to emphasize the social contradictions in England's moral fabric.[23] The structure of *The Color Purple* is a conventionalized melodrama of heightened emotionalism induced by music and heart-tugging moments. The film is two hours and thirty-four minutes long and contains almost two hours of music. The parts of the film that are not accompanied by music contain previously recorded natural sounds such as birds chirping, frogs croaking, and wind whistling through the cornstalks.

A potentially powerful scene is always juxtaposed with a comic routine. The transitions occur abruptly, because the film cuts from scene to scene instead of using dissolves. The transitional overlaps are those employing sound—voices, music, or sometimes train wheels and hands clapping. It is this aspect of the design of the film that gives it an ambivalent quality. At times it seems to preserve the tone of the novel—as when Mister's harsh treatment of the young Celie is graphically presented. The moment is lost, however, when there is an abrupt cut to buffoonery, most of which comes from the character Harpo. The character's comic antics and their strategic location lessened the power of such subversive moments as episodes of Mister's abusing Celie and those that show her loneliness and isolation. Two sequences in particular stand out.

The first occurs during the shaving scene with the young Celie and Mister. This sequence comes right after Mister has forced Nettie to leave his farm. As she leaves she points her finger and says that nothing but death can keep her from writing to Celie. Celie stands at the fence, crying and calling Nettie's name. There is a cut to an empty chair on the porch. We hear the sound of Celie's footsteps approaching the chair. She enters from the right of the screen; Mister enters from the left. As Celie begins to shave Mister he grabs her arm, telling her that if she cuts him he will kill her. Celie is terrified. While shaving Mister, Celie nicks him, and he jumps up and raises his arm to strike her. We hear the sound of the mailman approach, and Mister runs to the mailbox. Celie goes into the house and leans on the sink, taking deep breaths. She knows she has had a narrow escape, for if the mailman had not arrived Mister would have struck her.

After Mister reads that Shug is not coming, he yells to Harpo to saddle his horse and enters the house where Celie is cowering. She asks if she can see whether a letter has come from Nettie. This is a medium shot of Celie and Mister. Celie has her back to the camera, and this setup makes her look very vulnerable and small, whereas Mister appears much larger and older. Mister tells Celie that he never wants to see her at the mailbox—he has fixed it so that he can tell if it has been "messed with." Throughout this tirade he jabs his finger at Celie, forcing her backward. He yells at her, "You understand?" The sequence is one of sheer terror for Celie, and we have a sense of Mister's brutality. Immediately there is an abrupt cut to Harpo trying to saddle the horse, and the full impact of the action with Celie is lost.

Another example of the ambivalent structure of the film that conveys a mixed message of anger and comedy again involves a moment with Celie that is disrupted by Harpo's antics. After a comic

Mister (Danny Glover) prepares to strike young Celie (Desreta Jackson) but is interruped by the arrival of the postman, who delivers a letter from Shug

interlude in which the adult Celie helps Mister to get dressed for the arrival of Shug, he leaves, and she begins cleaning the house. She finds the scrap of paper with the word *sky* written on it, which reminds her of Nettie teaching her how to read. Celie stands at the window in close-up, gazing out with the piece of paper clutched in her hand. In the voice-over she says: "She say she write, but she never write. She say only death can keep her from it. Maybe she dead." The moment is held as Celie begins to cry. It is an impressive portrayal of the depth of Celie's loss that is shattered with the next shift to the arrival of Harpo and Sofia walking down the road to the house to meet with Mister.

The sudden changes to Harpo not only undermine the force of the scenes that precede his actions but are stereotypically racist.[24] Even beyond falling through the roof repeatedly, the subtle shifts in Harpo's language recall caricatures of black people from past racist works. When he attempts to saddle the horse for the first time, he misses the horse completely and says, "I'm gitting to it, I'm gitting to it." The viewer has been prepared for the language of the characters, and in many cases some of the words are spoken differently from the way they appear in the book. The word *mammy*, for example, is used sparingly. In the novel the stepfather, Fonso, uses the word *mammy* several times, whereas in the film he says *mama* rather than *mammy*. That he does so indicates Spielberg's partial effort to use as few commonly perceived negative words as possible. The shift in Harpo's words, then, can only be seen as intentional. When the grown-up Harpo saddles the horse he says, "Yessah, Pa, yessah. I's gitting to it. I's gitting to it." Nowhere in the novel is that kind of language used. Alice Walker carefully uses what she categorizes as black "folk language" to show how black people at a particular time and in a specific setting talked and in many instances still talk. She never resorts to the stereotypical words and phrases of the Joel Chandler Harris type, yet in the film the characters—especially Sofia, Shug, and Harpo—occasionally slip into these phrases. This is particularly true of Harpo. When Mister brings Shug home in the wagon Harpo asks repeatedly, "Who dis, Pa? Pa, who dis?" In the novel he merely says, "Who this?"

Spielberg's attempt to emulate the melodramatic conventions of Charles Dickens not only created a disruptive structure but displaced Celie as the central focus of the story. Spielberg constructed three scenes to show the connection with Dickens, with the result that Mister became the central character in the film. The scenes involve Celie or Nettie, or both, and the Dickens novel *Oliver Twist* (1837).

The first scene sets up the connection with the novel. In it Nettie is teaching Celie how to read. The book they are reading is *Oliver Twist*. The sequence begins with a medium shot of Celie and Nettie standing in a swing. We see only their shoes. Celie is hesitantly reading from the book, stumbling many times over the words. When she reaches the word *systematic*, she asks Nettie what it means. Nettie explains in such a way that Celie can relate it to something she does in her life: it's "like when you have a way of doing stuff, and you do it the same way every time." She tells Celie it is similar to the way they hang the sheets first so that—and here Celie joins in with her—they can "put the socks in the cracks."

As young girls, Nettie (Akosua Busia) teaching Celie (Desreta Jackson) to read, using Charles Dicken's *Oliver Twist* (1837) as the textbook.

The next scene occurs as Mister pursues Nettie on the horse while she is on her way to school. As the sequence begins there is a sound overlap that serves as the transition from the previous scene in which Celie and Nettie play their hand-clapping game. As they clap faster and faster, there is a cut to Nettie walking with her schoolbooks in hand. The sound of the claps blends into the sound of the horse's hooves as it trots faster and faster to catch up with Nettie. She turns around to see Mister on the horse approaching her as she walks faster and faster down an incline. The camera moves up into a crane shot, so that what we see is Nettie hurrying away from Mister on the horse. The feeling the scene creates is that she is vulnerable and helpless. There is a cut to Mister on the horse riding beside Nettie, and she fearfully watches to see what he will do. Mister goes through a series of playful routines. As the perspective shifts from Nettie's point of view to that of the viewer, there is a cut to the horse with an empty saddle. Nettie stops and looks; then Mister walks out in front of her. He takes off his hat, and there are purple flower petals on top of his head. Mister grabs Nettie's hands and begins a playful dance. As she attempts to pull away Mister whirls her into the bushes. There is a cut to a shot of the horse grazing, and then the sound of a sharp blow. Mister groans loudly, the horse jumps, and Nettie leaps from the bushes screaming and swinging her books wildly. As the books fly from her hands, there is a close-up of *Oliver Twist*. After a cut to Nettie running away in the distance, Mister rolls over into the frame holding his groin and saying, "I'll gitcha! I'll gitcha!"

The superficial intent of this sequence is to create for the viewer an association with the Dickens's novel; but the underlying message conveys something else. It emphasizes whom Spielberg considers to be the central character in the film. At the moment most women would consider to be a nightmare becoming a reality, what is privileged is the sound of Mister being hit in the groin, an image of the horse jumping, and, as Nettie runs away, Mister falling into the frame with his hands between his legs. Each time I saw this film, surrounded by others in movie theaters, most of the audience members reacted more to Mister's discomfort than to the fact that a young girl had almost just been raped.

The scene is similar to the one at the beginning of the film after Celie has been hit with the rock and Mister is having sex with her. The scene begins with a shot of belts hanging on a headboard. The camera slowly tilts down past a picture of Shug on the stand, into a close-up of Celie lying in the bed with her head wrapped in a bloodied bandage. The familiar rhythmic sound is amplified by the belts banging against the headboard. As we look at Celie, there is a grunt from Mister, and Celie is pulled upward. Mister's arm enters the frame, hits the headboard, and travels down Celie's face past her lips. Celie's voice is heard in the voice-over: "I don't cry. I lay there thinking about Nettie while he on top of me. And wonder if she safe. And then I think about that pretty woman in the picture. I know what he doing to me he done to her. And maybe she like it." The camera pans over the picture of Shug, moves back down to a close-up of Celie and holds on her, and then Mister falls into the frame sighing, "Jesus," as an indication of his exhaustion after intercourse with Celie.

A close-up of *Oliver Twist* as it lies face-up on the ground after Nettie swings her schoolbooks wildly in an attempt to ward off further attacks from Mister.

What should have been an image of repulsion becomes one that emphasizes Mister's gratification. Both these scenes suggest insensate cruelty that is neutralized by their representation and privileging of Mister's reactions rather than that of the victims.

The third *Oliver Twist*–type scene is the transition sequence in which the young Celie becomes the older one. This scene comes on the heels of the one in which the young Harpo saddles the horse. Mister yells out to Celie that he wants his supper when he comes back. We see Celie in a close-up as she responds pitifully, "Yessuh." In the background the shadow of a chair is visible. Celie turns around, walks to the chair—we see her shadow on the wall as she picks up the book—sits down, and begins to read from the Dickens novel. In the voice-over we hear her reading, while there are shots of a purple flyer blowing across the fields, the mailbox, porches, and the tops of houses. It finally settles against a door, face up. The flyer announces the expected arrival of Shug. There is a cut to the older Celie confidently reading the passage from the book. She reads so that the audi-

A moment of transition, as the young Celie is transformed into the older character. The young Celie hesitantly works her way through a passage from *Oliver Twist*.

ence will understand the symbolism that has been presented, that her life is not a good one and fate has dealt her an unfair hand: "For the next eight or ten months Oliver was the victim of a systematic course of treachery and deception. He was brought up by hand. The hungry and destitute situation of the infant orphan . . ."; and her voice blends into the action. Spielberg's sense of the novel *The Color Purple* that the life of a young black girl growing up in a world in which she has no access to power until she empowers herself is equivalent to the life of Oliver as chronicled by Dickens (or translated in film versions of his novels), reveals much about the overall mood of the film. It is one of "sweetness and light" rather than of horror and evil; it is stylized and stagy, as was much of the work of Dickens; and it played too much to the comic elements of life instead of dealing substantially with emotional issues. Some observers make the same assessment of Dickens—that he appeared to be depicting the ordinary life of the Victorian environment, but it was a façade of realism that emphasized the comic and contained stagy aspects of melodramatic conventions.[25]

A shadow of the older Celie (Whoopi Goldberg). In a voice-over, she confidently reads from the Dickens novel: "For the next eight or ten months Oliver was the victim of a systematic course of treachery and deceit."

The transition is now complete. As Mister yells at Celie offscreen, demanding that she help him prepare for his date with Shug, she responds: "Yes, suh?"

The film is frustrating to watch at times as it moves from scenes that are emotionally wrenching to those that are incomprehensible. This is a shortcoming not only of the film but of the genre of melodrama as well. According to Ellen Seiter in "The Promise of Melodrama: Recent Women's Films and Soap Opera," melodrama introduces injustice, evil, and chaos into its dramatic world but does not resolve the issues it portrays except by a "kind of narrative sleight-of-hand." Seiter observes: "Melodrama not only represents a troubled world; its message is itself troubling. In exposing evil and treating the subject of suffering, it raises contradictions which it cannot resolve in a consistent and sensible way."[26] Seiter submits that a critical question regarding the genre of melodrama is whether it will be subversive in its effect on an audience, prompting its members "to recognize oppression and social injustice," or whether it merely functions as a means of escape. That Spielberg structured the film melodramatically both drew an audience into the story and at the same time camouflaged its inadequate and confusing portraits of the three central black women: Shug, Celie, and Sofia. The humorous moments of the film provided comic relief, but the abrupt cut from the dramatic to the comic neutralized its moments of power. The ubiquitous music beneath the emotional scenes was intrusive in many instances but served to move many viewers in spite of themselves. Consequently, Spielberg's use of melodrama both enhanced the film and made its message slippery to comprehend. This is especially true of the way in which the women are presented. Thus what appears to be a story of black women in conflict with the men in their lives contains a vastly different subtext. As structured by Spielberg the film is a throwback to prior demeaning depictions of black women.

Because the film is a reversion to past racist works, a crucial question is whether Spielberg should have been its director. With his previous repertoire of escapist films tailored for a white, middle-class audience and his hallowed stature as the most successful producer and director in the business, could he present the story in a way that realized the intent of the novel? As we can see, he did not.

Unfortunately no black woman has been allowed to develop the track record that Spielberg has. Most industry professionals agree that only Spielberg could have obtained the financing to mount the kind of production that he did. Whether this was beneficial to black people or harmful in the long run remains to be seen. But the issues affecting the condition of black women in this society were debated nationally as they had not been before.

Spielberg as the director of the film did not aid the cause of black women. This is a critical point. The publicity surrounding the film motivated them to see it in large number, become involved in the issues it portrayed, and to become more aware of their status and the historical status of black women. But the movement to give black women a place of importance in this culture came from the women themselves. The film merely cast a spotlight on their efforts.

Paradox and Contradiction

That many black women have responded favorably to the film seems to be another instance of certain audiences having been manipulated by the mechanisms of mainstream media into accepting its repressive ideology without question.

I think the issue can be considered another way. The problem is not with the audience but with flaws in our theories of understanding audience reception of mainstream cultural forms. Audience researcher David Morley reminds us that subjects have histories that come into play at the moment of textual encounter. It is never a matter of one subject, one text, but one of multiple texts and multiple subject histories that will influence the way in which a specific audience constructs meaning from a specific text.[27]

Members of a social audience—people who are actually watching a film or television program—will utilize interpretive strategies that are based upon their past viewing experiences as well as upon their personal histories, whether social, racial, sexual, or economic. This is the cultural competency, the repertoire of background knowledge, that is brought to the act of making sense of a particular text. Black women's reactions to the film *The Color Purple* were a first glimpse into the fact that certain audiences interact with particular works differently. The assumption that reactions could be predicted became moot as black women confounded not only cultural critics but audience researchers as well. Black women's negotiation of a controversial mainstream film allowed researchers to understand that audiences had more control over their reactions to mainstream cultural forms and to other's opinions about how they should react than had been previously assumed, and that their historical and cultural knowledge played a significant role in their responses.

Courtland Milloy, a black columnist for the *Washington Post*, wrote a blistering article about the film and Alice Walker when the film first opened, even though he admitted that he had not seen it. Several months later Milloy wrote another article. This one was entitled "On Seeing *The Color Purple*." Milloy wrote that he went to see the film prepared to dislike it and to resist its emotional pull. What happened to him, he writes, was totally unexpected: "Never in my moviegoing experience have I seen whole rows of black women, teens to elderly, with . . . tears streaming down their faces one moment and eyes bright with laughter the next." Milloy makes an important observation about black women's reaction to the film. He wrote that "the audience . . . shook me up. Here we were watching the same screen, but seeing something completely different."[28]

Mainstream works, based as they are on dominant ideology encoding, have traditionally depicted black people negatively. That black women have engaged positively with the film does not mean that they are unaware of this fact. They have also seen where mainstream cultural products have either ignored their existence totally or honored them with persistently negative portrayals. Because these two factors are critical issues, what needs to be understood is how black women identified with aspects of the film and created meaning from it.

Literary scholar Deborah McDowell insists that Alice Walker deliberately and consciously wrote to an audience of black women.

Walker was aware that the majority of readers of novels in this country are white, but, in using the language that she does within the epistolary mode, she indicates her awareness of other readers. McDowell contends that Alice Walker's intended audience comprises mainly "Walker's 'sisters,' other black women." McDowell offers as support the structure and plot of the novel, which contains two black sisters writing to each other.[29]

McDowell also feels that Alice Walker's novel emphasizes, through its deliberate choice of subjects and images, that earlier black female writers had written without an audience "capable of accepting and appreciating that the full, raw, unmediated range of the black woman's story could be appropriate subject matter for art." According to McDowell, Alice Walker is able to accomplish her "revisionist mission" in *The Color Purple* because of "the social realities and literary circumstances of her place and time."[30] In other words, at the time that *The Color Purple* was published there were other black women actively working to reclaim the black woman's image and to alter substantively the oppressive conditions of black women's lives.

The preoccupations and concerns of these cultural workers have a correspondence in the lives of many black women. As such, the issues addressed in their works can be seen as constituting a repertoire of background knowledge that black women used as a discursive strategy for meaning construction of the film *The Color Purple*. This does not mean that the women who engaged positively with the film were aware of this heritage of black women's activism. It means, rather, that the issues that these women considered to be important were pervasive ones in many black women's lives such that the women were interpellated, or hailed, by a creative work in which these elements were present. Paradoxically, the film was constructed as the antithesis of the novel, and the meanings embedded within it are ones that are deeply ingrained in this culture. The struggle to resist the pull of the film and to extract progressive meanings is the same struggle that many black women have used to resist domination and oppression in everyday life. Thus black women's ability to read against the grain of the film and reconstruct more satisfactory meanings should not be undervalued.

When a particular audience forms an attachment to specific cultural products this is a correspondence that has been achieved, not a guaranteed outcome. The power of that correspondence should not be minimized, for it has potential to become a potent political and social force. Media audience researcher Rosalind Brunt suggests that social movements can "work in and through texts" and that there is a relationship to the "real world." Consequently there is no need to separate audience responses to cultural texts from what she labels "real politics." Brunt feels that cultural products may be one of the "key ideological forms" where there comes to light a "consciousness of conflict" and people are provoked to fight it out. Brunt further notes that by not separating the text from its use in the "real world" critics are directed away from the text as a privileged site of meaning, and audiences become more than mere receivers of others' messages.[31]

Thus cultural critics also accede power to members of the audience instead of granting total authority to the text and those who produced it.

CHAPTER THREE

Watching *The Color Purple*: Two Interviews

Given the similarities of *The Color Purple* to past films that have portrayed black people disparagingly, the fact that a large number of black women have demonstrated positive responses appears to defy explanation. Certainly my analysis of the film's ideological and formal construction by Steven Spielberg shows the subtle manipulations by which black people are indeed depicted in ways that have been harmful in the past. However, there are significant differences, in this specific instance, emanating from black female history and cultural experience that have induced a positive reading or a much more suitable reconstruction of a mainstream cultural product that needs to be considered.

It should also be noted that my examination of black women's responses to *The Color Purple* cannot be used in a one-size-fits-all manner. It would be a mistake to assume that any film or mainstream cultural product is without harmful effects simply because of audiences' ability to read around the text. That so many black women were vocal about their reactions to the film and defended it strongly and, more important, undertook a spirited defense against the attacks on Alice Walker would have gone unnoticed if other black women had not joined with them in a spontaneous, unorganized alliance to preserve their collective character. As black women cultivated resistance strategies during enslavement and fought against all manner of inequities and injustices during the early parts of this century, so too did they use the moment of the entrance of the film *The Color Purple* to advance a better understanding and knowledge of black women's historical and cultural legacy.

The oppositional impulse that has fueled black women's history of resistance is evident in their reactions to *The Color Purple*. The reactions are oppositional in two respects. First, the reactions contradict cohesive reactions by black people to past negative films such as *The Birth of a Nation* (1915), *The Green Pastures* (1936), *Gone with the Wind*, and *Porgy and Bess* (1959). In the case of *The Color Purple* the outrage against the film is not unanimous, for black people, and especially a vocal contingent of black men, are split and at times at odds over the film's effect on the condition of black people in this country.

The second way in which black women's reception of *The Color Purple* is oppositional is that it is a challenge to the mandate, given dominant media coverage, that black people should not have positive responses to the film. Two instances in particular stand out. The first concerned four black male panelists on *Tony Brown's Journal* who debated the effect of the film. Three of the men were united in agreement with Brown that the film was "the most racist depiction of black men since *The Birth of a Nation* and the most antiblack family film of the modern film era." When the fourth panelist, Armond White, spoke in favor of the film, declaring that something worthwhile could come from it, one of the others replied derisively that if White liked the film then he may as well be white.[1]

In another instance a clip of Whoopi Goldberg was shown on *The Phil Donahue Show* while Tony Brown was a panelist. Goldberg said that those who criticize *The Color Purple* as showing negative images of black men should also criticize the singer Prince for the disturbing images he showed of black women being dumped in garbage cans in *Purple Rain*. Brown responded that there were those who practiced the art of saying what white people wanted them to say.[2]

The stakes were high in the discussions concerning the effect of the film, and anyone who did not stand with those who criticized it were at risk of having their allegiance to black people challenged. That many black women clung tightly to their positive feelings about *The Color Purple* was significant in that it allowed them to extract meaningful elements when others were issuing decrees that there should be a wholesale rejection of the film. Although the women's reactions were severely condemned and little understood, these reactions can be seen in the tradition of black women's resistant history. Again, we can go back to Toni Morrison's *Beloved* for an explanation of the motivations behind black women's seemingly outrageous actions. Morrison talks of Sethe's courageous act of going against what society said she should do. As Morrison relates not just about Sethe but about other enslaved black women protecting their children in any way they could from the devastation of enslavement, "It was the right thing to do, but she had no right to do it."[3] Morrison explains what it meant for black women to take control of their family's lives in a society where the laws, institutions, and prevailing codes of behavior were intended to govern the women's actions:

> These women were not parents. People insisted that they have children. But they could not be mothers because they had no say about the future of those children, where they went; they could make no decisions. They frequently couldn't even name them. They were denied humanity in a number of ways. . . . So she [Sethe] claimed something she had no right to claim, which was the property, her property. And claimed it so finally that she decided that she could not only dictate their lives, but end them. And when one knows what their future would be, her decision is not that difficult to understand.

Admittedly, the reactions of a group of viewers to a cultural product is not the same as someone resisting years of brutalization and the prospect that her children would suffer the same fate. However, if we consider the cumulative effect of decades of derogatory representations of black women in mainstream culture and the subsequent transfer of the images as justification for debilitating institutional and social policies, then the symbolism of black women in resistance is more congruent. It is the same spirit manifested by black women during enslavement that impelled black women viewers of the contemporary film to speak out in support of their rights as audience and in defiance of how others felt they should respond.

An additional consideration is that as cultural consumers black women, along with everyone else in consumer culture, have been constantly enjoined to attend films, to watch television programs, to consume all manner of cultural forms in which their history, experiences, and bodies were characterized in a variety of demeaning ways. There is no evidence, however, that black women as a group ever exhibited the same response to previous mainstream works as that given *The Color Purple*. A partial explanation for this lies in the way in which black women were presented in the film. For the first time black women were seen in dominant media as a major focus of the work. Although, as my analysis detailed, black women were moved aside as the center of the story and a black man's experiences were privileged, black women were, nonetheless, constantly on the screen and were seen in ways not displayed before.

As an example, for a major motion picture, technicians took care in lighting, costume, and set design so that black performers did not fade into the background. Allen Daviau, director of photography for *The Color Purple*, explains that he and production designer Michael Riva and set decorator Linda DeScenna discovered a way of photographing black people that had not been attempted before. Darkening the set in addition to having the performers wear dark-colored costumes appeared to be a paradox, but it allowed more subtlety of lighting. This in turn separated the black performers from the background so that there was greater clarity in the images rather than a flattening out and competition with the background elements.[4]

This technical aspect contributed to black women's incentive to identify with the women in the film, because the characters did not appear *photographically* as caricatures—although the women I interviewed were not in agreement about the effect of the "look" of the film. One of the women expressed a feeling that was similar to one of the predominant criticisms by mainstream reviewers—that the novel was more "gritty," and Spielberg obscured its message by making the film look too nice. The woman who agreed with this sentiment stated that this offended her immediately when she first watched the film:

> I thought, Damn, this man [Spielberg] is trying to say, "Oh, look, they had a rough life, but wasn't it pretty." I mean, look at all the purple flowers. And he's saying, "Yeah, they had nappy heads and they had a hard life, but wasn't it pretty how the sun is coming in in all those shots." He romanticized it all the way through—and the music, it was that stereotypical old white romanticized music.

When I asked her if she wanted a grittier depiction of the characters' lives, the woman replied that she wanted a more realistic film.

It is interesting that those reviewers who criticized the "prettiness" of the film as being antithetical to the novel seem to be unaware of Alice Walker's often-expressed statement that the people she characterized in the novel were not poor, that they owned land, property, and dealt in commerce. So the presumed dark and somber ambience of *The Color Purple* would have to come from the minds of the viewers, because the characters as written by Walker were not in fact impoverished. It also speaks to many people's store of associations that whenever black people are rendered in a widely circulated work, if they are not presented as poor and downtrodden they appear "unreal" because there had been, up to that time, a scarcity of images in dominant media of well-to-do black people.

Another woman I interviewed had a contrasting view on the look of the film:

> I like the fact that it wasn't gritty. I think that if it had been gritty it would have been too much to handle. It was difficult to handle as it was; it was just real powerful. It was a lot to handle at one time. Sometimes you felt like someone had [here she makes a cutting motion across her chest] really exposed me. If it had been grittier it might have made that even more uncomfortable, or it might have made me back away from it so much that I couldn't feel it. It would have been too ugly. Because that's ugly; that behavior is very ugly. And I think if it had been realistic, it would have been too ugly for me to watch. And I wouldn't have seen it.

Yet another woman I interviewed spoke about the technical aspects of the film. This woman, however, talked about the subtle differences in the way in which the characters were presented. As the woman stated, Celie is photographed lovingly, whereas the character who plays Nettie, although just as dark and just as photogenic, is not. The contrast is a significant one because it illustrates two things. The first is that a director who is of the culture being portrayed is more likely to present all the characters in compatible ways, such as was the case with Dash and *Daughters of the Dust*. As director she took care and consideration in photographing not just the central character but all the people in the film, including the men.

The second part of the woman's comment relates to the way in which viewers can perceive the differences take note of them yet still find elements in the film they could enjoy and identify with. It is only when audience members are asked about their reactions that these perceptions come to light. Rather than castigate the women for their engagement with the film, I asked them to explain it, and they were able to do so. Consequently, the women can be seen as much more than "cultural dupes"—they are viewers who understand that they do not have control over image creation in mainstream media but that they do have control over how they will exhibit their responses. Thus the value of interviewing the women allows analysts to understand that audiences are not always the unthinking receivers of media messages but have the ability to manipulate their reactions in very distinctive ways. The issue then becomes what the women identified with and how that identification either was or could potentially be utilized, for progressive purposes.

For my research on *The Color Purple* I conducted two separate group interviews with black women who had seen the film. The first was conducted in December 1987 in northern California; the second was conducted in October 1988 in the Pacific Northwest. There were nine women in the first group and six in the second, for a total of fifteen women interviewed. Before the interviews I did a comprehensive review of the literature in an effort to chart black women's responses in newspapers, magazines, and journals and on radio programs. I also watched many of the nationwide television programs on which the film was discussed. These included two programs on *Tony Brown's Journal*, one of which was set up as a debate between black feminist Barbara Smith and black writer Ishmael Reed. I also watched *The Phil Donahue Show*, which presented black film historian Donald Bogle and Tony Brown as well as the lone woman on the panel, Michele Wallace.

I also had discussions with several of the black female scholars who were publicly defending Alice Walker's novel and black women's reactions to the film. A key person was Barbara Christian, who traveled extensively at the time of the initial release of the film in 1986, speaking to groups of black women in a variety of settings.[5] From this research and from conversations I was able to confirm my impressions that many black women had had an overwhelmingly positive reaction to the film.

At the beginning of the interviews I questioned the women in both groups about whether they were religious, because I needed to be able to gauge their reactions to aspects of the novel and the film that dealt with religious issues, such as when Shug, in the novel, talks to Celie about her feelings about God. When Shug asks Celie what her God looks like, Celie replies that she thinks of God as "big and old and tall and graybearded and white." Shug tells her that her description is the one that white folks use to describe their God, the one that is written about in their Bible. That is why their God looks like them. Celie tells Shug that her sister, Nettie, had written to her from Africa that Jesus's hair was like lamb's wool. Shug, referring to a much-noted hair and color bias among black people,[6] says to Celie about the texture of Jesus's hair: "If he came to any of these churches we talking bout he'd have to have it conked before anybody paid him any attention. The last thing niggers want to think about they God is that his hair kinky."[7]

Curiously, no one expressed a particular feeling about the religious parts of the novel. This is surprising, because it is evident that Walker is presenting a critique of pervasive religious attitudes among black people, and Walker's view of religion appears to be more one of pantheism than a belief in a great white deity in heaven. The women I interviewed had no reaction to Walker's representation of religion. There were, however, comments about religious moments in the film. A woman in each group mentioned the scene in which Shug leads the people who were at the juke joint down the road to the church, singing. Both the women thought the scene looked fake and was out of place in the film. In the second group two of the women disagreed that the scene was misplaced. They said that it reminded them of being in church, where people would come from outside and become part of the congregation. This drew comments from the other women: "I didn't ever think I would feel that way when I was in church. I noticed that when I was going through my deepest, hardest time, if I would go to church and get involved in the service, and they would start singing like that, I could feel the spirit."

To this statement another woman added that it was "God's spirit or somebody else's, but it was some spirit." The first woman responded that she did believe in a Creator: "I have a difficulty believing in the kind of God that I see lots of people worship. But I know there's a Creator. But my view is probably different from what they would say the Creator is supposed to be."

Another woman joined in the sentiments expressed by the women about their feelings about a God: "Nobody can have as many good things happen to them as have happened to me (without a whole lot of effort on my part) without something, some single spirit, some collective spirit, providing some support and guidance. I don't know if I believe in—what is it? The one, the two, and the three? The Trinity and all that, or a real, literal interpretation of the Bible, but I do believe there is something."

The women's expressed views about the religious parts of the film are important, because they indicate the complexities involved in audience studies, especially with groups in which there are few previous studies. There are no precedents or set guidelines, and the researcher runs into others' predetermined attitudes about how the participants' comments should be assessed. With groups who have been ignored in any analysis of media responses there is a tendency for outsiders to rush into judgment rather than consider the groups' background, histories, and social and cultural experiences. Thus when the women respond in unexpected ways their statements are dismissed rather than considered within the specifics of their lives. This is illustrated especially in the women's comments about the religious elements of the film. In considering their statements it is important to understand how religion has been an integral part of black history, even though it is contested terrain for radical scholars. As Stuart Hall reminds us, religion has been used to maintain ideological control over many societies in numerous epochs.[8] However, research data shows that religion is very important in black people's lives, with over sixty-five thousand black churches in the country with a collective membership of over twenty-four million people.[9] Although radical scholars question the viability of black churches and black religious attitudes, with so many black people involved in some kind of religious activity it is necessary to examine the historical evolution of their religious bonds rather than continually to condemn them. Cornel West, writing about the ways in which black people have fought against an array of forces aligned to thwart their progress and, more important, about how black people have constructed "cultural armor" to maintain a sense of hope and meaning in their lives, notes that the creation of black religious institutions was one of the "cultural structures of meaning and feeling that created and sustained" black communities.[10]

What this means in examining the comments from the women I interviewed is that it is important to go beyond a quick and superficial analysis of their statements and to consider their responses within the totality of their lives and within the full range of black women's past. Their statements may contradict radical sentiments, but there is no guarantee that those who claim to speak for the multitudes have any greater purchase on "truth" than the women I interviewed. As the earlier reference from John Fiske indicated, radical scholars are not always in step with those whom they are trying to engage. If more contact was made with those who participate in a range of everyday activities and who watch and view a variety of cultural forms, then there would be a greater understanding of the ways in which audiences (and a populace) negotiate their existence in a society not of their making but with some attempts at control.

The ages of the women in the first group I interviewed ranged from early forties to late fifties. All were employed or had worked at some point in their lives. One was retired. All except two had children. Three were born in the South and had moved away when they were young. One was born and raised in the Northeast, three in the Midwest, and one in the Southwest. All but two of the women had had some college education; four held advanced degrees.

The six women in the second group ranged in age from thirty to thirty-seven. Two of the women, along with their husbands, were best friends who socialized together frequently. All four were born and raised in the South, specifically in Georgia and South Carolina. Another woman in attendance was born in the rural South and had recently lived for a time in Atlanta, Georgia. One of the women had grown up in predominantly white neighborhoods in California, one was from Chicago, and another was raised in various cities in northern California and Oregon.

Three of the women in the second group were married, two were divorced, and one had never been married. Two had children. All had attended or were, at the time of the interview, attending college. One was a graduate student and another an undergraduate. Three held advanced degrees. All the women were employed, including those who were attending school. Two of the women worked at a large electronics firm in midlevel positions; one was a substitute elementary school teacher who had just moved to the area. One of the women worked as a manager of a small, community-based public service organization.

For my analysis of both sets of interviews I have changed the names of the women to preserve anonymity. The names given to the women in the first group are Christine, Stephanie, Cecelia, Lucille, Charlotte, Margaret, Danielle, Paige, and Constance. The names of the women in the second group are Morgan, Phyllis, Marilyn, Anne, Grace, and Whitney.

All of the women in the second group had read the book before seeing the film. In the first group about half the women had read the book first. All the women in both groups had read the novel and seen the film before the interviews. Six of the women in the first group had seen the film more than once while it was still in the theaters, and several had seen it again on video. Three of the women in the second group had seen the film twice.

Both groups were assembled for the specific purpose of discussing *The Color Purple* and other matters related to the status of black women in society. The responses from the women in the second group are especially informative because of the unique nature of the interview, which was conducted while the women were watching the videotape of *The Color Purple*. The discussion continued beyond the video as well, but their immediate, visceral responses were significant to my research because the women reacted to moments in the film that they may not have been able to recall later. Also, because all of us were watching the film together the women became comfortable enough with me present as researcher to make comments that they may have censored otherwise had the researcher not also been a black woman.

The setting for the first group of interviews was a metropolitan city with a markedly diverse economic and racial population. The location for the second set of interviews was a predominantly, almost monolithically, white city of about forty thousand people, located in the Pacific Northwest. The two major employers are a university and an electronics firm. It is an insulated community located some distance from two major metropolitan areas.

From the outset the women found moments in the film that resonated with elements in their lives. As the film opens Celie and Nettie, both young girls, play in a field of flowers. Fonso, their mother's husband, who they think is their father, approaches ominously and tells them to come in to supper. Celie smiles nervously as Nettie circles around her protectively. Fonso, looking at Celie, who is young, pregnant, and self-conscious, folds his arms across his chest and tells her: "Celie, you got the ugliest smile this side of Creation." Celie puts her hand up to hide her smile. Nettie looks at Fonso with anger and disgust and pulls Celie's hand down from her face.

The women react strongly to this scene. When Fonso tells Celie that she has an unattractive smile there were murmurings of disapproval from the women with whom I watched the film, and in the later discussions this was seen as a significant part for several of them. Morgan related that this scene made her realize that feelings she had about herself were also shared by others. She conveyed that it and other seemingly inconsequential parts of the film, "the little things," added up to her feeling as though she were looking in a mirror. Morgan noted that after Fonso commented to Celie about her smile she never smiled again without covering up her face. Morgan recalled observations that were made about her by important people in her life, such as her mother and her husband, that affected how she thought of herself. Relating this to *The Color Purple*, Morgan said that as she watched the film she realized that those attitudes belonged to her mother and her husband and weren't necessarily shared by other significant people in her life. Summing up the way in which the film affected her perceptions, she said that it was not a big moment that changed her life but "a lot of little issues coming from a lot of different places in the film."

Paige, from the first group, related this portion of the film to a later segment in which Shug tells Celie that she has a beautiful smile and should stop covering up her face. Paige said that she could relate to that part because the exchange with Shug made Celie's transformation at the end of the film so much more powerful. Paige recalled that everyone who loved Celie—Shug and Nettie—kept telling her to put her hand down: "That last time that Celie put her hand down nobody told her to put her hand down. She had started coming into her own. So when she grabbed that knife, she was ready to use it."

This comment refers to a scene near the end of the film when Mister and his family are sitting around the dinner table as Celie and Shug are preparing to leave for Memphis. Mister begins to chastise Celie, telling her that she will be back: "You ugly, you skinny, you shaped funny, and you scared to open your mouth to people." Celie at first sits quietly and takes Mister's verbal abuse. Then she asks him, "Any more letters come?" She is referring to letters that Nettie has written to her from Africa, which Mister has been hiding and Celie has recently found. Mister replies nonchalantly, "Could be, could be not. Who's to say?" Celie jumps up at that point, grabs a knife, and sticks it to Mister's throat.

In Paige's assessment of the significance of this scene, she says about Celie: "But had she not got to that point, built up to that point [of feeling that she was worthwhile], she could have grabbed the knife and turned it the other way for all that it mattered to her. She wouldn't have been any worse off. But she saw herself getting better. So when she grabbed that knife, she was getting ready to use it, and it wasn't on herself."

For many of the women in both groups this was considered a powerful moment in the film, because it marks a turning point for Celie, from someone who continually accepts abuse to a person who fights back against oppressive conditions. Comments from the

Black female viewers of *The Color Purple* were especially empowered by the female characters' assertive actions during the sequence featuring the family at the dinner table

women in the first group revealed the variety of emotions the women experienced while watching the film, as well as their view that if Celie had not changed, they would have had different responses. That she did was seen as empowering for the women because they felt she took charge of her life—as they saw that they had to do in the face of overwhelming odds. The women I interviewed did not consider themselves to be losers or in any way defeated by their life circumstances, and they liked the fact that a black woman was shown in a way they felt was similar to the way in which they dealt with adversities in their lives. Constance, in the first group, said that if Celie had not changed she would have been disgusted: "That just gets to me, about the roles of females. If they don't change, I don't want to watch it." Lucille added this observation:

> I had different feelings all the way through the film, because first I was very angry, then I started to feel so sad I wanted to cry because of the way Celie was being treated. It just upset

One of the women interviewed stated that Celie's retaliation against Mister's abuse marked a turning point, for then Celie evolved from being submissive to placing a higher value on herself.

> me, the way she was being treated and the way she was so totally dominated. But gradually, as time went on, she began to realize that she could do something for herself, that she could start moving and progressing, that she could start reasoning and thinking things out for herself. In the end I felt a little proud of her from the way she began and the way she grew.

To this statement Margaret commented that she was proud of Celie for her growth: "The lady was a strong lady, like I am. And she hung in there and overcame."

As their statements indicate, the display of Celie's strength, especially during the scene at the dinner table, was impressive and significant for the women. It was also a key indication of the ways in which the women reconstructed the film, because this scene was among those that had been altered from the novel. Additionally, this part was a graphic example of Spielberg's ambivalent structure for the film. Once again, moments of power were juxtaposed with comic and severely caricatured segments. This was especially true of the way in which Old Mister's antics and those of Harpo and Sofia were constantly interspersed with the women's actions.

In this scene all the women—Celie, Shug, Sofia, and Squeak—speak and exhibit power. For the first time in the film, in fact, Squeak insists on being called by her name, Mary Agnes, rather than "Squeak," as she has been called throughout the film. In the novel, this was actually the second time Squeak demanded to be called Mary Agnes. The first was after she was raped by her uncle, the white sheriff, after she went to the jail in a ruse concocted by the family to get Sofia released on parole. If a viewer could physically edit the film and remove the comic routines, as it appears that the women I interviewed did mentally, then the sequence featuring the women at the dinner table becomes a pivotal and empowering moment of the film.

Shug speaks first, informing Mister that Celie is going to Memphis with her and Grady. Mister replies that Celie's departure will be over his dead body. Shug answers, "You satisfied? That's what you want?" Celie then delivers her message that Mister is "a low-down, dirty dog. It's time for me to get away from you and into Creation. Yo' dead body be just the welcome mat I need." Her next declaration is the spark that wakes Sofia from her somnambulate, "confused" state. Celie tells Mister that he is no better than "some dead horse shit" and that his kids made her life there hell. She refers to them as "these fools you never tried to raise." Speaking over Harpo's objections, Celie informs him and everyone else at the table that if Harpo had not tried so hard to "rule over Sofia, white folks never woulda got her." She then tells Mister when he continues to berate her that until he does right by her everything he even thinks about is destined to fail. Mister sees this as a curse, so he yells at Celie: "Who do you think you is? You can't cuss nobody. Look at you. You black, you poor, you ugly, you a woman. You nothing at all." As Celie, Shug, Grady, and Mary Agnes begin to drive away, Celie raises her hand and issues the final warning to Mister: "Everything you done to me is already done to you." She finishes with an affirmation of her knowledge that she has indeed become a worthwhile person: "I'm poor, black; I may even be ugly. But, dear God, I'm here. I'm here."

As the women in the second group watched the film they analyzed Celie's transformation. They compared it to black women who tap into their resources to survive, and compared Celie to those who are so abused that they do not survive.

In the film when Nettie comes to live with Celie and Mister because Fonso continues to force himself upon her, she sees Mister's kids running wild over Celie. She tells Celie not to let the kids take advantage of her and that she should stand up for herself. Nettie, however, is hotly pursued by Mister. When she rebuffs him he gets angry and forces her to leave. Celie is distraught that Nettie must leave her and attempts to hold on as Mister tries to force the two of them apart. Nettie eventually runs down the road, but not without telling Celie that nothing but death will keep them apart.

As Mister orders Nettie to leave his property and Celie clings to her, some of the women felt that Celie needed to be stronger. Grace said that Celie needed to fight back; Morgan said that back then the women had a different kind of behavior. Phyllis said that Celie did not know that she could fight back, that she had low self-esteem.

Grace [observing Nettie leaving]: See, she is going someplace else.

Whitney: If you are confronted with a situation like that, in my mind, Celie *needs* to go someplace else.

Morgan: But Celie doesn't have the same spirit. Celie has no self-esteem. Zero.

Phyllis: Celie's already been beaten to the ground.

Whitney: I understand that. I also understand the bond between two sisters too . . . I would not leave that property without my sister. [She repeats her statement.] I would not leave that property without my sister.

Phyllis: It's easy to say you understand it, but if you haven't been there—see, I've been there.

Whitney: Well, none of us have been *there*.

Phyllis: Yeah, I've been there. I've been *there*. I've been in that very same situation. But it is a situation in which you can say something is supposed to occur; this is a survival situation. The women are trying to survive, see. They have no place to go. They don't have anything to look forward to. I mean, we do have options now. But they didn't have any options. They were somebody's chattel.

Morgan: I'm not saying that Celie would have gone anyway, but you always have an option.

Grace: I'm afraid I don't understand that, because I've never been in that situation; but don't you, even if you have been beaten to the ground long enough, say, "I'm better than this"?

Whitney: Yeah.

Phyllis: No, girlfriend, it don't work like that.

Morgan: After a point, Celie gets there—where she knows that she's better. But how long does it take her?

Phyllis: But everybody doesn't do that, either. Look around you at the women who are continually abused. All their lives they *look* for abuse. They actually *seek* abuse, because that's the way they define themselves. You can't see it because—I don't know—I think sometimes that some of us are very naive. And there's nothing wrong with that. There's nothing wrong with being naive. Celie doesn't think that if she cuts his throat, he can't kill her.

In the film the young Celie prepares to shave Mister because he thinks Shug is coming. As the scene begins we see the rocking chair on an otherwise empty porch. Celie enters the frame with the straight razor, and Mister enters from the other side with the towel, saying to himself, "My Shug is coming, and everything gonna be the way it should be. Come on, girl. I'm waiting." Mister puts the towel around his neck, and Celie moves the razor toward his neck to shave him. Suddenly, he grabs her arm and warns her, "You cut me, and I'll kill you!"

Whitney: She does think about it.

Phyllis: She thinks about cutting his throat, but she also thinks about the consequences of not killing him, which is another beating. Which is more abuse.

Morgan: I don't think that in this particular scene she even really thought about cutting his throat.

Phyllis: She's thinking about it; she's thinking about it now. But she's a young girl. She doesn't realize that if she cuts his throat bad enough he's not going to be able to hurt her. All she's thinking is that if she cuts his throat and he survives she's gonna have to suffer the consequences.

Whitney: She's thinking about it now.

Phyllis: Even if she nicks the man. [She pauses.] It takes a lot to come out of low self-esteem. It takes a lot.

Whitney: But not a whole lot to get in it.

Phyllis: Not a whole lot to get in it, you're right. All it takes is one word, one person, somebody that you think is supposed to be caring about you, somebody that you have the impression that they define who you are. And if they tell you enough times and they treat you enough like you don't mean anything, you begin to actually believe that.

Morgan: If people you value don't value you—

Phyllis: And I think, in a way, that's the way black people have been in the past. Because somebody told them that they were not worthy, and we believed that for so long that it kept us from doing some of the things we needed to do to progress out of that stage. Sometimes it means that you gotta die, but you have to have enough pride, enough self-esteem, to say, "I'd rather die than live in this."

Whitney: I understand her situation, and I understand as much as I can understand what's going on, but I still believe we always have choices.

Phyllis: Of course we do, but the thing is learning how to make those choices. Everybody doesn't learn how to make those choices.

Morgan: Some people don't even recognize that they had a choice.

While watching the scenes involving Harpo and his attempts to dominate Sofia, the women continue discussing black women who are survivors. In the film, after Sofia and Harpo fight, Sofia's family packs up her belongings and takes her and her kids away in the back of a wagon. Whitney says, "Celie ought to be right on the back of that thing. She needs to go on with that woman. Break camp."

Phyllis: You folks be talking about she should have gone with her, but you have to remember, girlfriend's mouth got her in jail for a while.

Whitney: That's true. Well, you gotta do what you gotta do. It's all about integrity.

Phyllis: First, it's about survival. Then it's about integrity.

When Sofia's troubles with the authorities were portrayed the women became upset and made very pointed comments. In the film Sofia and her boyfriend, the prizefighter Buster Broadnax, are in town with Sofia's kids. The mayor and his wife walk over to Sofia and her kids, and the wife begins to make a fuss over them. In the background the mayor is heard drawing the attention of some white townspeople passing by to "Miss Millie, always going on over the coloreds."

Marilyn: Those who work with white folk.

[Someone says, "Lord, have mercy." Someone else says, "Kissing all on his face" (the scene in which one of Sofia's kids wipes the kiss off).]

Phyllis: But, you know what—if you kiss their kids, they just be wiping that shit off.

[Everybody laughs and agrees.]

Whitney: Thing is, don't do it, you hear?

When the mayor's wife says of Sofia's kids, "Y'all so clean," Grace parrots her by saying, "So clean." Everyone is angry at the mayor's wife for thinking that they would not be clean.

Morgan: At least she had sense enough to know she was totally out of control.

JB: Yeah. With her kids?

Morgan: Yeah [suggesting that Sofia at least understood her temper enough to know to make sure her kids were safe].

The action of the film shows the mayor's wife asking Sofia if she would like to work for her as her maid. Sofia replies, "Hell, no." The mayor's wife asks her what she said, and Sofia repeats her statement. The mayor becomes angry and walks over to Sofia, questioning her about what she said to his wife. When Sofia repeats, "Hell, no," he slaps her. Sofia, in turn, punches the mayor, who falls down. At that point all the townspeople run over and surround Sofia. She calls to Buster and Swain to get her children away as the townspeople yell and call her names. One white woman taunts, "You black slut. Who do you think you are?" When a white man says to Sofia, "Who do you think you are, you fat nigga?" the women watching are visibly upset.

Whitney: He enjoyed that.

Phyllis: You know, we didn't get no respect [i.e., when the sheriff knocks Sofia to the ground with his gun butt].

Whitney: Whew, Lord.

Marilyn: His fist would have been enough.

[Everyone is upset. Phyllis and Morgan start crying.]

Whitney: This is what broke me up.

[Morgan and Marilyn agree.]

Marilyn: Then to put her in jail—and she ended up working for them anyway.

At this point in the film it is Christmas, and Sofia has been released from jail on probation and is in the custody of the mayor and his wife. One of her jobs is to teach the wife how to drive. The mayor's wife drives wildly and recklessly, and as she and Sofia careen through the town the people on the street scatter out of the way. As they approach the store to do their Christmas shopping the mayor's wife is chatting gaily and weaving from one side of the street to the other. Sofia sits in the car with her head down and looks totally defeated. Marilyn is angry about what is happening in this scene.

Marilyn: Why would she choose to have Sofia in her life?
Grace: As punishment. That's the ultimate punishment—you've got to wait on me for the rest of your life. That's the ultimate punishment.
Marilyn: But would you want someone—
Whitney: —but, see, you're thinking the way you would think.
Marilyn: That's all I can do.
Morgan: You're just not that sadistic.

As Sofia and the mayor's wife enter the store, the mayor's wife hands Sofia her shopping list and directs her to get the items listed. Sofia only has one good eye; the other was smashed by the sheriff when he hit her with the butt of his gun. As Sofia tries to read the list, Celie, who has been silently observing the mayor's wife ordering Sofia around, approaches her quietly. She takes the list from Sofia and begins to place the groceries in a shopping bag. While this takes place the mayor's wife is talking nonsense to the owner of the store about Mars and how she would like to know what it's like to live there.

Phyllis: Fool.
Whitney: God forgive me, but I'd kill that woman. I'd kill that woman dead. You hear me?
[Grace starts laughing.]
Marilyn: The film made her look like an asshole.
JB: Well, you know, one of the criticisms about that part is that they made it seem like the white woman was the exception—just a silly little white woman. Her comment about Mars, and stuff like that, rather than that was routine treatment. What do you think?
Marilyn: Well, I certainly know better. I certainly know that she probably represents the majority. No, I don't think they make her less exceptional.

Anne: I think they do. Because all of a sudden you see the town. You see all the white folk in town. You didn't see all the white people in town before. And all of a sudden they're there. And she's the one who's the center of this whole thing. On the whole you don't see them.

Whitney: There are certain black neighborhoods like mine [i.e., where she grew up in South Carolina]—you can stay there today and not see white people.

Grace: In my neighborhood [i.e., where she grew up] we never saw white people. I lived in an all-black neighborhood. I didn't really see white people, even when we went to town. The section in Atlanta was black in the sixties when I grew up.

Whitney: And it's still ninety-five percent.

Grace: So my only real interaction with whites was when I went to college. And I think that was black parents' way of protecting their children from all the racism. It was not quite as severe as this.

[Whitney is agreeing throughout.]

Grace: I think that was their unconscious way of protecting us from all the things that would come along.

JB: Where did you go to college?

Grace: At Georgia State, which is predominantly white.

JB: How was it? Going from an all-black neighborhood—

Grace: It was more of a shock than coming out here.

[Whitney, Phyllis, and I react to this.]

Whitney: You betta take that back—

Grace: Yeah. Let me change that. It was different because I had a support group.

Whitney: You could go home.

Grace: Yeah. When it would get three o'clock I was back in the black community, so all the changes I went through at Georgia State were like, Okay, I can do this for six hours, and get my support, and go back.

Whitney: That's right.

At another point in the discussion Whitney elaborated on Grace's point.

Whitney: You talking about integration, I happen to think personally, that *Brown vs. the Board* was probably the worst thing that ever happened to our people.

Phyllis: I agree. I went to segregated schools in elementary school. I started out at a Catholic school with white students, and yeah, I was speaking French and doing little Catholic things and all that stuff, but there was something about going to an all-black school . . . the teachers—

Grace: —they cared—

Phyllis: Everybody cared. If I screwed up in school—

Grace: Before you would get home they would tell your mamma.

Phyllis: Everybody would. And that is that carryover from Africa; we have lost that. And that is so sad. Because the kids now, they have no respect for life experiences. They have no understanding of what it takes to struggle. We give our children everything, we put them in these upper middle-class houses, we buy them cars. My son got mad because he asked me for a car and I told him I wasn't buying him doodley-squat 'til I saw some grades coming in. It is expected that we give them everything; they expect us to go out and buy the Guess jeans, the Swatch watches, the Reeboks, and all that stuff. They don't know how to wait for anything—it's instant gratification; everybody wants it right now. And these white kids, the way they talk to their parents—if they were my children, they would not have teeth in their mouths. They might not even be living now.

At this point Whitney makes a comment that seems not to relate to what Phyllis is saying; however, the tape is still playing, showing what is happening with Sofia and her probation with the mayor, his wife, and family.

Whitney: You know another thing—part of me is grateful that she [Sofia] slugged that man [after he slapped her].
Whitney: That she had the courage—
Grace: —to release that tension.

Although the majority of the women in both groups had talked more about Celie's growth and Sofia's strength, Danielle, in the first group, felt that Shug was a better "role model" in the film. She insisted that the other women were off the mark in characterizing Celie and Sofia as the major catalysts for the other women in the story coming into their own, because she felt Shug provided the incentive for all the other characters to change. As Danielle declared: "She [Shug] was the catalyst for everything. I really don't think Celie would have risen above her situation or recovered from it had it not been for the power of this other woman. So I identified very much with the sisterhood."

Danielle was also angry with those critics of the film who characterized the bond between Shug and Celie as a homosexual relationship. As she spoke there was strong agreement from the other women, especially from Danielle's mother, Margaret. Danielle stated

> I was very offended by things people were saying about this movie. When people started talking about homosexuality and lesbianism, that really offended me. As I read the book both times, I really didn't have any reaction that "this was a lesbian situation." [There is continual agreement from the others in the group. Margaret states several times, as Danielle is speaking, "Sisters, sisters."] As I read it and as I felt it, the woman [Shug] was actually showing her how to love and how it feels to be loved. [Margaret underscores Danielle's sentiments by saying again, "Sisters, sisters."] Because she [Celie] had no self-concept, her self-esteem was zero. She's just mentally put down. And so I think Shug had enough love in her to share with this other woman. I think Shug made the supreme effort to show her how to love. And I really didn't

> think it was lesbianism or homosexuality. I liked it because I like to see black women reach out to other black women, lift each other up, hold each other up, be there when we need each other.

When the scenes in which Shug kisses Celie were shown, it was helpful to watch them in the presence of the women in the second group. Their reactions were important to observe as the scenes were taking place. When Shug first appears in the film after coming to live with Mister and Celie, Whitney, in the second group, declares: "She's the only one to really control him." Phyllis states, "Naw, he fool enough to be pussy-whipped. He controls himself. She just says the words that pull the string." When Shug first sees Celie and tells her that she is indeed ugly, Whitney and Grace consider this a mean putdown. Grace replies, "She must be from Atlanta." As Celie is helping Shug in the bath when she is recovering from her illness, the women begin to discuss their feelings about Celie's and Shug's relationship.

> Whitney: The book played a little bit more on the relationship between those two women. [Everyone agrees.]
> Morgan: I think that would have been hard for them to bring to the film.
> Whitney: I think the little bit they did bring was pretty hard for a lot of people to accept.
> Morgan: Shoot, it was hard for me.
> JB: To watch?
> Morgan: Yeah.
> JB: Why?
> Morgan: I'm just not real comfortable with that.
> Grace: But she needed that.
> Whitney: Yeah.
> JB: Was it hard for you to read it in the book?
> Morgan: Not as much in the book.
> Whitney: Because you didn't see it so graphically?
> Morgan: Yes.

Grace: But she needed that, she did.

Whitney: Yeah. Like Phyllis was saying. Regardless of where it's coming from.

Morgan: It wasn't that I thought it was a bad thing.

Whitney: You weren't prepared for it.

Morgan: I just wasn't prepared for it, and it was not *my* thing. And it's so different from *my* thing that it was hard for me to relate to it.

Whitney: I found it really difficult to deal with when that white man hit what's-her-name, Harpo's wife, than I did that part. That was difficult for me to deal with, sitting in a theater surrounded by white men. It was difficult.

Phyllis: I guess the reason why I didn't find it offensive was that there was some actual caring there.

[Whitney and Grace agree.]

Whitney: I didn't find it offensive. Not at all. I was just uncomfortable. Just awkward.

Phyllis: I didn't find it uncomfortable.

JB: To watch it?

Morgan: Yes.

Whitney: I would, probably.

Phyllis: That's something that's private.

Morgan: Yes. I guess that's it. The only reason that I don't find it uncomfortable with men and women is that I've seen it so much. When I first started seeing women and men on television and the movies involved in very intimate behavior I found that uncomfortable, too, because I felt like I was peeking in somebody's window, where I had no business being. And I guess I saw that as being similar, and I wasn't accustomed to it.

After Shug sings in the juke joint and everyone begins to fight, Shug leads Celie away from the fight and into her dressing room. Celie emerges shyly from another room, wearing the red dress in which Shug performed. Shug tries to get her to loosen up by playing some lively music and showing Celie how to move her body. Celie giggles self-consciously and keeps putting her hand up to her mouth. Shug asks her why she's always covering up her smile and tells Celie to show her some "teef." Celie begins to smile shyly and again puts her hands up to her mouth. Shug comes behind Celie and puts her arms around her, holding Celie's hands to prevent her from bringing them up to her mouth. As Celie begins to laugh freely, Shug tells her, "See, Miss Celie, you gots a beautiful smile."

Shug next tells Celie that it's time for her to leave, time for her to start traveling again. Celie grows quiet and sad, and Shug wants to know what's disturbing her. Celie hesitates, then says, "He beat me when you ain't here." Although Shug admits that Albert is a bully, she wants to know why he would beat Celie. Celie replies, "He beat me for not being you." Shug wants to know if Celie minds her sleeping with Albert, and Celie asks her incredulously if she enjoys it. Shug tells her she has a passion for Albert and wants to know if Celie doesn't also enjoy it. Celie tells her that during sex with Mister she just pretends that she isn't even there. Mister pays no attention; he just climbs on top of her and does his "business." Shug says that seems like someone is just going to the toilet on her, and she tells Celie that she is still a virgin. Celie tells her she is because no one loves her, and Shug lets her know that she loves Celie. Shug then begins to kiss Celie, first on the cheek, then on the forehead, then gently all over her face, then on her mouth. Celie smiles and begins to cover her mouth, then brings her hands down to her lap. She smiles broadly and kisses Shug back. Then Celie and Shug kiss and touch each other. During this segment of the film the women comment throughout.

> Phyllis [in response to a statement about Celie's lack of confidence and Shug's abundance of it]: No, girlfriend, that ain't true. Shug may have had low self-esteem, too, and demonstrated it a different way.
>
> Grace: By being arrogant.

Whitney and Grace find the part of the film when Shug says to Celie, "Show me some teef" amusing.

Whitney: Show me some teef. *Teef*, honey. [Everyone laughs.]
Marilyn [in response to Celie's laughing]: There you go.

During Shug's and Celie's scene in Shug's dressing room the women watching become very quiet. Most of their reactions are when Celie says something poignant like, "He beat me when you ain't here. . . . He beat me for not being you." When Shug tells Celie she is still a virgin, Celie replies that it is true, "'cause don't nobody love me." Morgan begins to cry. After Shug and Celie kiss, no one says anything for a while, then Phyllis and Grace comment.

Phyllis: I think that's really as far as she thought it was going to go [referring to the kiss].
Grace: I don't think she knew what was going on.
Whitney: I don't think she realized the magnitude.
Phyllis: I don't think she was ready for what happened next.
JB: Who wasn't, Celie?
Phyllis: Yes. I don't think she was ready.
Morgan: I don't think she had any concept of having that kind of relationship with anyone.
JB: Not that it was female or anything?
Morgan: I don't think that probably played any part with her . . . and Lord knows, with her I can see where she would not get excited about a man.
[Whitney, Grace, and Phyllis agree.]
JB: Do you see this as a lesbian relationship either in the book or in the film?
Morgan: In the book I did, not in the film.
JB: You did in the film?
Morgan: In the book I did. In the film I did not.
Whitney: I agree. I see it in the book and not in the film.
Marilyn: I agree.
Morgan: Because it wasn't enough in the film to make me necessarily feel that way. It was just suggested. If you had not read the book, it's possible that you missed the point.

Later, as we were approaching the end of the interview, when I asked the women if there was a particular scene in the film that they felt was especially significant, both Grace and Whitney referred back to the moment when Shug kisses Celie. Grace said, "Even though it was an intimate scene between her [Celie] and Shug, I liked that because she began to feel, 'I'm somebody special—I'm not like everybody has been treating me.' "

Still later, when I was interviewing another group of women about their reactions to *Daughters of the Dust*, the issue of the relationship between Celie and Shug was again discussed, and one of the women made an observation that had not been considered during the incendiary environment of the film's first release: "I think that all those people who made such a big deal out of Shug and Celie, you have got to wonder what their motivation was. If some black people didn't want to label the relationship as homosexuality, then it doesn't become an issue. I think if other people want to make it an issue, they should just go right ahead. But I don't think they should make the whole film be about that if other people saw different things in the film."

This woman's assessment of the attempts to categorize *The Color Purple* as a lesbian work is similar to the analysis that black lesbian feminist Barbara Smith gives of the work. Smith ascribes the mass acceptance of the relationship between Shug and Celie by a heterosexual audience to the form in which Alice Walker presents the story. Smith commends Walker for addressing the issue in the first place but sees the novel as a fable rather than a "realistic" portrayal of the lives of lesbians in a culture that would react with hostility to two women having the kind of relationship that Shug and Celie openly display. In a society where homophobia is so rampant, if two women were to interact as they do in the fictionalized story, Smith feels there would be drastic repercussions. She also refuses to categorize the relationship between Shug and Celie as a lesbian one because she feels that is not a designation they would give themselves. As she concludes about the women, "As a black lesbian feminist reader, I have questions about how accurate it is to identify Walker's characters as lesbians at the same time I am moved by the vision of a world, unlike this one, where black women are not forced to lose their families, their community, or their lives, because of whom they love."[11]

In the extended and prolonged public discussions about *The Color Purple* questions were raised about whether the black women who were emotionally attached to the film were able to distinguish between the film and the novel. I asked the women in the second group to talk about their reactions to both the novel and the film.

Morgan: I didn't really want to see this movie at first. I had enjoyed the book so much, I was afraid I was going to see the movie and have that experience ruined. And I was really, *really* reluctant to see it. So when I did, I felt it complemented the book, and it didn't detract from it. I think they did a really good job. I still can't understand how someone can watch this movie without reading the book. I can't imagine what kind of perspective they would have. To me the book without the movie would be okay; it's hard for me to see how they could see the movie without the book.

JB: A lot of people didn't read the book.

Morgan: I know. I couldn't watch this movie in the state of mind of a person who hadn't read the book. When I watched the movie for the first time, it's like if you had some favorite song from when you were a kid and heard it again many, many years later, something that you associated with something very special. Reading the book was like that for me. With the book, it was an original event, and the movie was like kind of a reminder, of revisiting or reliving it.

JB: Did you feel that most black women or most black women that you talked to liked the film?

[General agreement.]

Phyllis: Overwhelmingly.

Morgan: Yes. In fact, I had to beg, plead, plead with my mother to go see it—she was afraid to see it because she felt there were too many things, from what she heard about the movie, that were too closely related to her experiences. She just didn't want to relive that. And so I pleaded and I begged and I said, Mother, go. Just go by yourself. And she finally went and saw it and had a real positive feeling about it. I kind of felt sometimes like it was mine. Not that it was mine such that nobody else could have any of it. It wasn't an exclusive ownership in that way, but it was mine.

Phyllis: I think it was a catharsis for me. Because it was some of those things I had actually lived, some of those things I had actually seen other people live. I liked being able to sit there and see it on the big screen. It was important for other people to view that, to make them aware that this is really happening, folks. For critics to say that this is a fantasy—I had a real problem with that, because it's just like saying that the "Cosby Show" is a fantasy. I know that just like the things that have occurred in this movie are real, the things that happened in the "Cosby Show," I know families like that—who kid around, joke around, have all that love. Even considering black college life; there's a lot of stuff that goes on in "A Different World" that actually happens on black campuses. It's almost as if people are negating some part of my existence when they say that this movie [*The Color Purple*] isn't real. It opened up a lot of wounds for me, it made me go inward, it made me do a lot of thinking.

Anne: I got angry that Spielberg, white man . . .

Phyllis: . . . had to do it . . .

Anne: . . . did it. I got really upset with that. I felt violated in that sense.

Phyllis: I was just glad somebody did it.

Grace: I didn't feel angry. I'm glad somebody did it. If he had not done it, I don't know too many other people who would have even tried—

Whitney: —or who would have had the money or the financial backing.

I asked Anne to elaborate on her point about Spielberg mishandling the film.

JB: You didn't like *The Color Purple*?

Anne: I didn't like it the first time I saw it. I saw it, and then I rented it this summer, and I looked at it, and I liked it. I thought, Now why didn't I like it the first time? The first time I didn't like it, I think, was because I was offended so much by this white man portraying these black people. There're black directors out there, there're black people out there. Damn it, let them get through.

Marilyn: But who was the movie made for?

Anne: It was made for white audiences.

Marilyn: Okay.

Anne: And that really made me angry, because here I was sitting in an audience of white people, except for one row . . .

Phyllis: Who controls the movie money?

Anne: White people, but . . .

Morgan: She's not talking about the intellectual aspects of it—I mean we can all intellectualize things and still get pissed off.

Much of the criticism of the film revolved around white people's perceptions of black people and the feeling that black people's progress would be stymied because of the supposed harmful images presented in the film, such as those about black people's physical characteristics, skin color, hair texture, and so on. I asked the women their feelings about this aspect of the film.

JB: What were your feelings about any of the things that the film dealt with that was unique to black people? They kept saying that Shug's hair was nappy, [that she was] black as tar; when Celie was combing the children's hair. Did that—

Whitney: Did that bother me?

JB: Bother you watching it [in the company of a predominately white audience]?

Grace: That to me is the thing that makes me proud, that makes us different. It always has; I guess that's the way my mom brought us up. That it's all right to be dark and your hair is nappy; that's a good thing. So, it doesn't [bother me]—I'm proud of that.

Whitney: Yes, I am too. I didn't even think about it.

Morgan: When I watched it [here], I just tuned all that out. Just tuned out the rest of the audience. And I left; I went to my car, and I went home. I think maybe when I got out there was a sense of . . . it might have been different if I had been watching it with a black audience. I wouldn't have felt that I needed to rush and get home if I didn't want to interface. I didn't want to see *all* those people, probably that I would have seen from work and would have had to interface and deal with those kinds of issues.

Whitney [agreeing throughout]: Yes, yes.

Phyllis: You felt like you wanted somebody you could talk to, that you could share it with?

Morgan: That would have been nice. I would have been afraid [seeing the white people that she knew] that I would have had to explain something, where I would have been expected to explain something. I didn't feel like explaining shit to nobody.

Whitney: Right, right.

Morgan: You don't get it, that's your problem, not mine.

Phyllis: Right, right.

JB: I'm not Encyclopaedia Britannica.

Morgan: Right. I just didn't feel like being this week's representative for all black America.

Phyllis: Of the black race.

Whitney: [They would ask] "What did you think about it?"

Morgan: Yes.

Grace: Sometimes that gets real old.

I asked the women to respond to the prolonged discussions about the effect of the film.

Whitney: You mean the male-female thing? . . . Well, I talked to Howard [her husband] afterward, and he didn't feel threatened by it. I really didn't see the big deal.

Grace: I didn't, either.

Whitney: I think it was much ado about nothing.

Morgan: I never understood it, either.

Phyllis: I heard a lot of guys say this portrayed black men as very negative creatures, not questioning if the shoe fits, you got to wear it. If it was not a threat to you and you did not feel that's the way you are, then it should not have bothered you. But they still felt that the greater society would view them as wife-beaters and philanderers and what have you. To be absolutely honest with you, having been in Atlanta for the amount of time that I was there, seventy percent population [that is black], I have to admit that there were a number of brothers who lived up to that.

Whitney: Well, the greater population, if you talking about whites, believe we got tails and horns, too. So they are going to think what they want to think.

Phyllis: That's true, but I guess that's why I feel comfortable with the portrayal—because I've seen black men in my own life who reacted to adversities and to a lack of a feeling of power the very same way that these men in this movie acted.

Morgan: In my mind it just seemed like this was one set of people and their circumstances. And that didn't reflect on anybody else.

Whitney: We see bad [people in] movies all the time. Everybody is not like *The Godfather*, it's just a movie.

JB: But did you feel that the controversy itself affected the film or the way people saw it? Did you feel—even though you didn't think the controversy was worthwhile, was it a very large issue, do you think?

Phyllis: It was blown out of proportion.

Whitney: I felt violated that we let it get out of the family.

I asked the women in the first group to respond to the disparaging statements made about the film. Margaret said that she felt white people were behind the disputes and that they were putting words in the black men's mouths. Someone said that the NAACP (National Association for the Advancement of Colored People) was behind a lot of the protests against the film. Margaret replied that there were white people in the NAACP and that black men had sold out with their protests: "You know, a piece of silver . . . they'll sell us out. People will sell us out for money."

Danielle added: "Why don't they protest what's on television every week? Fred Sanford and all of them." She said that many people who did not like the film felt it was an airing of black people's dirty laundry. Paige said that there was nothing wrong with that: "We don't always have to pretend that everything is hunky-dory. It could be that if I tell somebody and they tell somebody else, then maybe I can get some answers to some problems I have."

Danielle followed up on her charge that *The Color Purple* was selected for criticism while other more detrimental films were not: "Where was all this hue and cry when the Blaxploitation films came out?" She also questioned films such as *Sounder*, which did not generate any protests and in which the black man is also depicted as a loser:

> Listening to us talk here I'm beginning to see that it's [the protest over *The Color Purple*] a sexist thing, and that upsets me because black people in general are oppressed. We're in this together. We worked in the same fields together; we walked in the same chain coffle together. It's just sad, because we all know that we wouldn't be here without the black woman having strength.

Constance discussed the charge by some critics that neither the book nor the film was realistic. She said that someone who had seen the film declared to her that no man would allow a woman to take a razor to his neck after he had treated her so badly. Margaret replied with some heat: "They will beat you up, black both your eyes, and then go get right in the bed and go to sleep." This remark prompted Paige to add: "And then will have the nerve to want you to cook them something to eat." Danielle talked about why some black men abused black women. She referred to incidents that her mother, Margaret, had related about her father:

> My mother asked my dad how come he would jump on her. Sometimes when she hadn't done anything he would just jump on her, for GP.[12] She asked him some years after they split up, and he told her he didn't know any better. That when he sat around with the guys . . . the guys would talk about how you had to keep a woman in line, you had to whip her ass every so often. And so he told Mamma that's what he thought he was supposed to do to make sure he could be the man around the house.

Anne, in the second group, referred to the contentious discussions when she talked about seeing the film in the local theater with most of the black males from the college basketball team seated behind her:

> It was also crowded, and I thought it would be really interesting to see what their reactions [would be]. There was a lot of shouting [when she saw the film], and I had just read about the controversy a couple of days before I had seen it. I thought that the guys would get real quiet and timid because of the way that the males were being portrayed. I thought that perhaps this would happen, because I heard that big mass thing going on and all these men getting angry. But they seemed to get into it, and I thought I could understand why. How often are black people recognized in this community?

Marilyn followed up on Anne's statement about why black audiences react differently to films featuring black characters than do other audiences. She also made a critical observation about how black audiences watch films in contrast to other groups of viewers.

Marilyn: That's right. I got the same impression from seeing *She's Gotta Have It* and *School Daze*. I thought that *School Daze* was a really extremely silly film, but it's the kind of thing that does great things for the morale of young black people. I saw it in Seattle, and there were maybe four whites in the theater. It was like the difference between going to a white Catholic mass and going to a black Baptist church. You know how you go into a theater, and folks sit there quietly—well this theater was live. Everyone was just yelling and screaming and laughing and dancing in their chairs. But it just does great things for our morale.

JB: To see us in films?

Marilyn: Yes, it's just fun.

Because of the pervasive absence of black people in mainstream media there is a tendency to enjoy seeing black people in television programs and films rather than critically evaluate the works. The concern for many critics of *The Color Purple* was that this was the trap, "the trick bag," into which black women fell—that they became so enamored of seeing black women on the screen that they could not distinguish a harmful image from just the pleasure of seeing black women in roles other than comics or domestic workers. I asked the women about this perception.

JB: To see yourself, to read about yourself [in media], is exciting, but how about if you see yourself negatively? Are you ever conscious that when a film is made by a white filmmaker that there is going to be something in it that will portray us negatively?

Morgan: You see it on TV all the time. Like, what's that silly show that's set in Boston? "Spencer"—the black character on that—Hawk—is a joke. And it's insulting. I mean, every time I watch it, I think, Oh, God. When I see things like that that are very negative or stereotypical, and or incredibly one-dimensional, then I'm insulted.

A strongly contested dimension of the claims made about the effect of *The Color Purple* was that it altered the way many black women perceived their lives and their relationships with others. Although the women I interviewed were ambivalent about the long-term effects of the film, Phyllis felt strongly that it had indeed changed many black women's outlook: "I was in Atlanta when the movie came out. I noticed that the movie started women doing a lot of talking, a lot of reevaluating of how they dealt with the men in their lives—if they were going to either buckle under or stand up. And I noticed that a lot of women began looking at what direction they wanted to take." Marilyn picked up on Phyllis's sentiments and expressed her thoughts about another part of the discussion that was also challenged—that after seeing *The Color Purple* many black women sought out other books by black women writers: "In a way it was a validation. I think it was a validation for the way . . . our lives had to be lived. The book was the main incentive for me to want to read more, and see more of black writers. I know a lot of black women who didn't read the book, and they had to rely on the movie. And the movie was very validating of our lifestyle." Morgan related her own experiences of how, although she had not previously read many works by black women, once she read *The Color Purple* she was motivated to read more. Morgan also made a connection with other books she had read but had not considered their impact on her. The significance of her comments is that it underscores the claim that the impact of the novel and the widespread coverage of the film was so great that it provided an atmosphere that enabled the women to listen to black female activists who placed the issues that the novel addressed within a broader context of their past.

Morgan: It's funny; I found *The Color Purple* by accident. I read the book probably two years before I saw the movie. I had never heard of Alice Walker. I was in the bookstore, I saw this book, it looked kind of interesting, so I picked it up.

JB: You had never heard of Alice Walker? Had you heard of any other black woman writer?

Morgan: Maya Angelou and—

Marilyn: Toni Morrison.

Anne: Shange.

JB: *colored girls*?

Phyllis: Now that moved me, too.

JB [to Morgan]: Can I ask you if both your parents are black?

Morgan: Yeah, they both are black. . . . I had to think about that a second. Last time I looked they both were. [She continues her comments about reading the novel.] I mean, I just picked up this thing that I thought was going to be an interesting novel and got *sucked* in.

Marilyn: That's what happened to me. After that I read *In Search of Our Mothers' Gardens* and other books.

JB: After you read *The Color Purple*, you went out and sought out other books by [black female writers]?

Marilyn: Yes, I did.

Morgan: I did after reading that one because I had read other black stories. Now that I think about it, those were some of the ones that I really did like the best.

Marilyn: Have you read *In Search of Our Mothers' Gardens*?

Morgan: I read parts of it.

Marilyn: That was a wonderful book.

Morgan: I read a little thing here [by other black female writers] and a little thing there, and some of it I didn't like because it was so hard. It was so . . . angry. Some of it just seemed real angry.

Phyllis: Who was the woman who wrote back in the forties?

JB: Zora Neale Hurston. *Their Eyes Were Watching God.*

Morgan: Yes. I liked that story.

I asked the women in the second group to sum up their feelings about the film.

JB: If you could describe the film in one word, or just a couple of words, what would you say?

Marilyn: It's about time.

Anne: Sorry it had to be a white man. I'm sorry it had to be a white man to do it.
Phyllis: I'm just grateful that it came out.
Morgan: Personal, I guess.
Anne: I guess I'm really bitter that way. I'll have to think about it.

Anne's sentiments were shared by many critics of the film who would have preferred a black filmmaker translating Alice Walker's novel. As much as that may have made a significant difference, the effects of the existence of the film were still important. And black women's reactions to it were a crucial part of that effect even though their reactions were themselves criticized. However, this again emphasizes that the ability of an audience to negotiate their responses is as important as the acknowledgment of their skill in doing so, as the following example illustrates.

One of the strongest criticisms of the film concerned the metamorphosis of Shug as she was in the novel, strong and self-reliant, into the insecure, oversexed daughter of a minister, as she was portrayed in the film. I asked the women in the second group about Shug's having, in the film, a father who was a preacher. Phyllis felt that it deepened her character, and Morgan felt that it made her more well-rounded. Grace added that it revealed a vulnerable side to her, because, even though she was strong, there was a part of her that was really hurting. I asked if they felt that Shug was too strong in the novel. They did not feel that, but they reiterated that Shug was someone who had been hurt deeply and felt rejected and that her lasciviousness was her way of dealing with it. I asked if they liked her better in the film. Whitney replied: "We like her the same either way."

In the first group I asked the women to respond to the charge from some radical critics that Shug was deliberately changed in the film to neutralize her power by having her constantly seek a reconciliation with her father. The other women fervently agreed with the comment made by Christine: "It didn't have that effect on me. Shug was still a strong woman. It didn't neutralize her to me. Now, if that's what they [the producers] wanted to do, they missed the boat, because it didn't do that to me. You go back and tell the critics they missed their point."

During the course of the later interviews about the groups' reactions to *Waiting to Exhale* and *Daughters of the Dust* I shared with the women some of the criticisms asserting that because the black women who participated in my study of the film were articulate, they could not possibly be representative of the majority of black women in this country. Once again, the women displayed a shrewdness about their status in society and about the way black women are viewed by others. One of the women wondered if the critics knew that a person could be intelligent but not necessarily well educated. Another stated that she knew of too many people who had an abundance of academic degrees, yet when they speak they say nothing. Still another commented that many people react with surprise when they hear black people speak sensibly because, too often, that is not what is allowed to be presented in a public forum. She then asked a rhetorical question toward which the other women responded with spirited agreement: "Don't you think we would have come off sounding stupid if someone other than another black person was doing research on us?"

CHAPTER FOUR

Daughters of the Dust

When a work is so densely seeded within black culture, a lot of people who are not from the culture will say that they find the film inaccessible or they find it is not engaging. What they are saying is that they do not feel privileged by the film. So they choose not to engage or allow themselves to become engaged.

—*Julie Dash, in an interview with the author*

From the slow, leisurely pace of the film's unfolding to the strategic placement of visual references to earlier black artists, director Julie Dash establishes the creative provenance of *Daughters of the Dust*. It is a film deeply saturated in black life, history, and culture and is intended to honor those traditions from which it is spawned. By very conscious tributes to the photographs of Harlem photographer James Van derZee, the religious folk dramas of early black filmmaker Spencer Williams, and the unorthodox cinematic vision of black director Bill Gunn in *Ganja and Hess* (1973), Dash constructed a work that places black people at the center of the story.

Van derZee's portraits were first "discovered" by the public at large during an exhibition of photographs entitled "Harlem on My Mind" at the Metropolitan Museum of Art in 1968. Van derZee was eighty-three at the time and had lived and worked in Harlem since the turn of the century. A self-taught photographer, Van derZee trained himself through experimentation with the use of different kinds of cameras as well as with the varieties of developing and printing methods. Although the pictures that Van derZee took were a means to earn a living, he exhibited such care in the composition of each individual portrait that the photos were later considered to be works of art. One of the techniques he used was multiple imaging, in which, through double printing, one photograph was superimposed on another. A striking example of this technique is the now famous funeral photograph of the daughter of the minister of the largest black church in New York. Blanche Powell, daughter of Adam Clayton Powell, Sr., and the older sister of the man who would become the first black elected United States congressman from New York, died when she was not yet thirty. Van derZee had previously taken a photograph of Blanche Powell as a young girl, and this he superimposed on the one of her lying in her coffin.[1]

Dash emulated Van derZee's multiple-image technique in the composition of her film. Through lap dissolves that end with one shot superimposed on another—what Dash terms "layered dissolves"—she re-creates a technique that has its origins in the work of one of the first, if not the first, black photographers. The beginning of the film is an example of this superimposition: through the careful composition of individual shots, and through editing in such a way that the scenes become iconic portraits, the images resonate beyond their duration on the screen.

As the film opens, after the initial credits are shown, a prologue explains that the setting of the story is the Sea Islands located off the mainland of South Carolina and Georgia. The inhabitants are descendants of black people captured from Africa who have chosen to live in isolation and have retained much of the culture that was brought by the earlier Africans. The island people are called Gullah. On this, their last day on Ibo Landing before their migration north, there is a family gathering in celebration of the move. The feast is conceived as a Last Supper before the family takes its leave of the island. The time is 1902.

After the prologue there is a series of slow dissolves over a background sound of the wind blowing and then a close-up of a pair of hands covered with soil that is being blown away by the wind. Toward the end of the dissolve the hands begin to spread apart, and their image is superimposed on that of a fully clothed woman washing herself in a river. That image is held for a time before the start of the next dissolve, over what appears to be a nightstand in a bedroom. There is a slow pan left, to a bed with gossamer netting over it. Two people are lying in the bed. There is another slow dissolve to a wide-angled shot of the mouth of a very large river, where a boat appears very small in the distance. The next dissolve ends in a shot of a woman standing majestically in a boat that is maneuvered by three men, and is followed by a dissolve to an extreme close-up of a St. Christopher medal worn around the woman's neck. After the fade to black the title of the film appears.

The changing of the scenes is accomplished precisely and is synchronized so that the images at the end of each dissolve correspond to the words spoken in the voice-over. The person who is speaking, we later learn, is the one standing in the boat. The voice-over timed to the shot of the woman bathing in the river begins with these words: "I am the first and the last, I am the honored one and the scorned one." There is a period of silence until the voice-over of the bedroom scene states: "I am the whore and the holy one; I am the wife and the virgin; I am the barren one, and many are my daughters." After a quiet interlude the voice-over accompanying the image of the woman standing in the boat reveals: "I am the silence that you cannot understand; I am the utterance of my name."

For Dash, each dissolve means something; it is more than a transition device signaling the passage of time. The dissolves are used to convey important information, such as in the opening of the film. They are also a homage to Van derZee and the method he used to compose his photographs featuring the black inhabitants of Harlem during the early decades of this century.

The words spoken during the dissolves are taken from the collection of Gnostic scriptures in the volume *Nag Hammadi Library*. The passage is entitled "Thunder: Perfect Mind." It is used to introduce the audience to the fact that this is a black woman's story, telling of the fate of black women since their journey across the sea. The juxtaposition of the images noted earlier with "Thunder: Perfect Mind" invokes the symbolism of this passage. Parallelism, antithesis, and paradox are conveyed by the contrasting phrases: first, last; honored, scorned; barren, multiple progeny; silence, utterance. "Thunder: Perfect Mind" is interpreted as a revelation discourse that is unique in its use of a female figure as the speaker. It is understood as encompassing the active, intelligent element in all things. Through reason, the female figure is able to provide instruction, to those who listen, about the course of true life.[2]

The hands covered with soil serves as a play upon the title of the film, which Dash took from a passage in the Bible. Although the words from the book of Ezekiel refer to "ye sons of the dust" Dash paraphrased it as "daughters of the dust."[3] The old woman bathing in the river symbolizes rebirth and the integral connection of the old with the new. Later the theme will be expanded upon with the introduction of the Unborn Child, who has been beckoned from the "otherworld" by the matriarch of the family as a way of healing the growing dissensions among the people of the island.

The sleeping couple are at odds because the husband, Eli, is uncertain that the child carried by the wife, Eula, is his. He wants her to reveal the name of the man who raped her; Eula refuses. The woman in the boat represents those black women who have lived life as it has been handed to them yet have not lost contact with their past or been broken or bowed. For this reason she stands proudly in the boat. The dissolve to the close-up of the St. Christopher medal recalls old photographs of black women at the turn of the century. It shows that every culture has its talisman, whether it be "scraps of memory" contained in a tin can, as for the great-grandmother, or charms worn around the neck, as for the worldly granddaughter. The old woman, Nana Peazant, will later ask her granddaughter, Yellow Mary, in a tone tinged with skepticism, what she is wearing around her neck. She queries her, "What kind of belief that is?" She then asks her with concern, "Do it protect you?" as she leans her forehead against Yellow Mary's while her hands are placed lightly on her shoulders.

Later in the film an additional layer of information is added when the woman who was standing in the boat, Yellow Mary, tells Eula, the character who has been raped by a white landowner and is now pregnant: "At the same time, the rape of a colored woman is as common as the fish in the sea." This is the first and only time the word *rape* is used to describe what has happened to Eula. Not only is the word not spoken but the action is deliberately concealed. Dash states that the historical facts of the sexual carnage of black women by white men is a story that has been referred to so many times that it has lost its potency and its ability to enrage. For this reason, she felt it was important to deal with the aftereffects of the rape, to show how the couple and the family handle it; therein lies their demonstration of the strength needed to survive.[4]

To further enhance the horrors of enslavement and lift the images from the mundane and the ordinary, Dash felt it was necessary to show the family's hands permanently stained from the poisonous indigo dye that was the source of riches for those who had captured the people on the island. Dash reveals that she knew the permanent imprint of the dye was historically inaccurate, but she felt it was imperative to reconstruct the familiar symbols of enslavement—the scars on the backs and the chains around the hands and feet—and recast the images to re-create the shock associated with the enormity of the acts of enslavement.[5]

The baptismal procession to the river is another cinematic reconstruction that has a dual purpose—both to honor the religious "passion plays" of early black filmmaker Spencer Williams in his films *Go Down Death* (1944) and *The Blood of Jesus* (1941), which feature similar processions, and to provide a contrast and comparison of religious beliefs between the people on the island. The black people in the procession are following the new mores of Christianity learned from their sojourn in this country and are antagonistic to the beliefs of the Islamic religion practiced by Bilal Muhammed, the last black person brought over from Africa, who still maintains his African traditions and practices.

In the final third of the film two scenes are intercut to reveal this blending of the past and present and its significance for the future of the people of the island. The scenes involve Yellow Mary and Eula sitting under an umbrella on the beach and Bilal Muhammed walking past a line of Baptist worshipers as they follow their leader in a baptismal procession to the river.

Yellow Mary is lying down in such a way that Eula can lean back comfortably against her under the umbrella. She tells Eula about a pink satin case that she saw once on her travels. The case had a handle on one side that could be turned so that music played. Yellow Mary tells Eula that even though she could not afford the case, in her mind she possessed it and put all her bad memories in the case and locked them there. She said: "So I could take them out, look at them when I felt like it, and figure it out, you know. But I didn't want them inside of me. I don't let nothing in that case or outside that case tell me who I am or how I should feel about me." After Yellow Mary finishes talking she and Eula turn their heads to the right, and that image is held in a medium shot before a cut to the Christians walking to the river.

The people in the procession are dressed in white robes. The lead person is cradling a Bible in both hands. The shot is framed so that the worshipers walk straight toward the camera and out of the frame just as there is a cut to an old man passing, holding a prayer rug. The leader of the Christians says the man's name three times—"Bilal, Bilal, Bilal Muhammed"—and enjoins the man to come with them to the river. As the leader raises his hand in a gesture of entreaty, he says to Bilal, "Come wash away your sins in the blood of the lamb Jesus." As Bilal completely ignores the procession and continues on his way, two other men in the group respond to his actions angrily, making sarcastic comments to his back: "Let him go, Deacon. Bilal's a 'salt water, Negro.' He has no shame." The other man replies in kind, "He's the master of the sun and the moon." After the taunts and jeers at Bilal the procession continues on its way out of the frame, and a long shot of open space is held until there is a cut back to Yellow Mary and Eula under the umbrella. They have now been joined by Trula, Yellow Mary's lover.

Yellow Mary tells Eula that it is time for her to depart from the island to go to Nova Scotia. She feels it is an appropriate time for her to leave; she shares her plans in a veiled reference to her life as a prostitute: "I never had too much trouble making a dollar, you know. Never needed nobody to help me do that. I can't stand still,

In *Daughters of the Dust*, director Julie Dash constructed several notable sequences as a tribute to earlier black filmmakers. These scenes of the baptismal procession to the river are a homage to Spencer Williams's *The Blood of Jesus* (1941).

The walk to the water in *Daughters of the Dust*.

got to keep moving, new faces, new places. Nova Scotia will be good to me." There is a cut back to the baptismal party at the river as a woman is dunked under the water. Another cut shows the other Christians standing on the banks of the river with their hands held high, rejoicing as the woman is baptized.

The scenes of the baptism hold particular significance in the film for they both refer back to the films of Spencer Williams, especially *The Blood of Jesus*, and rework a worn-out tradition first used in the film *Hallelujah* (1929). The baptismal scene in *Hallelujah* was commented upon by a *New York Times* reviewer as a faithful rendering of "the peculiarly typical religious hysteria of the darkies and their gullibility . . . their hankering after salvation, the dread of water in the baptism."[6] In the film the director, King Vidor, has the black actors jump around hysterically, as if they were overcome by religious frenzy after their encounter with the water.

The opening scenes of *The Blood of Jesus* follow a procession of worshipers walking slowly behind a minister flanked by two

The baptismal procession in *The Blood of Jesus*

The Blood of Jesus.

A dignified baptismal scene from *The Blood of Jesus*, sharply contrasting with a similar moment in King Vidor's *Hallelujah* (1929)

women as the group advances toward the water. Those who are a part of the ceremony are dressed somberly in dark clothing, while the people who are to be baptized are in white gowns. Gospel singing provides an accompaniment to the march to the river. When the baptismal ritual begins one of the women begins to line out a hymn with the others following her lead as the minister and a deacon lower a woman into the water. Williams's film exhibits a fidelity and dignity to the proceedings that had not been shown in films directed by white people. According to cultural scholar Adrienne Lanier-Seward in "A Film Portrait of Black Ritual Expression: *The Blood of Jesus*," Williams's work set a precedent as a model example of black cultural expression in film.[7] Lanier-Seward feels that Williams deserves to be remembered for the way in which his film "employed structures and themes from Afro-American folk drama and religious expression to simultaneously entertain black audiences and acknowledge the culture's expressive style" (p. 198).

The baptismal sequence in *Daughters of the Dust* is an acknowledgment of Williams's contribution to the history of black films. In Dash's tribute the same formal style is used as the baptismal party heads toward the water. There is an additional quality in *Daughters of the Dust*, for it is clear that the Christian believers are under scrutiny (by the filmmaker) as they reverently adhere to the tenets of their new religion. There is also a subtle commentary on contemporary black people who likewise disparage those who would practice a religion much older than Christianity. That the baptismal procession is intercut with the scenes of Yellow Mary and Eula on the beach is indicative of the director's sentiment that everyone handles the crossing over to the "new" world, with its harshness and brutality, in whatever manner they can and still retain their sense of themselves and their integrity; therein lies their solace and comfort. As Yellow Mary re-creates her grandmother's tin can of memories in her vision of the pink satin case holding her demons until she is ready to handle them, so too does Bilal Muhammed exist in a land not of his choosing but in possession of his own traditions, principles, and beliefs.

As Dash discovered during her research for the film, Bilal Muhammed was an actual person who lived on the Sea Islands in the 1800s. He practiced his Islam religion and prayed five times daily. His papers and diaries are still on permanent exhibition at the Smithsonian.[8] In 1902, the time of *Daughters of the Dust*, Bilal's five daughters were still living on the islands, practicing their religion. Dash featured the character Bilal Muhammed in the film because the historical person had never been acknowledged in any other film produced by a black person, and she felt he needed to be remembered.

The way in which we are first introduced to the character provides a continuity in the overall construction of the film. Just as Bilal is employed as a contrast to the religious fanaticism of the people attending the baptism, so too does he link up with Dash's goal of utilizing cinematic techniques practiced by black filmmakers from the past as a way to honor and remember them. Thus, she juxtaposes Bilal Muhammed's scenes with those of the young women on the beach.

The women grouped together are seen earlier in the film with Yellow Mary and Trula sitting in a large tree as Eula gazes up at them. The scenes in the tree are influenced by the work of black director Bill Gunn in *Ganja and Hess*. Gunn's film now holds something of a cult status among film aficionados, but it was suppressed for many years because the distributors did not feel that Gunn had made the film for which he was contracted. The film was made during the boom period of the black action adventure films, and the distributors wanted to exploit that market while it was being made. The instructions were to make a film about blood. Blood there is in *Ganja and Hess*, but Gunn's project is more than that, for the film concerns an anthropologist, Dr. Hess Greene, who has contracted a rare blood ailment from an artifact he collected on one of his field trips to Africa. Dr. Greene becomes a vampire who survives by sucking blood stolen from blood banks or taken from human beings. Dr. Greene's assistant is George Meda, played by Bill Gunn, an artist who has been institutionalized and is still fighting madness. Meda's estranged wife, Ganja, comes to look for him at Dr. Greene's estate, but George has died, either by successfully committing suicide or being killed by Hess Greene. After Ganja arrives and finds George's body, she joins Dr. Greene in his life as a vampire, and continues it even after Dr. Greene repents and dies.

Gunn's film is an unconventional one that challenges the traditional tenets of filmmaking and the routine understanding of cinema. According to Manthia Diawara and Phyllis Klotman in "*Ganja and Hess*: Vampires, Sex, and Addictions," one of the attractions the film holds for contemporary black film critics and filmmakers is Gunn's questions regarding the black artists' responsibilities in a white controlled art environment and the artists' desire to utilize the resources found within black life.[9]

The scene from *Ganja and Hess* that resonates in *Daughters of the Dust* concerns George Meda sitting in a tree with a rope looped over a branch of the tree and loosely tied around his neck. The tree is in Dr. Greene's yard. When he goes to look for George and finds him sitting in the tree he is concerned that George will commit suicide on his property and the police will be summoned to interrogate him, the only black resident of the neighborhood, and thus make him vulnerable because of his vampire secrets. In the scene Hess Greene is looking up at George in the tree, and all we see are George's legs swinging slowly back and forth as he shares his anguish with Dr. Greene.

In the tree sequence in *Daughters of the Dust* both Yellow Mary and Eula tell of their troubles as we see Trula's legs hanging down from the tree, swinging slowly back and forth. As the sequence begins, Yellow Mary and Trula are in the tree, while Eula gazes up at them as they share a cigarette and laugh merrily. There is a cut to a close-up of Eula, who says to Yellow Mary: "As much as I like to fish, I'll never put a pole in that water." Eula tells the story of the young "salt-water girl" who was drowned by her owner. Yellow Mary chides Eula for her parochial ways, saying, "I thought this was supposed to be *Ibo* Landing"—a reference to one of the sustaining myths of the island, according to which the captured Africans, after their arrival on land, walked on water back to their homeland.

Although Eula looks puzzled by Yellow Mary's gentle jibes at the backwardness of the people on the island, she does not seem offended. She tells Yellow Mary of her experience the night before, in which her long-dead mother came to her and took her by the hand. She speaks of the Gullah custom of placing a letter under a glass of water under the bed to summon forth the spirit of those who have died. Eula says that because she needed to talk to her mother, she came to her.

Even though Yellow Mary exclaims over the superstitions of the isolated people on the island, she is still in the grip of Eula's need to find a resolution for her problem with Eli. She eventually questions Eula about whether she has told Eli who raped her. After Eula shakes her head, Yellow Mary tells her she has done the right thing: "There is enough uncertainty in life without having to sit at home wondering which tree your husband's hanging from." Yellow Mary reiterates her charge: "Don't tell him anything."

As the three women remain by the tree Yellow Mary explains to Eula how she came to be "ruint," as she is labeled by the other women on the island. The other people know she is a worldly woman who has earned her keep through prostitution, and they also sense that she and Trula are lovers. Of both relationships the people of the island disapprove. In a remarkable moment in the film, as Yellow Mary sits in the tree there is a close-up of her in profile as she tells Eula how she happened on the life she lived. She shares with Eula the story of her baby being born dead—"And my titty was full of milk. We needed money, so I hired out to a wealthy family." Yellow Mary nursed their baby, even after they moved to Cuba, and they refused to let her return home. She tells Eula, "That's how I got ruint. I want to go home, and they keep me. They keep me. So I fixed a titty. They sent me home."

Yellow Mary's treatment by the family in Cuba parallels Eula's rape by the white landowner. Although she doesn't talk about it, and it is absent from the film, Yellow Mary was herself raped by the husband of the family for whom she worked. This led to her becoming a prostitute to earn the money to leave the family. In the eyes of the people of the island this is part of her depravity, as is her relationship with Trula, the woman she brings home to the island. It is indeed a sexual relationship; the women are lovers. Dash based the relationship between the women on research that she undertook for the film. According to her studies, many of the prostitutes at that time were lesbians or bisexual, and the women traveled together, perhaps as a means of protecting themselves from the hazards of their profession.

Trula also served another purpose in the film: the introduction of her character added additional tension to Yellow Mary's homecoming and provided insights into the character of the people on the island. It wasn't simply that Yellow Mary is a prostitute coming home to her family; and it wasn't just that she was with another woman, or that this woman was truly light-skinned, whereas Yellow Mary has worn that nickname all her life, until she finally wears the name with pride. By bringing someone not from the island into the islanders' midst, Yellow Mary revealed aspects of their recidivist natures. For as much as the ancient African traditions, folkways, and principles of the people on the island are celebrated in the film, their insularity, their pettiness, and their obstinate holding on to many destructive ways are also examined.

The Myth of Ibo Landing

The setting of the film derives its name from three stories, or myths, that have been handed down since the arrival of the inhabitants of the island. The three myths about Ibo Landing—or, as Dash states, two myths and one reality[10]—relate to the fact that the African captives from the Ibo tribe refused to live enslaved. One account of the myth has the captives walking on top of the water all the way back to Africa; another describes how the captives flew over the water back to Africa; the third account, which Bilal Muhammed substantiates in the film, is that the captives walked back into the water, shackled and chained, and drowned themselves. Thus, although the name of the island is a mythical one, every inlet on the Sea

Islands is labeled Ibo Landing because they are all seen as the place where the captives, one way or another, resisted. According to Dash, the myth of Ibo Landing provides sustenance for a tradition of black resistance.

In *Daughters of the Dust* the myth of Ibo Landing is used to bring resolution to the trauma between Eli and Eula. The elements involved in the resolution are the myth, the Unborn Child, and the wooden figurehead of the torso of an African warrior floating in the river, whose function in the film is to symbolize the loss of status of the African people in this country and of all that was sacred to them in their homeland. It is a replica of a figurehead used on the prow of a slave ship, and Dash utilized it as an unspoken reminder that this was the first thing the African captives saw as they were being led onto the boat that would carry them away from their land. Fifty years after enslavement, the figurehead lies floating and rotting in the water as a constant relic of that time.[11]

The Unborn Child symbolizes the belief in the connection between the "otherworld" of those who have lived before and are now dead, and life in the present. During the flashback of the earlier inhabitants of the island working as slaves on the indigo plantation, there are scenes of the workers pounding the indigo solution and dipping the fabric in vats of hot, steaming dye. The Unborn Child is among them, trailing her finger among the containers of blue dye. In a voice-over she talks about the nobility of her ancestry and her beckoning to Ibo Landing: "We were the children of those who chose to survive. Years later, my ma told me she knew I had been sent by the old souls."

After the flashback to the indigo plantation the Unborn Child returns to the present of the family picnic, looking through a wish book with Myown and tracking the objects in the book with her blue-stained finger. The Unborn Child notes whimsically, "I was traveling on this very true mission. But sometimes I would get distracted." There is a charmingly quixotic quality to this part of the film, in which the sacred belief that those who reside in the realm of the spiritual are vitally connected to the people in the present is symbolized by a five-year-old girl who is knowingly caught up in the normal activities of a child that age. This ambience is enhanced as she remains the same throughout the film, costumed in the same white dress with the same blue ribbon in her hair, as she travels between both worlds.

After the sequence between past and present is a cut to a group of children running in slow motion up a path, followed by the Unborn Child, who scampers along behind them. After a cut to a close-up of the river the camera tilts slowly up over the water. At the completion of the dissolve Eula enters the frame from the left, looking back wistfully over her shoulder. In a voice-over the Unborn Child reveals: "My ma said she could feel me by her side." There is a cut to a bird circling in the sky, then another to a medium shot of Nana Peazant breathing deeply and looking out over the land. In a voice-over the Unborn Child tells how she came to Eula and Eli: "I remember the call of my great-grandmother. I remember the journey home." A cut takes us to a long shot of the graveyard, adorned with the bottles, pots and pans, seashells, broomsticks, twisted metal, and other grave markers that were the personal effects of those who died. In a voice-over the Unborn Child says, "I remember the long walk to the graveyard, to the house that I would be born in . . ." There is a slow dissolve to a superimposition of the graveyard with a man riding a bicycle along the beach, moving leftward across the screen. The voice of the Unborn Child continues, ". . . to the picnic site." She begins to speak more slowly, and her words become more drawn-out at a slow dissolve to a superimposition of Nana Peazant leading a group of children, carrying chairs upside-down on their heads, over the sand dunes and on to the picnic area. During the overlap the voice of the Unborn Child says, "I remember. And I recall," as the waves seen in one shot become a part of the background for Nana Peazant's leading the children over the land.

In *Daughters of the Dust* references to the past are usually made through scenes in which a character travels left across the screen or looks off to the left.[12] In this sequence the boy on the bicycle riding left across the screen emphasizes a gesture toward the past as Nana

Peazant enters the frame. With the waves forming a backdrop to the scene the intent was to symbolize the Middle Passage, in which the captured Africans were brought on slave ships to the land of their captivity. The chairs carried by the children upside-down on their heads symbolize crowns and are emblematic of the grand and glorious civilization that once was Africa. As the Unborn Child states that she remembers and recalls, the significance is that the past is fused with the present moment, for she is a new member of the Peazant family, summoned by one who was an active participant in that past. The suggestion is that it is necessary to cling to the parts of the past that are vital to understanding the present and that there is knowledge to be gained from those who have lived before.

This intertwining of the wisdom learned from the past with its influence in the present is again visible as Eli follows the Unborn Child to the graveyard. There is a cut to a close-up of Eula pensively watching Eli enter the graveyard and become seized by emotion as he falls to his knees at his mother's grave, then another to an extreme close-up of Eli bent over before the grave. The camera pans slowly over his body as there is a dissolve to the figurehead floating in the water and then a dissolve to Eula facing left with her arms raised as her body undulates to receive the Unborn Child, who comes skipping along in slow motion, merging with Eula's body. After a cut to two figures on a bicycle traveling across the sand to the left of the screen, there is another cut to a medium shot of the Ibo Landing sign on the bank of the river, then another to a close-up of Eula's shoes, as the camera tilts slowly up her body and she begins to recite the Ibo Landing tale.[13]

Eula is passing the tale along to the Unborn Child. The version of the myth she uses is the one in which the Ibo walk back across the water to Africa. As Eula tells the story Eli returns from his sojourn with the spirit of his mother at the graveyard, walking slowly and deliberately toward the river. In the distance the figurehead is visible, resting in the water. Eula relates how the Ibo departed from the ship and took a look around, studying the place carefully: "And they saw things that day that you and I don't have the power to see. Well, they saw just about everything that was to happen around here." The Ibo foresaw the coming war and what was to happen to their descendants there on the island. As Eula speaks we see Eli begin to walk out in the shallow water toward the figurehead. A shot of Eula in the foreground, Eli standing in the water in the middle distance, and the figurehead resting in the water in the background is held for a time. Eula continues relating the myth: "When those Ibo got through sizing up the place real good and seeing what was to come, my grandmother said they turned, all of them, and walked back into the water. Every last man, woman, and child." There is a cut to a close-up of Eula as she smiles proudly and looks down as if she were in the company of a small child. Intercut with shots of Eula speaking are shots of Eli kneeling down by the figurehead, cradling it in his arms, then pushing it farther out into the water. There is a dissolve to a moving camera shot of Eula watching the figurehead as it floats down the river, followed by another dissolve that ends in a close-up of the figurehead, and then a cut back to Eli walking, with his back to the camera, toward where Eula is standing. He kneels down in front of her, grasps her around the waist, and clutches her tightly.

At the beginning of the film, Eli's great-grandmother, Nana Peazant, advises him to contact the spirit of the ancestors, so that they may guide him during his turmoil over the rape and pregnancy of Eula. She tells him that he won't ever have a child that wasn't sent to him—that "the ancestors and the womb, they one and the same." Even though he was not ready to heed Nana's words, she makes the connection for him: he comes to see for himself, through Eula's retelling of the myth, the present-day entrance of the Unborn Child and the force of the figurehead and its poignant history. Nana tells Eli: "There's a thought, a recollection, something somebody remembers," as a signal that her story will invoke a contemplation from the past. She continues: "We carry these memories inside of we. Do you believe that those hundreds and hundreds of Africans brought here on this other side would forget everything they once knew? We don't know where the recollections come from. Sometimes we dream them. But we carry these memories inside of we." Nana provides Eli with a benediction when she tells him she is trying to help him contact the spirit of the ancestors, that if he could learn to beckon them they would come at unexpected moments to guide him. She tells him, "Let them feed your head with wisdom that ain't from this day and time." Nana Peazant reminds Eli: "Those in this grave and those what across the sea, they with us. They all the same, the ancestor and the womb."

"God's My Witness . . ."

Nana Peazant's "recollection" is enacted earlier in the film when we first hear the voice of the Unborn Child telling us that her story is older than she is: "My story begins on the eve of my family's migration North. My story begins before I was born. Nana prayed, and the old souls guided me into the New World." But Nana's belief that the spiritual exists in the living present is contested by two of the women: Haagar and Viola, each of whom has a clearly defined function in the film.

Haagar is first seen running the tip of her toe through the broken bottles on the ground. The bottles are from one of the bottle trees beside each house, each bottle of which represents someone who has died. The bottle trees provide protection and goodwill for the inhabitants of the homes. Eli has smashed this particular tree, after his conversation with Nana in the graveyard. He is frustrated because his lifelong belief in the power of Nana's charms is being challenged by his inability to come to grips with Eula's rape. While Haagar is out near the destroyed bottle tree the Unborn Child enters the frame and tugs at her dress. She gazes wistfully up at Haagar, waiting for her to acknowledge her spirit. Haagar's disbelief is so strong and so willfully held that she makes no contact with the Unborn Child, who turns around and runs merrily on to the rest of her mission.

Haagar gazes up to the top of a huge tree, and as the camera tilts slowly down from the top of the tree to a long shot of Haagar, she beats her hand against her chest, proclaiming grandly, "God's my witness. When I leave this place I'm never again gonna live in your land."

This particular moment in the film is reminiscent of the famous penultimate moment in *Gone with the Wind* in which, after the South had lost the war and those who formerly were living grandly are now left without even the bare necessities, Scarlett O'Hara falls down at the foot of a gigantic tree and vows that, as God is her witness, she will never be hungry again. Scarlett's declaration in one of the most heralded films of all time is a declaration of the tenacity of those who would stop at nothing, even to the point of feeling appointed as "owners" of other human beings, in the service of their belief in an innate superiority. In *Daughters of the Dust*, Dash reverses Scarlett's declaration: it is a repudiation of the antebellum South and all that it represented.

The film is constructed around such moments, with all the grandeur and pomp usually devoted to those securely lodged within mainstream culture. A radical reversal takes place as black people form the center of the story instead of being used as background window dressing for the chronicle of others' lives. When Haagar displays her strength of will at the foot of the tree and issues her challenge to all, she stands as a symbol for those whose stories have never been told. As her particular history unfolds throughout the film it echoes previous black women's lives—specifically her speech to the women gathered at the picnic site preparing the food for the celebration feast.

After scenes of Iona and St. Julian Last Child, the last Cherokee nation–born child remaining on the island, talking and embracing on the beach, there is a cut to a medium shot of the Newlywed Woman leaning back against a tree, gazing off into the distance. Haagar begins to glance around and call out for Iona. She turns away, frustrated at Iona's absence, and then begins to criticize Nana Peazant in front of Viola, Nana Peazant's granddaughter, who is lying on a blanket reading her Bible, and the Hairbraider, who is shucking ears of corn. Haagar tells them that Nana needs to stop going off by herself contemplating the objects from the past in her

Haagar Peazant (Kaycee Moore) declares her intention: "God's my witness! When I leave this place, I'm never again gonna live in your land."

tin can of memories. She follows up with the thought that perhaps Nana Peazant is not in her right mind. Viola defends her grandmother, chastising Haagar, "You're laughing at an old woman, Haagar Peazant." Viola reminds Haagar, "Just like Eula, you married into this family. But she's our grandmother. Ain't nothing wrong or harmful in that tin can she carries." After Haagar and the Hairbraider mimic what seems to them to be a familiar chant about Nana's "scraps of memories," Viola tells them that she is aware that Nana is carrying a lot of baggage from the past and that she needs to put "her soul in the hands of the Lord. But she built her life around this family. She's old, and she's frightened. What does Nana know about the world outside? Nothing. Nana was never educated. All she knows are simple things, things people told her a long time ago."

The Hairbraider insists that Nana must go with them to the North. At this point Haagar becomes even more agitated and states adamantly that Nana and her old ways need to remain on the island. Haagar walks defiantly toward the other two women, one hand on her hip and the other grasping a carrot that she is preparing to cook, jabbing the air with the carrot to emphasize her point. She states, "I might not have been born in this family, but I'm here now. And I say, Let Nana Peazant stay behind. That's what she wants. We moving into a new day. She's too much a part of the past." The Hairbraider responds that Daddy Mac, Nana Peazant's son, had better not hear Haagar saying what she just said. Haagar becomes even more belligerent, telling them, "I'm a fully grown 'oman and I don't have to mind what I say. I done born five children into the world and put two of them in the ground alongside they daddy. I work all my life and ain't got nothing to show for it. And if I can't say what's on my mind, then damn everybody to hell."

Haagar is mired in the same parochial mentality as the other residents of Ibo Landing. She is naive in her optimism that there is a much better life for them away from the island. She is as frightened of new things as Nana Peazant is, as we witness in her treatment of Yellow Mary when Yellow Mary returns from her world travels with her can of "store-bought" biscuits. But Haagar stands tall for her rights and is fiercely protective of what is hers. For that reason her children are named Myown and Iona. She tells the other women, "My children ain't gonna be like those old Africans, fresh off the boat." She feels it is a new world that they are moving toward: "I want my daughters to grow up to be decent somebodies. I don't want my girls to have to hear about all that mess." Haagar issues a warning: "I'll lock horns with anything and anybody that tries to hold me back." Because of these sentiments—that the old ways are harmful to her children—she is determined to stop them from joining the others in kissing the "hand" that Nana has prepared as a charm to protect them on their journey to the North. Haagar demonstrates her sense of commanding all that is hers at the end of the film, when Iona runs off to join St. Julian Last Child and they ride away on the horse. Haagar protests loudly to everyone that she owns the child and thus can dictate what her actions should be.

Haagar also displays a strength of purpose and a toughness of will that reveals how she was able to survive the tortures of life there on the island. In her declaration at the foot of the tree and her speech to Viola and the Hairbraider on the beach she is reminiscent of such black women as Sojourner Truth, who demonstrated the same courage and endurance as she told of her life under slavery. Sojourner Truth also spoke of bearing children who later died under the rigors of slavery, and of working hard and feeling the lash of the whip. In *Daughters of the Dust* Haagar and the other black women answer affirmatively and proudly Truth's centuries'-old question—"And ain't I a woman?"

Each of the women in the film also serves to represent the full scope of black women's lives and experiences. In contrast to the limited depictions of black women formerly available in mainstream cultural forms, *Daughters of the Dust* presents the varieties within black womanhood. Nana Peazant places her faith in her ancestors and the relics from their past lives; Yellow Mary clings to her St. Christopher charm and her strong conviction that she can always make her way in the world; and Eula sets a letter beneath a glass of water under her bed to summon the spirit of her mother to guide her. Haagar believes firmly in herself and doesn't need any of what she terms "that hoodoo mess." Viola, more than anyone else, has entrusted her life to the belief systems of the dominant culture.

Viola has moved away from the island and become a devout Baptist missionary. Viola's style of dress and coiffure reveal that she is a tightly corseted woman with not a hair out of place. Her stern visage as she constantly interjects her religious homilies—"Mind now, the Lord is a-listening"—is a mask behind which she hides her self-doubts, her fears of abandoning her traditional mores, and her womanhood. At the end of the film, when it becomes evident that those who are leaving for the North are truly parting with Nana Peazant and the home of their birth, Viola begins to unravel. Her hair comes undone, and her blouse pulls halfway out of her skirt. She protests that old folks are supposed to die and go to heaven, not be left behind grieving for their lost kin. When Viola realizes the value of her grandmother's traditions and folk beliefs, she finally kisses the "hand" that her grandmother has fixed as a gesture of reconciliation of her past with her future.

Viola's burgeoning understanding and reevaluation of her past is accompanied by Mr. Snead's appreciation of his African background. Mr. Snead is a photographer and an anthropologist who has come with Viola to document the Peazants' last day on Ibo Landing. He has an ulterior motive, however, of assembling an exhibition of his photographs when he arrives back in the North, to showcase his collection of photographs of "primitive" people. For Dash, he represents the viewing audience—those who perceive the people and the culture she has depicted as exotic, foreign, and something to be looked at under a microscope.[14]

But Mr. Snead undergoes a transformation during his sojourn with the people on the island. His sense of superiority and his scientific outlook are eclipsed as he reaches an awareness that these are the people and traditions that are part of his heritage. After Mr. Snead takes a series of photographs and talks with several people, he appears overjoyed and grabs Viola in a hug and whirls her around in a circle. She reproaches him, saying sternly, "Mr. Snead!" while pulling her arms from his grasp and attempting to put herself back together. Mr. Snead asks Viola if he may talk with Bilal Muhammed; he wants to know if he is family. Viola desists, however, for she sees no value in talking to Bilal Muhammed: "That old heathen. He's not important." She goes on to explain to Mr. Snead that everyone on the island is family in some way, but, she adds, "Unfortunately, so many like Bilal are so backward. They believe everything that happens is caused by conjure, magic, or their ancestors." Viola inserts her own religious sentiments self-righteously: "They don't leave nothing to God." Mr. Snead finally talks with Bilal Muhammed and learns the true story of the Ibo and how they drowned themselves rather than live enslaved. While he takes the portrait of the entire assembled group of Peazants, Mr. Snead is so overcome that he shouts to them, "Look! Look up! And remember Ibo Landing!" Later, Daddy Mac adds his recollections to those of Bilal about what he learned from his elders. In the scene the men sit spread out along the beach. Present are Eli, lying down looking around contentedly; Bilal Muhammed, standing by a tree and gazing out at the water; and Daddy Mac, kneeling on one knee as he leans in to talk with Mr. Snead, who sits spread-legged on the sand, having given up his studies of the people to really learn from them. Daddy Mac tells Mr. Snead he was taught that "woman is the sweetness of life." Daddy Mac describes the beauty of black women and their "lovely" voices and repeats his assertion that "woman is the sweetness of life." He concludes the litany of instructions from his elders, telling Mr. Snead, "And that's what I remember." After his conversation with the men, Mr. Snead readily joins in the ritual kissing of Nana's "hand" and then walks quickly over to Viola, grabs her, and kisses her on the mouth.

In the film Mr. Snead becomes a changed person. He is no longer a voyeur stationed outside the community, minutely examining the people and their assumed backward ways, wanting only to exploit them under the guise of scientific studies. Rather, Mr. Snead becomes a true believer. His transformation is matched by that of Viola, who formerly interacted with her family with a bemused tolerance. She appeared to be harboring a secret desire to convert them from their heathenism to a better appreciation of the finer points of "civilization"—evident as she demonstrates through the scenes in which she tries to teach the young girls the "proper" way to sit and comport themselves gracefully. Although Viola chastises Haagar for demeaning Nana Peazant's supposedly pagan practices, Viola is just as disdainful of Bilal Muhammed's religion. Her strict, tight-laced dress and demeanor suggest that she is rigidly holding herself in. Viola suppresses not only her background but her sexual self as well, displacing it onto her strict religious beliefs.[15]

Viola's attempts to restrain her sexual feelings were not unusual, for many black women of that era attempted to present themselves as refined and genteel in response to the pervasive sentiment that black women were loose, untamable sexual creatures. The Club Movement initiated by black women at the turn of the century worked to counter these historical misrepresentations. Literary works such as

Iola Leroy (1892) by Frances Harper and *Contending Forces* (1900) by Pauline Hopkins are two examples of fictional works engaged in the effort to eradicate this false image of black women.

Daughters of the Dust is the first film to explore the issue of black women and the ways they responded to images of themselves as sexually immoral. The presentation of Viola and her starched, restrained, religious countenance provide a stark contrast to Eula's rape and to Yellow Mary. Their two stories, coupled with Nana Peazant's history, are a dramatic reconstruction of one of the most devastating myths about black womanhood.

". . . We Never Was a Pure 'Oman"

Dash talks about the process of taking historical moments and depicting them in a different way, of "showing black families, particularly black women, as we have never seen them before."[16] In this way events come to have more meaning than they would in a strictly conventional presentation of the story. There are two scenes in which Dash had planned to depict the reality of slavery that were different from their routine presentations. One was actually shot but not included in the final edit; the other, written but not shot.

The first scene is a flashback to Nana Peazant as a baby who has been taken from her mother and sold to another plantation. Nana's mother had cut off a lock of her own hair and sewn it into a baby's blanket to send along with the young girl, so that when she was old enough she could take the lock of hair out and remember her mother. The image that was to be used to convey the mother's feelings of loss, of the need to maintain a connection with the child who had been taken from her, was the milk that flowed from her engorged breasts. After a baby is born the mother produces milk, even in the absence of the child. To show the mother's grief, Dash constructed a scene in which the milk seeps from the mother's breasts through her dress and drips to the ground. In place of tears the milk flowing from her breasts was to serve as a symbol of the mother mourning the baby that was taken from her.

The second scene revolves around Yellow Mary and her experiences with the white family in Cuba, where she worked as a nursemaid. There is a flashback to the Cuban bedroom, where Yellow Mary nurses a white baby as the baby's father fondles her other breast. At the point where Yellow Mary talks to Eula about the rape, as she is sitting in the tree, there was to be continual cross-cutting with the Cuban bedroom scenes.[17]

It was a conscious decision not to show the rape of Eula, because that segment of history has been graphically presented many times. With Yellow Mary the parallel editing accomplishes a different purpose, a stark black and white contrast that amplifies her predicament of having faced the personal trauma of losing her child and needing to escape what has been forced upon her. That Yellow Mary becomes a prostitute to gain her independence emphasizes that she is the one in control of her life rather than at the mercy of those who felt they had a divine right to the use of her body.

Although the two proposed scenes were not part of the finished film, they are present as a subtext, underscoring the need to remember the specific details of black women's history. As Dash relates, "It is the specifics that are so important, that add resonance to what we as black filmmakers do. And we have to be very careful that we don't lose our original voice in the writing, in the editing, and in the final cut. We have to be very careful because what to us reads as resonance, to others can be read as an error."[18]

In the finished film the original voice of black women and their life histories is seen in the final moments, when Nana Peazant, Yellow Mary, and Eula demonstrate the ways in which black women cope, survive, and, most important, triumph despite centuries of abuse.

After Bilal Muhammed and Daddy Mac share with Mr. Snead their teachings about black women, there are loud cries from Nana Peazant as she sits among the women. She is distraught, pressing her hands against her breasts and shaking her head from side to side. Everyone becomes alarmed, trying to determine the cause of her anguish. Nana stands and begins to run away from the group.

Yellow Mary clasps her in an embrace as they rock back and forth on the sand, and tries to comfort Nana by assuring of her need for her and her desire to be among the people who realize who she is. She tells her, "I need to know I can come and hold on to where I come from. I need to know that the people know my name. I Yellow Mary Peazant, and I a proud 'oman, not a hard 'oman." Yellow Mary tells Nana, "I want to stay. I want to stay with you here."

Yellow Mary has been out in the world that the others of the island are so eager to enter—been in it and found it wanting. Although, as it becomes increasingly clear, staying on the island means separation from Trula, who will travel on to Nova Scotia, Yellow Mary remains with her grandmother and takes solace in the familiarity of her past.

Nana Peazant herself is confused about the others' need to leave the island. She asks them, "How can you leave this soil? This soil, this what our loved ones—they here in this soil." Even though they persist in going, Nana tells them, "I love you 'cause you mine. You the fruit of an ancient tree."

As the people are gathered around them, Eula takes up the charge that Yellow Mary and Nana Peazant began. She has heard the not-so-subtle comments about Yellow Mary's being "ruint"; she has seen the way they have treated her since her return to the island. Eula reminds them that Yellow Mary was responsible for providing the money that kept one of their kin from jail. Eula probes further into the prejudices and biases of her family. She asks, "You so ashamed of Yellow Mary 'cause she got ruint. Well, what do you say about me?" She then makes a statement that is the overarching theme of the film: "As far as this place is concerned, we never was a pure 'oman. Deep inside we believe they ruin our mothers and their mothers what come before them." Eula speaks passionately of the routes black women have taken to protect themselves, of their battle for a sense of their own importance, and of their value to themselves and their families. She says, "And we live our lives always expecting worse, 'cause we feel we don't deserve no better. Deep inside we believe that even God can't heal the wounds of our past or protect us from the world that put shackles on our feet." She reaffirms for the women that their past was forced on them and that their future may not be as soiled. She tells them to let go of that past while holding on to the resources from their ancestors: "We are the daughters of those old dusty things that Nana carries in her tin can." Eula reassures them that they deserve whatever good comes from the roads they take in life, "because we all good 'oman."

Eula's soliloquy is as much directed to those members of the family surrounding her as it is a tribute to the black women who have not let their inheritance from enslavement rob them of their heritage of resistance and survival. Eula talks about the sustenance black women gain from the support of other black women and reminds them that this is a necessary part of their survival: "If you love yourselves, then love Yellow Mary, because she a part of you. Just like we a part of our mothers."

Black Women in Otherworlds

"As a black woman," states Julie Dash, "you take for granted that you are never going to see certain moments—certain private moments—on the screen."[19] For this reason she makes a conscious effort to bring the audience into the film, to convey a closeness, rather than try to distance the audience from the film. Three sequences in particular illustrate Dash's assertions. The first example of the intimacy, of the subtle shadings provided by a director who is part of the culture being portrayed, involves Yellow Mary and Nana Peazant. The careful attention to the choice of words spoken, the positions taken by the actors as Yellow Mary crouches on her haunches before Nana Peazant in her regal chair, the contrasts of the women's styles of dress, and the familiar manner in which they touch and stroke one another—all are intricate aspects of a mise-en-scène that places the viewer within the midst of the women's emotional moment. The motion from two-shot to close-up and the poise and control of the actors in the reaction shots all blend together to create an aura of warmth and poignancy as Yellow Mary tells her grandmother, "I wanted to surprise you, Nana." The weight of years is heard in Nana Peazant's gentle reply: "No surprises here, Yellow Mary." Without censure, without expectations, without judgment, Yellow Mary's grandmother strokes her hair and gazes affectionately into her face, making sure that her excursion to the New World has not destroyed her inner being. When she is satisfied that all is well, Nana Peazant leans in toward Yellow Mary and places their foreheads softly together.

The second example contains a series of shots of Yellow Mary with Eula or interacting with Trula that culminate in the three of them sitting together on the beach under an umbrella. After Yellow Mary recalls for Eula her experiences in Cuba, there are shots of her and Trula walking along the edge of the water. The music accompanying them is soft and soothing, providing a gentle background as Yellow Mary touches Trula's hair and bows her head to look up at her face, then the two embrace and gently rock back and forth. In the next shot Trula walks off by herself as Eula and Yellow Mary enter the frame, trailing along behind her. The three of them find an old, discarded umbrella lying disintegrating on the shore. The music continues as they twirl and spin the umbrella. After a dissolve we see the three of them sitting on a fallen tree. The image is held as the camera slowly pulls back.

It is a remarkable moment in cinema when all these elements converge—the music, the cinematography, the editing—to create a loving portrait of three black women. The moment resumes as Yellow Mary and Eula sit under the umbrella while Yellow Mary gives Eula an example of shutting off the demons in her mind until she is prepared to cope with them.

The closing scenes of *Daughters of the Dust* are an epiphany, providing coherence and balance to the opening scenes of the film. In the beginning the female voice-over speaks of being the first and the last: "Many are my daughters." At the end of the film, the lingering evocative shots of four generations of black women walking along the water's edge are a fitting conclusion. Nana Peazant has lived to see the birth of the newest member of the family.

Nana Peazant (Cora Lee Day) and Yellow Mary (Barbara-O) share an intimate moment upon Yellow Mary's return to Ibo Landing.

Yellow Mary (Barbara-O), Eula (Alva Rogers), and Trula (Trula Hoosier) finding sanctuary in one another's company while relaxing on the beach.

Multiple generations of Peazant women strolling along the water's edge at the end of *Daughters of the Dust*.

The Unborn Child (Kai-Lynn Warren) running along behind her elders at the end of the film.

Daughters of the Dust is not simply a tale of black women reclaiming their past. As a work deliberately conceived as a film about black women, with black women intended as its primary audience, it intervenes strongly in a tradition of derogatory portrayals of black women in dominant cinema. It is thus a powerful component of a cultural movement toward the empowerment of black women.

CHAPTER FIVE

Black Women Reading *Daughters of the Dust*

Because of financial exigencies *Daughters of the Dust* was released on a staggered schedule rather than simultaneously in many theaters across the country. Part of the reason was the cost of producing the 35mm negative and prints that were necessary for commercial exhibition.[1] Additional expenses included producing the 16mm negative and prints for exhibition at colleges, libraries, and museums; for the film was heavily and successfully promoted in that market as well. Because of the small number of copies available, the film was shown in one market, or in only a few, at a time, then sent on to the next engagement. Something of a juggling act resulted as the film did turn-away business in one location or another, and the exhibitors wanted to keep it longer than planned in order to make the most money while the audience was still primed to see the film. Subsequent exhibitors' schedules were disrupted, because everything was coordinated to correspond with the film's openings: newspaper reviews, interviews with the director on local radio and television stations, opening night receptions, and so on.

Word-of-mouth advertising becomes crucial when a film is released in this manner, because interest must be sustained beyond the opening weekend, the Thursday, Friday, Saturday, and Sunday of the usual exhibition cycle. For this reason the financial and eventual critical success of *Daughters of the Dust* was even more impressive, because audiences throughout the country waited for the film to open in their respective areas. Even though it showed on only one or two screens per market, *Daughters of the Dust* sold out the house in most of the areas where it was shown. At one point *Daughters of the Dust* had the highest per-screen average for the week, beating out such films as *The Hand that Rocks the Cradle*, *Fried Green Tomatoes*, *Father of the Bride*, and *Grand Canyon*.[2]

Its showing in New York, where extra screenings had to be scheduled both during its initial run at the Film Forum and afterward, when it was transferred to the Village East Cinemas in Greenwich Village, was important. Nationally, all the key metropolitan newspapers—the *New York Times*, the *Washington Post*, and the *Chicago Tribune*—reviewed the film, and the morning television talk show hosts interviewed the director. After the audiences in major market areas—New York, Chicago, Boston, and Washington, D.C.—served notice through their attendance in overwhelming number that the film was an event not to be ignored, the television movie critics gave favorable reviews of the film.

The fact that the film survived in spite of the handicaps of the first negative reviews and the problems obtaining a distributor points to an area of film scholarship that bears further investigation. Much has been written about the presentation of images of black people throughout motion picture history. However, little attention has been given to the ways in which the composition of audiences determines which films will be produced in the future or to what extent the economics of consumption influences the content of succeeding films. Two particularly noteworthy studies of black film attendance are relevant to this analysis of the cultural and economic impact of black women and their responses to *Daughters of the Dust*, because they illuminate the ways in which particular audiences have maneuvered around the dictates of the film industry and the manner in which the industry has responded.

Black Film History

Historically, during each period in which black audiences were able to attend films there has been a corresponding increase in the number of films produced by black filmmakers.[3] These have not always been films that black critics considered reputable, but many attempted to depict black people's lives faithfully and responsibly. At each point, however, the established film industry worked to exploit this audience for maximum profit while simultaneously containing whatever subversive thrust remained in works created by black filmmakers. The industry accomplished this through several means: a decline in the amount of financing, coupled with inadequate marketing and publicity for films created by black filmmakers; a lack of support from exhibitors located in important areas; the making of black-themed films by established white producers; and, in an especially critical area, unflattering reviews in widely read mainstream publications.

Mary Carbine's study of the first black-owned theater in America, located in Chicago, is useful because it demonstrates how black audiences employ what she terms "tactical consumption" to create a "specific dynamic of reception that mitigated against the hegemony of mass culture."[4] In other words, the fact that black audiences attended mainstream commercial films in large number did not mean that they subscribed to the dominant ideology presented in the films. In her historical study of black film attendance, Carbine investigated a black community that thrived in Chicago during the early part of this century. Her findings are important because they challenge previous scholarly film analyses that attempt to minimize the ability of specific social groups to use cultural products in culturally specific ways.

Carbine goes further in her insistence that although text-based examinations of black characters and themes are revealing, they are limited because the emphasis remains on black people as "constructs of a text or victims of Hollywood racism." A more productive approach is one that examines audience consumption and exhibition practices with an eye toward the ways in which black people working in combination as cultural workers and consumers, as performers and spectators, can "invent their own cultural forms and practices."[5] Of particular significance in Carbine's analysis is the way she demonstrates how black entertainment was sustained by black efforts through advertising in black publications and in venues specifically located in places frequented by black people. She thus proved that black cultural forms, or cultural forms of interest to black audiences, have long been profitable if black cultural consumers are made aware of their existence.

A second study demonstrating the power of black audiences is James Miller's analysis of the impact of black film attendance during the early 1970s. Miller shows how theaters that were located in downtown areas of major cities systematically discouraged black patrons from attending. As white patrons moved to the suburbs, and theaters located in shopping malls became the dominant venue of film exhibition, revenues declined in downtown theaters until the black action films of the early 1970s attracted black patrons there. To recoup lost revenues from the disappearance of white audiences the owners of downtown theaters actively targeted black audiences. Consequently, according to Miller's research, not only did black people begin attending films in large number but, additionally, they even saved one prominent Hollywood studio from extinction.[6]

From the astounding financial success of the early 1970s black action films *Cotton Comes to Harlem* (1970) and *Shaft* (1971) Hollywood studios began to churn out films directed at young, black, urban audiences until the films' attraction waned and other films with similar formulas directed at white audiences began to make money. Miller suggests that what the success of the 1970s films taught Hollywood producers is that there was a black film audience that contributed substantially to the industry's profits.

Hollywood producers also learned that black people constituted a large part of the audience even for films whose themes were not exclusively black.[7] Thus according to Miller the industry recognized that it did not need to cater to black audiences, because this segment of the population attended films nevertheless.[8] Therefore Hollywood producers no longer felt they needed to appeal to a black sensibility or a black consciousness whenever they sought a black audience. Even as some critics protested against the derogatory portrayals of black culture, Hollywood knew there was a black population guaranteed to spend a great deal of money to attend films. Consequently, little attempt was made to create works that would present an enlightened view of black life. Hollywood films that featured black themes needed only to have a crossover appeal for white audiences, because it was assumed that black audiences would attend anyway.

This rationale was borne out in what Miller feels is a particularly illuminating example—*The Color Purple*—with repercussions for almost a decade of film production. Miller sees the film as one that was designed for mass consumption by white audiences. He concludes that the commercial success of *The Color Purple* would thus lead to "a renaissance of films about black subjects."[9]

Miller's prophecy appears to have been on the mark in the years following the release of *The Color Purple*, for there was a boom in films directed by young, black, male filmmakers. However, these films were mostly tailored to a formula that appealed to white audiences and, more important, to the expectations of mainstream critical reviewers. Some of the films provoked extended media discussions. The *New York Times* devoted prominent space to analyzing what the editors of the newspaper viewed as the detrimental societal effects of Spike Lee's films. The monthly news magazines presented selective coverage of what they perceived as violence in theaters where *Boyz N the Hood* was shown. When films directed by black filmmakers did not meet the white expectations of subject matter these films received minimal coverage, little effort was made to advertise or distribute them to theaters attended by black people, and they eventually died a quiet death. Significant examples are Charles Burnett's *To Sleep with Anger* (1990), Wendell Harris's *Chameleon Street* (1990), and Charles Lane's *Sidewalk Stories* (1989).

Commenting on this trend of financing (and publicizing) the films by black directors that depict the lives of young inner-city males, Jacquie Jones noted that this practice may "threaten the viability of other types of mainstream black cinematic expression."[10] She suggests that films that are not about teenagers and crime and that attempt to delve more deeply into complex aspects of black life will meet with resistance in obtaining distribution. Perhaps the greatest harm, though, comes from the tendency of certain types of films that garner establishment approval to set the standard for which films are considered noteworthy. As Jones concludes, the promotion of young urban "hood" films to the exclusion of films by other filmmakers "promises to codify a range of behaviors as uncharacteristic of the black experience as those represented in films made by whites."[11]

What this meant for *Daughters of the Dust* is that the film carried with it a burden of expectations regarding its entrance into the history of black film production. Many black film critics and scholars were aware of a film in the making by one of the most respected black women filmmakers, but hardly anyone knew the film's specific content, and fewer still had seen the form it would take. All, however, were cognizant of the importance of the production of what would become the first commercial feature-length film by a black woman. Although later reviews of *Daughters of the Dust* were overwhelmingly laudatory, the first articles in key publications addressed specific elements and thus established the terms on which the film would subsequently be evaluated.

Because of the way in which the film was released—that is, area by area rather than nationwide—the first reviews had the potential to govern its success or failure. That the film became economically successful, especially relative to its production expenses, does more than simply open the door for films by other black female filmmakers. The example of *Daughters of the Dust* also reveals specific audiences' power to challenge what they consider to be the ultimate constraints on what is presented as appropriate subject matter for black film audiences and, further, what constitutes topics that black audiences feel are worthy of spending money to see. An analysis of the most identifiable cluster of reactions—those of black women—provides insights that may lead to the production of similar films that contradict establishment sentiments and redress past structured absences within mainstream film.

From February through June 1992 I interviewed three groups of black women—a total of eighteen—about their reactions to *Daughters of the Dust*. All the women lived on the West Coast, although not all were born there. The majority of the women had been born and had grown up in the South and had moved to the West Coast as young adults.

I was living on the West Coast doing research on black women and their reactions to different kinds of film when I learned that *Daughters of the Dust* had finally secured a distributor. At that point I decided to concentrate my interviews exclusively on the women's responses to this specific film. For the interviews I was fortunate enough to obtain a videotape copy of *Daughters of the Dust* from the New York public relations firm KJM3, for the film would not be shown in area theaters for several more months.

Four of the women in the first group I interviewed participated in one of the sessions on *The Color Purple*. As part of the current research project I began attending the same beauty salon that members of my research group regularly frequented. By going often, I was able to become acquainted with many of the black women who went there. They were aware of the type of research I was doing, but I was careful not to tape anyone without her permission or to ask questions related to the project without prior consent or without stating that I considered what she was saying to be relevant to my study. When I decided to concentrate on group interviews for *Daughters of the Dust*, the women from my previous study readily agreed to watch the copy of the film I had obtained from New York and to discuss their feelings about the film with me. I invited other regular patrons of the beauty salon to participate as well. Three consented, but several others were reluctant to commit their thoughts to tape.

The seven women who took part in the study were aware that they would have to allot a significant portion of their day to the project. We arranged to meet on a Sunday afternoon for an early dinner and to go on from there. The names of the seven women in the first group are Cecelia, Paige, Constance, and Christine (who also participated in the earlier set of interviews on *The Color Purple*) as well as Kathy, Marianne, and Justine, who were new to the group. The women ranged in age from late thirties to middle fifties, with the majority in their middle to late forties. The women were all solidly middle-class in income. Three held management positions, one at an electronics firm and two for the city government. Three were longtime elementary school teachers, and one taught vocational education at a community college. Four had advanced degrees, two had bachelor's degrees, and one had some college education but no degree. Three were married, and the other four were divorced. All had children, and four had grandchildren. All had lived on the West Coast for a number of years.

The session lasted for several hours, including the time spent viewing the tape and the discussion afterward. Before starting the film I gave a very brief overview, stating the film's setting and time and noting its significance as the first commercial film by a black female director. Aside from this information, the women knew little else about the film. From my experience with one of the groups interviewed about *The Color Purple* I was prepared to let the women speak during the film, but this group surprised me by saying almost nothing while the tape was playing. They asked no questions about the language, the characters' relationships, or anything of the sort. There were exclamations at portions of the film that moved them, and at certain moments several of the women began to weep, but otherwise very little was said. In fact, the women were so quiet that I became a little unnerved and began to assume that perhaps they actively disliked the film or found portions of it offensive. At the end of the film the women were completely silent, until one declared, "That's the most beautiful movie I have ever seen," prompting an outburst of conversation from the others.

The first question asked was "Who was the woman in the yellow dress?" (The dress the character Trula wore was actually peach-colored but appeared yellow in the videotape.) The fact that Trula and Yellow Mary were lovers did not receive as much attention in the critical reviews, nor was it given as much emphasis in any of the commentaries about the film, as the relationship between Celie and Shug did in *The Color Purple*. I wanted to see where the question was headed, so rather than answer it directly I attempted to elicit from the women their thoughts on who she was. Several minutes of conversation concerning the departure of Yellow Mary and "the woman in the yellow dress" to Nova Scotia, and other seemingly inconsequential matters, followed, until Marianne stated bluntly, "I thought they were lovers." Cecelia immediately concurred: "Yeah, I did too."

JB: Say some more about that.

Kathy: You know, I sort of had the feeling [that they were lovers] at the very beginning, but I wouldn't let myself think that. Isn't that funny?

JB: Why wouldn't you let yourself think it?

Kathy: I don't know. Because they were both so very pretty and so very feminine, that's why I wouldn't let myself think it. And now that you mention it, it's just quite possible.

JB: If you think that they were lovers, how does it make you feel?

Cecelia: It didn't bother me at all.

Kathy: It didn't bother me one way or the other.

Paige: You didn't let yourself think they were lovers, so you must have had some kind of feeling about it.

Kathy: I didn't want to think that I was misunderstanding the movie. I didn't want to be seeing something that wasn't there.

Without prompting, the women continued to discuss the relationship between Trula and Yellow Mary. I did not sense that they were critical of the fact that the women were lovers; they seemed more concerned about understanding what was going on.

Constance: I thought they had some kind of relationship, but I also thought that Yellow Mary wasn't satisfied with that relationship, because she kept talking about men.
Marianne: She kept talking about finding a good man she could lean on or something.
Constance: I thought there was maybe some connection there but that she was still not comfortable with it [i.e., the relationship with Trula].
Kathy: She [Yellow Mary] didn't seem to be too comfortable with herself, really. She was in a lot of turmoil.

The women in the second group were also uncertain about the relationship between Yellow Mary and Trula. These women, though, went a bit farther with their discussion and discussed the way in which the relationship was presented by the director and how this affected their reactions.

The seven women in this group were highly educated women who lived in the vicinity of a major West Coast university. The area could not be considered a college town, but many of its activities and businesses were influenced by the presence of the university nearby. The women ranged in age from their mid-twenties to their mid-forties. One was a university professor, one was a high school teacher, one was employed in a medically related field, and the other four were graduate students working toward their doctoral degrees.

Before the interview I had never met any of the women. They were interviewed in March 1992 and had seen a copy of *Daughters of the Dust* in a classroom setting while it was being promoted prior to its opening in their area. The women all knew one another; they were members of a research and study group that met regularly to discuss various issues related to black people and black scholarship. I had heard from a friend that the women had seen *Daughters of the*

Dust and were willing to participate in my research project. After making initial contact with one of the women, we set up a time for the interview, and I traveled to the area for the interview.

Because the women had already seen the film this session was discussion-only; we did not view the film again. The interview lasted approximately five or six hours.

The women in this group were younger than the others I had previously researched and also more involved in higher education than any of the other black women. They also kept abreast of cultural activities affecting black people and were more accustomed to critically analyzing, rather than simply discussing, issues. The women's names were Gwen, Tracy, Helen, Leah, Dorothy, Eileen, and Agatha.

Although this was not the first topic discussed it is relevant to the conversation that the women in the other group had about "the woman in the yellow dress," as the character Trula seems destined to be forever designated.

Leah: At first I thought, for a brief moment, that she might have been Yellow Mary's daughter, but then I realized that they were—

Dorothy [finishing for her]: —special friends—

Tracy [finishing further]: —were close.

JB: Did you wonder about the relationship while you were watching the film, or afterward?

Dorothy: There were a couple of moments [while watching the film] where you said, "Oh, oh," where you knew—

Leah [interrupting]: —where there was recognition—

Dorothy [completing her thought]: —where you knew what was going on. And afterward we talked about it just to confirm.

Leah and Agatha commented that they liked the relationship between Yellow Mary and Trula. Leah added, "It was done in such a way as to make it seem less obvious on the one hand, therefore creating a different kind of text about it. It just seemed a part of and a different dimension of the family or the group." Dorothy felt the way the relationship was handled was not intrusive and did not interfere with their paying attention to the rest of the film. To this Leah added the observation that Trula was used as the outsider, the one who provided a contrast to the rest of the group there on the island.

My analysis of the function of Trula in the film, as a catalyst for the subsequent actions of other people on the island and as a mirror to illuminate the attitudes and characteristics of the other women, is based upon repeated viewings of the film and from my interview with the director. Leah's comment is insightful, because she had seen the film only once and had read very little about it. One of the recurring pans that *Daughters of the Dust* received from established reviewers was that it was difficult to understand and thus audiences would be turned off and refuse to attend. One of the reasons that the organizers of the Cannes Film Festival gave for rejecting the work was that they did not understand the film.

Julie Dash, referring to the sentiments expressed by white male reviewers, insists that white men promote films about young black males in urban areas because they can pretend to be a part of the environment without actually living there and without having to experience those social conditions in any way but vicariously. She adds, "Most white men don't want to be a black woman for two hours. It's [i.e., vicariously being a black woman] two hours too long."[12] Dash also feels that if white men are not the center of the film, either as subjects or as objects of black male anger, then they are turned off and refuse to have anything to do with the story.

The women in the second group talked about the absence of whites in general, and of white men in particular, in *Daughters of the Dust*. Helen said that she was not expecting to see any white people in the film, so it did not have a major impact on her. Agatha replied that the white man was actually present in the film—he just wasn't present physically. She suggested that the rape was his presence. Leah wondered how the others could assume that the rapist was white, because there were no white people seen on the island. Helen replied that she never thought of the rapist as anything but a white man, after which Tracy and Dorothy analyzed that aspect of the film.

> Tracy: I didn't know where he came from, but I knew he [the rapist] was white. I had a strong suspicion at the beginning when they first started talking about it, and then when that sister [Yellow Mary] came back, she made a comment that it was a good thing she [Eula] had not told her husband [who the rapist was] because he would be found hanging from a tree. Well, black people don't hang each other.

Dorothy thought the absence of white people—"the white man," as she put it—was very effective, but at the same time she wondered at the absence of people other than the family. She stated that these two parts of the story were left for the viewer to fill in. On the one hand the absence of white people affected her, but on the other hand she kept trying to figure out where the rest of the people were. Dorothy also raised the point that life on the island was shown to be so idyllic that she wondered "why anybody would ever want to leave this place. That continued to be a question for me. If it's so good, why leave it?"

Leah and Agatha disagreed about the idyllic representation of the family's life. Leah countered that the scenes from the past revealed that the family had to work the land extremely hard to survive there. She then commented on the scenes set in the present in which the family was shown preparing the feast: "That island didn't just grow corn and okra and all of the other things they had in that gumbo. You have to work pretty hard to have all that stuff." Dorothy, however, was not convinced and felt that part of the film needed further explication: "It's one thing to be out in your garden and pick okra and tomatoes and all that. It's quite another to be out there toiling for somebody else's profit. And that's the dimension of the movie that is really cut away."

Dorothy's view of the film's incoherence and lack of continuity was one of the predominant criticisms in the first important reviews—that the film suffered from an insufficient back story, was ahistorical, and presented such an idealized portrait of the Peazant family that viewers would question their motivation to leave the island for what would surely be a harsh life in the North. These are issues that lend themselves to further examination in the other women's reactions to the film.

In this respect the comments from the women in the third group are significant, because these women experienced the regular process of film attendance: they heard about the film on television programs, read the reviews in local newspapers, then saw the film in the theaters. Their reactions were more likely to be affected by the pre-publicity, because they were not seeing the film on the occasion of a research project or in a classroom setting, they would have an opportunity to discuss the film with others, and they would form impressions about the film over a longer period of time.

The third group of women was also unique in that it contained a grandmother, mother, and daughter from the same family, and a good friend of the family as well. I had met one of the women at a meeting and had overheard her talking about *Daughters of the Dust* on several occasions. When I spoke with her about the film I learned that she was so taken with it that she had made special arrangements for her mother, son, and two daughters to see the film on Mother's Day. I was so intrigued with her comments that I asked if I might interview her and her family for my project. She agreed and asked whether her friend, who had also seen the film as soon as it arrived in their area, could be a part of the interview as well. We then set up a suitable time, and I traveled to the city to interview them.

Elizabeth, my initial contact, was a forty-eight-year-old mother of three who was employed as an administrative assistant in a large company. Her husband had died sixteen years earlier; she had raised her children by herself with some assistance from her mother. The oldest child, Rebecca, who was present for the interview, was eight when her father died. She remembered helping her mother with the younger children while Elizabeth worked and, later, when she went back to school to complete her college degree. Rebecca was then working and living with her grandmother in order to save enough money to return to college.

The grandmother, Mildred, was seventy-two and had been born in the South but had moved when she was eight to a large Midwestern city to live with relatives after her parents died. There she met her husband. The two later moved to the West Coast in the early 1940s and had lived there ever since. Her husband, then retired, had worked as a Pullman porter while Mildred worked as a domestic and nurse's aide most of her life.

Cynthia, the fourth member of the group, worked as a secretary in the same company as Elizabeth, and the two had been friends for a number of years. It was obvious that Cynthia visited the family frequently and had a warm relationship with them. She was thirty-two, the divorced mother of a two-year-old son, and had completed her B.A. six years previously and was considering quitting her job to go to graduate school. She revealed during the course of the interview that *Daughters of the Dust* had had a profound impact on her and was pivotal in her decision about graduate school.

The interview lasted five or six hours and took place on a Sunday afternoon in June 1992 in a West Coast suburb. Elizabeth, who had seen the film three times, talked about going to see it the first time. She said that although she was excited about finally seeing the film, she did so in anticipation of having to work so hard to figure it out that by the end of the film she was exhausted. Nevertheless, Elizabeth said she found the film to be worth the effort of unraveling its story—so much so that she decided to take her family and then see it again herself. The first time Elizabeth saw the film was different from the next two occasions. The second time she took her family. On the third occasion she was accompanied by a man who was interested in seeing the film. Referring to the third viewing, Elizabeth stated with a laugh: "Shit, it was a disaster because all he said was 'So what?' He didn't understand anything, so I didn't even talk about it to him. But I saw even more the third time than I had the two previous times." She explained what she saw:

> The next day after I saw it, I kept seeing all these beautiful scenes of the beach and the sand. Last Thanksgiving we spent the week . . . on the beach, and that was a special time for us as a family. And I remember seeing the same kinds of scenes, the water and the people on the beach. The things that really were interesting to me was the fact there was a basic story; there's a story inside a story. And you really had to kind of study it to figure out all these other little avenues. But they kind of represented all that goes on in the black community. There was the sister-in-law who said, I don't want my children to know about these African ways, and there are people today who do not want to think about Africa and the fact that we're from Africa. Then there's the woman who comes home, and she has a reputation, or seems to have a reputation, of a woman who's not as proper as the other daughters—because she's not married, and there's a hint there that perhaps she could be a lesbian. I mean, I picked that up. That may not be true.

On this point Cynthia exclaimed, "Oh, I wondered about that." I asked the women what kind of feelings they had if they assumed that Yellow Mary and Trula were lovers. Elizabeth replied that she didn't have any particular feeling but that when she related what she felt to the man she was with he became confused and said that perhaps Trula was Yellow Mary's daughter. Cynthia said that at first she thought the women were best friends. Elizabeth said that it seemed obvious from the beginning that the women were lovers. Rebecca agreed. Elizabeth added that when she and her family went to see the film a man sitting next to them "freaked out" when he realized that Yellow Mary and Trula were lovers. The women laughed because the man was so upset about it. The women did not appear to have any particular feelings about that part of the film. Elizabeth stated that she "felt okay" about the relationship and did not dwell on that part of the film any more than on other parts. Cynthia said she could see how Yellow Mary could have a woman lover if she were a prostitute, because there was so much violence in the profession that it seemed logical to her that she would love a woman.

Elizabeth continued relating her initial response to the film and her feeling that it was an uncomplicated story but that she had to see it several times to figure it out. I asked her if it bothered her that she did not understand parts of the film. She said that it did only in the sense that she wanted to know what was going on; but she also felt that the film contained lessons from the past that black people should apply to their present circumstances: "Each of the characters, it seemed, had a little part that was reminding us that we are getting ready to move into the year 2000, which is almost a hundred years from where they were. It seems like it's a history, it's a reflection, and it's so simple. You go to the theater and you want something to be very complicated, but really it's so simply laid out for us."

The women in the group who watched the videotape held attitudes similar to Elizabeth's in that they too were less concerned about filling in the missing parts of the plot. To them what they saw was evocative and prompted them to use their imaginations to flesh out the story. Justine related that she was sad to see some of the family leave but gratified that some stayed, because of the rich traditions on the island. She felt those who left probably would not have the life they dreamed about, and their history would be diluted. Kathy echoed her sentiments: "People have been migrating from the South for years, and when they got where they were going it wasn't all heaven. Same thing with people coming to California, with all the stories of oranges growing on trees. It's not exactly what people think it's going to be. When they get here it's not as good." Paige added that those who left the island would look back and wish their children had been born on the island. She noted that Yellow Mary had warned the family that the world beyond their birthplace was not the progressive world they envisioned.

The women in this group seemed to accept the story as presented to them with the feeling that it contained similarities to their own lives. Constance picked up on Paige's statements about the rituals the family had preserved from enslavement that carried forward to black people living in other parts of the country. She talked about growing up in a government-subsidized housing project and the diversity among the black people who lived there: "It wasn't like living in a closed neighborhood. When you lived in the projects you saw everybody." She shared her observations about living among the kinds of people represented in the film and about the varieties of superstitions and beliefs: "You know people yourself who still believe in some of those things. I don't care what they've done, I don't care what church they go to and how much they say amen—they still believe in hoodoo."

When Marianne related that her relatives in Louisiana were still immersed in their Geechee rituals Kathy said she felt that everyone had their own forms of superstitions: "It's no different from us now if a black cat crosses in front of you. Some people might say that's inconsistent with Christianity and you shouldn't believe in it, but sometimes you do."

More so than any of the women in the other two groups, these women were very religious, with a strong belief in traditional Christianity. In fact, the interview time was set for the early afternoon because all the women went to church almost every Sunday and were active members of their churches. Their comments on the religious aspects of *Daughters of the Dust* were intriguing because of the way different types of beliefs were examined in the film. In the earlier interviews on *The Color Purple* I had observed the fluidity of the women's reactions to the religious attitudes expressed in the novel and film, again evident in the women's response to *Daughters of the Dust*. Both works were severely critical of established religious tenets, and *Daughters of the Dust* provided an even greater religious conundrum in that it presented beliefs that ranged from open agnosticism to Islamic practices to Christian fanaticism. For devoutly religious black women who followed traditional religious practices, their assertions about both *The Color Purple* and *Daughters of the Dust* revealed how they engaged with the works. They seemed to be less rigid in their stance than other readers and more accepting of the critiques presented. Two examples from the interview are especially pertinent.

As we were preparing to watch the film there was a spirited discussion of the recent trial of heavyweight boxer Mike Tyson, charged with rape. The women had very strong feelings about what was being written in the newspapers and stated on the television talk shows. Kathy was highly critical of a group of black ministers who thought Tyson was being treated unfairly. When the ministers expressed their support for him in a televised news conference Kathy was especially incensed: "What pissed me off worst of all is those ministers. Now, I have had it with them—talking about how the judge should be lenient with him [Tyson]. They're standing up there at the National Baptist Convention talking that kind of mess. I said, Well, this is a damn shame. It is." Constance, who had watched the same news conference, interrupted Kathy to explain to the other women that not all the ministers were in agreement: "Not all the ministers said that; it was not all of them. Didn't you hear one minister say, 'Wrong is wrong; this [Tyson's action] was wrong'?" Kathy was not appeased; she continued condemning the other ministers and made a pointed observation about how she felt their statements reflected their attitude toward black women: "This was at the Abyssinian Baptist Church, and that's one of the largest black churches in New York. He's [the minister of the congregation] the one who said, 'Wrong is wrong.' What motivated these other ministers? They were at the National Baptist Convention. Do you know how many black women they represent? More women than men." Kathy's criticism of the ministers contradicts the routine presentation of black women as blindly faithful and easily led rather than independent in thoughts or actions. The women in the group recognized the critique of this characterization in their assessment of the character Viola, who, possessed of a strong religious zeal, returns to the island committed to overturn what she perceives as the heathenism of the other members of the family. When Christine isolated the various beliefs represented in the film, "Christianity, the hoodoo, the atheist, and the one who didn't believe in any one of them," Marianne pointed out Viola's fanaticism. When I asked them how they felt about Viola, Marianne said she felt that Viola was struggling with her beliefs and with the fact that the other people on the island were not embracing it as she was. Kathy jumped in at that point with the observation that people like Viola, who are in turmoil about their own convictions, typically try to convert everybody else. Kathy asserted that the others were tolerant of Viola's belief but that Viola went "head over heels" to try and make them believe as she did.

Although these women's comments appeared to be consistent with the filmmaker's intentions, not all the women interviewed felt they were in sync with the director. Dorothy, in the second group, disagreed with several of the others that the visual images complemented the aural ones and aided in understanding the unfamiliar language. Leah felt that the language was not the only means through which to understand the film: "The film itself was so visually explicative that even though there were times when I didn't understand what they were saying I could understand the context." She mentioned one moment in particular: "When the woman, Eula, did her soliloquy, just sort of went off on everybody, I didn't understand everything she was saying, but I understood what she must be saying. And I understood that it was a pivotal point, and I understood that everybody was really listening to her. I didn't understand every word she said, but it didn't detract from the film."

Dorothy found the film to be less understandable and felt that often the images did not in any way relate to the dialogue: "Just the images themselves, as I remember them kind of going across the screen, didn't have much to do with the overall progress of the story." Although Dorothy thought many images were repeated excessively, she did concede that the repetition was one of the subtle ways the audience came to understand the language. When Helen said she didn't have a problem with the language Dorothy responded that it was because she was from the area and was accustomed to the accents. Most of the women agreed that there was no need for subtitles and that they would have distracted from the film's emotional intensity had they been used.

Leah remarked that in a different viewing of the film it might be more important to comprehend every word, but, as she stated,

"There was a way in which aesthetically there was so much going on for me in the movie," that she was not concerned about discerning every word. Tracy, working through her thoughts about the feelings the film provoked in her, added the following:

> I can't pinpoint the parts that were emotional for me exactly, but I do know that at several points I did cry. It reached a place—I think it may have had something to do with going back and remembering the slaves. And the level of intimacy and acceptance that was there. Even with all the battling that was going on, there was still a level of acceptance in the community that was there, and it was very strong emotionally for me.

The women in the first group agreed that the look of the film was special and that there were moments that would stay with them for a while. Kathy felt that some scenes were "priceless. Like the one with the great-grandmother and Yellow Mary, the way they were sitting very close together like that. I think that was very touching, and it moved me." Constance cited the scene in which Yellow Mary and Trula sit together in the tree, talking to Eula: "That was just gorgeous. And they were having such a good time sitting in the tree smoking."

Kathy interrupted Constance at this point to state that "nobody was ever hurt by smoking a little weed." At this Paige asked, "How do you know they were smoking weed?" When Kathy became confused and thought that perhaps she had misunderstood the scene Paige provided her own explanation: "I know they were having a good time, and a cigarette don't ever make you have that good a time."

Constance spoke of how the women smoking in the tree related to her southern roots: "The way I remember it is my grandmother smoked something that smelled very much like marijuana for her asthma. So I knew the smell of marijuana at a very early age. And I knew they used that down in the South. They had a name for it, jimson weed or something, and it smelled very much like marijuana.

And I remember my grandmother smoking that stuff, so I knew they were smoking something in the same family."

The women in the first group agreed with those in the second group that subtitles would have been intrusive. Marianne said the language wasn't a problem; the viewer just had to concentrate. Christine said that the language added to her enjoyment of the film and made her want to see it a second time. When I informed the women that the film would probably go into distribution with subtitles because there was a concern that audiences would find the Gullah dialect too intractable, Constance and Christine offered provocative observations. Constance said she watched a lot of British television programs and couldn't always decipher what the actors were saying, especially if they were portraying people from an area where there was a strong regional accent: "All it means is that I have to be real attentive, or I'm going to miss something." Christine suggested that perhaps the distributors thought that white Americans would not understand the film, so they felt the need for subtitles. She added, "The difference is that we do not mind paying attention or having to hear it again."

The women's statements were in line with Julie Dash's assertion that cultural products emanating from certain cultures carry a stamp of legitimacy, whereas a film produced by a black person, especially a black woman, must follow a prescribed formula:

> To tell the truth, I had problems with *Miller's Crossing*. It made me realize that I've done that all my life, pushed through on accents until I understood them. Why is it with *Daughters of the Dust* that people seem almost offended by it? When they bring it up, I tell them, "Release on it, you'll understand it in a minute." You may not understand every sentence but you'll surely get the general idea, the sensibility of the whole thing. We've grown up translating. We've had no other choice.[13]

The women I interviewed reacted very strongly to having the choice of seeing a film coming from a black woman's sensibility. Although there may be differences between the creative intentions of a film-

Yellow Mary (Barbara-O) and Trula (Trula Hoosier) sharing a smoke.

maker and what audiences eventually perceive, Dash's motivation for constructing particular scenes is important because of the critical discussions concerning their effect. There are, she says, predetermined mandates, established through years of representations of black women in a variety of cultural forms, about how they should be presented. To violate that mandate is to risk censure. If black women are not shown as "objects" who have been raped, or who are beasts of burden, or breeders and nurturers, then they have no use value in mainstream cinema. Dash asks rhetorically, "When was the last time you saw a film about a black woman who is a trapeze artist? It's out of the question." Other images of black women that contradict dominant strictures are ones that show the women in control of their lives. Dash continues to talk about what appears beyond the pale in representing black women: "Forget about black women having a zest for life, a productive life, successful in whatever they want to accomplish. That's too much." She concludes, "Historically, African-American women never had the luxury of being simply a *woman*."[14]

One particular image that Dash felt was especially empowering, given that black woman are rarely shown in mutually reciprocal romantic relationships, is that of Iona, Haagar's daughter, riding off on the back of the horse behind St. Julian Last Child, so that they could live their lives together. This image was particularly significant to Leah, in the second group of women: "I was hoping for it, waiting for it, and was anticipating it and was going to be damn upset if he didn't come and get her. And the fact that he does come for her, gets her, and they ride off into the sunset is just very satisfying."

The women in the third group also responded to the scene with Iona and St. Julian Last Child. Cynthia and Rebecca found the moment especially moving; whereas Elizabeth felt for both Haagar and Iona: "I cried for both the mother and the daughter, because I knew what that [i.e., Iona leaving Haagar] meant."

Some critics found other moments in the film unnecessary, irrelevant, and tedious. Examples include the many long takes of black women interacting with one another, the slow-motion camera shots of black women gamboling on the beach, and the portraits of the various groupings coupled with the intensity of the women's actions. However, the women I interviewed considered the scenes memorable and evocative.

Rebecca, in the group that had seen the film commercially, said it reminded her of looking at old photographs, which was special because there were no films featuring black people set in that time period. She spoke of having a similar experience while working on a stage play at a local theater: "I was working on *Ma Rainey's Black Bottom* last summer and trying to get the costumes together on that. We had some old books of different decades and time periods and clothing. That was probably the closest thing I ever came to that period when the clothing was like that."

Both Rebecca and Elizabeth observed the significance of the variety of hairstyles presented in the film and noted that it was especially striking because black women were rarely shown representing such diversity. Cynthia expanded upon their comments, relating them to her background and to the direct influence of such diversity on her life. She began by talking about what it meant to be

An evocative and moving image for black women viewers of *Daughters of the Dust*.

Iona (Bahni Turpin) and St. Julian Last Child (M. Cochise Anderson) riding off to begin a new life together.

considered black in this country, in contrast to the Caribbean, where her parents were from and whose traditions they followed:

> My father is from Suriname, which used to be a Dutch colony in South America, and my mother is from Trinidad. When you get into the Caribbean, everyone is so ethnically mixed, that [even though] I consider myself to be a woman of color, I consider myself a black woman, the perspective is different here in this country from in the Caribbean. Because there you acknowledge all of who you are. Whereas I find that here—and it's partly the legal system that has been established in this country—if you're one thirty-second of African blood, you are considered black. It's not really like that there; there isn't really the emphasis on race, [although] there is in other subtle ways. So I also acknowledge the other things that I am.

Cynthia spoke of her racial and ethnic background as being a combination of African, East Indian, Portuguese, Dutch, "and probably there might be some other things, because you don't know when you get back into your generations." Because her parents were from the West Indies where such ethnic diversity existed, her cultural development was different. Her parents began straightening her hair when she was five, and she had continued to wear it that way until recently. Cynthia stated that her parents' standard of beauty was based upon the ethnic group with which they felt the family should identify, which was more of a European standard than a black one. Thus it was a struggle for her to cut her hair and stop chemically straightening it. As she stated, "I think I'm coming into a period of my life where I'm feeling more powerful, feeling more self-assertive and taking control of my life rather than just being controlled. And part of that is just more self-awareness of being a black woman." Cynthia said it was a big step for her "to just cast aside societal judgments about what's considered beautiful. It's part of accepting who you are."

When I asked the others in the group if seeing *Daughters of the Dust* had an influence on them independent of their feeling that it was a worthwhile film, Rebecca answered that films did not really have that much of an effect on her and that although she found *Daughters of the Dust* a powerful film, it did not affect other parts of her life beyond that. Cynthia responded differently. She said that after seeing the film she decided to stop perming her hair and elaborated on her reasons:

> It's something I've been thinking about for so long, and I just didn't have the courage to do it. I thought, Well, I'll wait until I'm a student, because then I'll be out of the workplace and won't have to deal with those people who are going to have comments about my hair, and in school it's a more liberal environment. But I saw that movie and I thought, God, look at how beautiful those braids are. I have cousins who grew up wearing their hair like that, cousins in South America who have this long, beautiful black hair, and they grew up wearing braids. But my experience growing up in the United States, and being separate from that, and having my hair straightened when I was five years old, I've never had that experience. And I thought it would be nice to just know what my hair was like. It sounds so trivial, but that movie definitely had an impact on that.

Daughters of the Dust may not have heralded the millennium for black women or eradicated the harmful effects of every derogatory representation within the history of film. But it will have a sustained, long-term effect, for its impact is similar to that of early black female writers. This is not to make a case for constructing a paradigm for analyzing the works of black women filmmakers identical to the one that has functioned so effectively in examining the tradition of black women writers. But the social conditions and political circumstances driving the works are worthy of comparison. A poignant example is Gwendolyn Brooks's novella *Maud Martha* (1953). Brooks holds the distinction of being the first black recipient of a Pulitzer Prize, which she won for her volume of poetry entitled *Annie Allen* (1949).

Literary scholar Barbara Christian categorizes *Maud Martha* as a transitional work because of its location within the continuum of black female writing. The treatment of its subject matter and the form in which it is presented also mark a turning point within black women's literature. For the first time, in fact, the depiction of an "ordinary" rather than extraordinary black woman is rendered. The book would later influence other writers' characterizations of black women—specifically Paule Marshall's *Brown Girl, Brownstones* (1959) and Alice Walker's *The Color Purple*. The book's protagonist, Maud Martha Brown, is a plain, dark-skinned black girl who leads an unexceptional life but quietly faces the many small challenges of being a black women in American society. Brooks tells the story through the thoughts of Maud Martha. It is thus a private tale with an interior, solitary, and ruminative ambience. It is not a chronicle of a black person confronting a hostile white world but an exploration of the inner character of an individual. The effects of racism are implicit, rather than overt, throughout the work. In this respect, it stands in sharp contrast to the other, more widely heralded, novels published the same year: *Go Tell It on the Mountain* (1953) by James Baldwin and *The Outsider* (1953) by Richard Wright.[15]

Maud Martha, a novella rather than a novel, is a short book consisting of vignettes covering significant moments in Maud Martha Brown's life as she grows up during the 1930s and 1940s. A review of the novella is significant to this analysis of *Daughters of the Dust*. *Maud Martha* is an unexpected kind of depiction of a black woman's life. As a novella, the book's form was different from that of other stories of black life written at the time, and thus it varied sharply from other novels by black people. This made for a complex critical reception at the time of *Maud Martha*'s publication.

Christian's very useful analysis of *Maud Martha*'s effect is helpful in considering the potential long-term influence of *Daughters of the Dust*. Christian uses Georg Lukács's analysis of Solzhenitsyn's novella *One Day in the Life of Ivan Denisovich* (1953) to address the impact of *Maud Martha*'s form. According to Lukács, novellas are written at the end of an epoch or the beginning of a new historical period. Christian refers to his concepts *noch nicht* (not yet) and *nicht mehr* (no longer) to identify the artistic phases in which novellas appear. Their specific characteristics give them an elusive significance:[16]

> For in its focus on a single character or situation rather than the totality of a society, and in its economy of presentation, the novella may summarize the essentials of a period that has just ended and be an exploration into attitudes that are just forming. The writer, then, although not consciously intending to write a novella, may find that in trying to express the moment of transition from one mode of interpreting reality to another, the present cannot be expressed in the novel of the past, nor is the totality of the new reality understood enough to transform it.[17]

Daughters of the Dust is not presented in a short form, nor did it fade gently from public view, as did *Maud Martha*, which went out of print immediately after publication and remained unavailable to a mass readership until its recent reprinting. However, *Daughters of the Dust* did emerge during the resurgence of black-directed films of the late 1980s and early 1990s and is drastically different in subject matter and style. For these reasons it has a complex stature within cultural criticism, for it portends a break both from mainstream white representations of black life and from black male–directed films about black culture. *Daughters of the Dust* privileges black women's history and emphasizes the manner in which black women have survived and overcome through their own resources. These factors, combined with the director's skill and expertise in visually presenting black women in exquisitely composed configurations, works to position *Daughters of the Dust* as a foundational text in this transitional moment. Dash, justifiably, refuses to accept the film's designation as an experimental, avant garde, or art house film, labels that attempt to distance the film from its desired audience. Dash conceived the film as one that would be accessible to the primary audience at which she aimed it—black women. She does not demean the film's audience by assuming a condescending stance or presenting images beyond viewers' range of historical memory. *Daughters of the Dust* taps into black women's common background, thrusting traditional representations aside, to re-create images more in line with black women's lives. For this reason, what are perceived as the film's shortcomings emanate from its appearance within the transitional moment of its difference. Its presentation of a new cinematic reality for black women may not immediately transform their representation in film or other cultural works; but it does lay the groundwork for future cinematic works about black women, which will also not retreat from a progressive, subversive portrayal.

Additionally, the popular appeal of *Daughters of the Dust* demonstrates yet again for those who were able to see it a specific audience's ability to transcend the criticism. Thus a space has been opened up for black female activists to build upon the momentum of many black women's favorable reactions to the film. As the statement by John Fiske quoted in the introduction indicated, popular art may not be revolutionary, but it can be progressive by offering "points of pertinence" to the everyday life of a populace.[18] The comments from the women interviewed in this book offer insights into the specific ways in which the film related to many black women's experiences. In this respect audience studies can augment the understanding of a specific cultural and historical moment as part of a broader movement toward black women's empowerment.

Conclusion

In *A Minor Altercation* Jacqueline Shearer examines the early 1970s conflicts in Boston, Massachusetts, resulting from a court ruling that the Boston school system was operating racially and educationally imbalanced schools. When the court ordered citywide busing of schoolchildren as an immediate remedy, battles between black and white parents ensued.[1]

Shearer dramatized the story, presenting the hostilities from the perspectives of two families—one white, the other black. The daughters in both families had been suspended from high school because they had fought each other over what was perceived to be preferential treatment when one of the girls was placed in a highly sought-after computer course. Shearer thought that trying to give each side equal representation deflated the conflict. In her mind the real issue was racism, and Shearer wanted to place more emphasis on the plight of the black mothers because she felt they were in the frontlines on the busing issue, fighting for the rights of their children to have access to the best education available.[2]

When Shearer produced and directed the "Keys to the Kingdom" segment of *Eyes on the Prize II* in 1989, she finally told the story of the black mothers in Boston. Using footage obtained from television news programs that followed the confrontations, Shearer shows compelling instances of the women facing up to the hostile white-controlled school board. The board took the lead in organizing white parents in their protests, trying any number of tactics, including throwing rocks and eggs at school buses carrying black children. At one point, the white parents overturned police cars being used as a shield to prevent them from storming into a high school to get at black students who were locked inside.

In the heat of the conflict one black mother expressed doubts about the wisdom of initiating the desegregation suit that led to the black children being bused: "It killed me to see our black students go through that procedure." Another spoke out defiantly that she would not teach her kids to hate, even though the white parents in South Boston were teaching that lesson to their children when they encouraged them to throw rocks and chant derogatory names at the black students bused into the area.

Shearer's media representations of these women exists as striking testimony of the ways black women have historically used tactical maneuvers against oppressive forces challenging them and their families. These women were not helpless, nor were they compliant pawns of the machinations of power in society. They stood up for their rights and were successful.

Shearer was a pioneer black female filmmaker. One of her abiding principles, in her extensive media endeavors, was that political activism is an integral part of media production. The development of the skills needed to create a cultural product should be tailored toward achieving social change. Shearer's two documentaries are vivid examples of the cultural merging with the political to expose the political possibilities inherent in specific historical moments.

Currently, as even greater challenges are confronting black women, the need for cultural and political resistance is intense. Socially constructed images of black women are being used once again to reinforce oppressive social and public policies affecting them. Within the constantly shifting representations of black females in mainstream media, the image of the dependent black, single mother is becoming attractive to dominant ideologues. Because of resistance from a forceful movement of black women, other images have lost the ideological potency of particular moments. Representations of black women's sexual character, the strong-willed matriarch, the domineering spouse no longer carry the force they once did. Thus others are needed by those who are working to maintain the political status quo.

In a revealing article entitled "It's a Family Affair: The Real Lives of Black Single Mothers" Barbara Omolade maintains why the image of the pathological black single mother is necessary for white politicians and social scientists. She asserts that single black mothers are a convenient scapegoat for changes that are occurring in society in general and in the white family in particular. Omolade points to a steady increase in white female–headed households, an increase in the number of white children who are born out of wedlock, a rise in the rate of white teenage pregnancy, and instances in which white women are solely responsible for rearing children and providing support.

Omolade contends that "historically, problems in the white family have been attributed to individual failure while problems in the black family are seen as evidence of collective black pathology." This rationale, she submits, has become a legitimation for continued racism and economic injustice: "In attempting to separate racial from economic inequality and blaming family pathology for black people's condition, current ideology obscures the system's inability to provide jobs, decent wages, and adequate public services for the black poor."[3]

The "Demonic Black Woman Narrative"

In spite of the widespread availability of the information that forms Omolade's cogent analysis, the image of the dependent black woman has become so attractive that it is being used in a variety of seemingly inappropriate circumstances. Cultural scholar Wahneema Lubiano provides an insightful and carefully thought-out analysis of the ways in which those in power utilize the cultural accretions associated with the term *welfare mother/queen*. Lubiano considers this image to be a part of the storehouse of social constructions that she labels "the demonic black woman narratives." All the images are designed to undermine the hegemonic potential of black women.

In her powerfully argued essay "Black Ladies, Welfare Queens, and State Minstrels: Ideological War by Narrative Means," Lubiano considers the ways in which narratives of race and gender are essential to the operations of power. By strategically inserting these narratives within highly contentious dialogues, the political status quo attempts to block any movements toward change.[4]

Lubiano outlines how the category of "black woman" is invested with an emotional intensity, through narrative strategies that "have been constructed over time and transformed to fit the requirements of maintaining the present terms of the U.S. political economy" (pp. 332–33). In her analysis, Lubiano shows how two specific narratives concerning black women were deployed during the confirmation hearings of Clarence Thomas and used to combat the force of Anita Hill's testimony. To invoke associations of pathology, traditionally weapons used against black women, the narrative construction concerning Anita Hill was framed with that of another woman connected with Thomas: his sister, Emma Mae Martin. Earlier, in his first set of hearings, Thomas had described his sister as chronically dependent on welfare, thus implying that his background was one of individual initiative in elevating himself from poverty. Thomas's portrayal of his sister was less flattering.

By framing Anita Hill together with Emma Mae Martin, Thomas ignited a set of historical narratives that those in power used to present black women as instruments of the destruction of the American way of life. According to Lubiano, Emma Mae Martin became the specter of welfare dependency, while Anita Hill became the embodiment of affirmative action. Hill's Yale University education and status as a university law professor prompted her critics to level this claim.

That the same set of associations were not attached to Thomas, another Yale Law School graduate, was due to his employment of the Horatio Alger–type success myth of individual effort leading to success, along with the tale of his grandfather's being the motivating force behind his achievements. In perpetuating Thomas's presentation, his supporters were also able to condemn black women. Their weapon was an invisible though predominant text concerning black women—the 1965 Moynihan Report, which placed the blame for what it maliciously categorized as the "failure" of black families squarely on black women's shoulders. Lubiano sardonically assesses the vicious power of this mythmaking process:

> Thomas and his grandfather became, within the economy of these myths, the bringers of order, of law—against chaos, against anarchy—the male figures so desperately needed in (and missing from) Moynihan's "black family." Thomas' mention of his grandfather functioned to invoke nostalgia for a golden age when black men were real men (and present in their families), a nostalgia that could find its desired object in Thomas himself, the present day embodiment of that age. (p. 334)

Further proof of Lubiano's analysis of the function of the demonic narratives concerning black women is evident in the example of law professor Lani Guinier and her battle to correct the misrepresentations of her views regarding civil rights. The story is a familiar one: Guinier was nominated on April 29, 1993, by President Bill Clinton for the position of assistant attorney general for civil rights. By early June Clinton had withdrawn her nomination because of the aggressive campaign mounted by conservative Republicans opposing Guinier's nomination.

The conservatives utilized a version of a familiar narrative of black women in their efforts against Guinier. She was cast right from the start as a "Quota Queen" because she advocated ensuring that within a democracy all voters should have access to equal treatment. As Guinier eventually explained her views, she did not recommend quotas but did believe that when the majority wins it should not tyrannize the minority through policies of exclusion.[5]

Through a calculated effort to present Guinier negatively, the conservative right labeled her the "Quota Queen." They were aided by newspaper columnists and media commentators who repeated the description and expanded upon it. The momentum was generated by the attempt to contain the force of yet another powerful black woman in a public role by referring to her in such a derogatory manner. As one observer noted after Clinton withdrew the nomination and then made the incomprehensible statement about his affection for Guinier and willingness to lend her money: "He was treating her like a welfare queen—read Quota Queen—looking for a handout. It had the instant effect of putting her in a subservient position and him in a position of great generosity."[6]

Although these attacks against Anita Hill and Lani Guinier are personal and not without an effect on them as individuals, they also activate a constellation of societal apparitions about black women that have been used throughout history. The whole idea of "strangeness," and thus something to be feared, gained additional force through the oft-repeated description of Lani Guinier: "Strange name, strange hair, strange writings, she's history."[7]

That these narrative constructions of black women are on the rise, and so blatantly so, speaks volumes about the power structure's desire to contain what it rightly perceives as black women's threat to its dominance. It also speaks to the need for constant vigilance by black women in constructing their own narratives.

Even as others have repressed their stories or distorted their experiences, black women's words are being used effectively to reconstruct past derogatory mythmaking strategies. Two recently recovered narratives are especially important because they present the lives of black women during slavery through the writings of the women who lived through it.

Our Nig (1859) was written by a free black woman, Harriet Wilson, living in the North. The work is considered the first novel written by a black person in this country. Henry Louis Gates, Jr., the editor of the reprinted work, maintains that Harriet Wilson created the black woman's novel.[8] Beyond its significance as a literary first, *Our Nig* documents the inhumane treatment that black women in the North, who were not living in slavery, also suffered. *Our Nig* graphically illustrates that these women were also treated like property and those for whom they worked could do whatever they wanted to them. However, the author of the novel also shows the process through which the protagonist, Frado, discovers she has the inner resources to fight back.

When Frado, after enduring years of brutality, learns that she can resist, she does so. Thus Harriet Wilson underlines the fact that black women in earlier eras were willing to go to their deaths in defiance of their subservient roles.

The second recently reprinted narrative was dismissed for decades as a fraud because historians felt the story was fiction written by a white author. *Incidents in the Life of a Slave Girl* (1861) was written by a black woman named Harriet Jacobs. She was forced to use the pseudonym Linda Brent, because members of her family, and those friends who helped her escape from slavery twenty years before the publication of her book, were still living in slavery. Jacobs presents a well-written, deeply moving story of her life under slavery. *Incidents in the Life of a Slave Girl* is thought to be the first slave narrative whose primary purpose is to emphasize the sexual exploitation of slave women.[9] Jacobs's understanding of the "peculiar institution" and its capitalist and ideological underpinnings does much to reveal a different side of black woman's experiences.

Establishing Their Own Voice

Reclaiming and reconstructing narratives authenticating black women's histories helps to countermand other strategies working to oppress them. Within the last several decades, black female activists have increased their efforts toward excavating black women's social, cultural, and political past.

Novelist and social critic Toni Cade (Bambara) edited a landmark volume of critical essays, *The Black Woman* (1970). Others works soon followed, including *Sturdy Black Bridges: Visions of Black Women in Literature* (1979), and *All the Women Are White, All the Blacks Are Men, But Some of Us Are Brave* (1982), a guide to the creation of black women's studies programs and an invaluable reference work from those who had long been teaching courses about black women.

The work of black women writers was even more widely disseminated in several path-breaking works: Mary Helen Washington edited two early landmark anthologies of black women's writings, *Black-Eyed Susans* (1975) and *Midnight Birds* (1980), and Barbara Christian produced one of the first examinations of the tradition of black female writing in the long form, *Black Women Novelists* (1980).

The necessary work of placing black women's cultural texts in the public sphere continues in the studies of black female filmmakers, film critics, and scholars. The pioneering work of filmmakers Madeline Anderson, Monica Freeman, and Jacqueline Shearer is documented in the studies of filmmaker and critic Michelle Parkerson, literary scholar Valerie Smith, and film scholar Gloria Gibson-Hudson.[10] Gibson-Hudson is restoring the films of black women who made films in the early part of the century, an effort that will bring to light the contributions of women such as Eloice Gist, Zora Neale Hurston, and Eslanda Goode Robeson, who have been passed over in traditional film scholarship.

Books such as the present volume add black women readers to the tradition of black female cultural and social activism. As part of an interpretive community, black women cultural consumers are not simply viewers and readers but cogent and knowledgeable observers of the social, political, and cultural forces that influence their lives. Adding their voices to black women's cultural work helps to develop what Patricia Collins refers to as a "black woman's standpoint"—a standpoint shared by many black women. The idea of a standpoint connotes a perspective specific to black women, which helps to clarify the meaning of black women's historical oppression and provides insight into methods that black women can use to resist it.[11] Collins, among others, is adamant that black women have a clear understanding of their oppression and have struggled continuously against its various forms. Collins refers to the useful construction by black sociologist Deborah K. King, who suggests that black women face "multiple jeopardy" because of their status as black, female, and, for the most part, lodged in a specific class hierarchy. According to King, this multiple jeopardy is not additive in the sense that the forms of oppression are cumulative. This "incremental process" leads to a nonproductive conclusion that one factor can, and should, supplant the others. A more useful analysis examines each form of oppression, multiplied by the others. In other words, King insists, "the equivalent formulation is racism multiplied by sexism multiplied by classism."[12]

Black women's perspective on their material conditions has impelled them to value the ways in which they represent themselves, for others' characterizations have distorted their history and attributes. Collins sees an integral connection between the history and social conditions of black women and the structure and content of the way in which they represent their perception of their status in society. In the face of a commonality of oppressions, black women do possess aspects of a common history, but there are different and varied expressions of these commonalities, which, Collins suggests, come from the "diversities of class, region, age, sexual orientation shaping individual black women's lives." Therefore even though a specific black female standpoint exists, the variety of expressions can reveal that the specific "contours may not be present to black women themselves." Research, then, on black women's lives will help to "clarify a black woman's standpoint for black women."[13]

Notes

Introduction

1. For overviews of the reviews see Daniel Max, "McMillan's Millions," *New York Times Magazine*, August 9, 1992, pp. 20, 22, 24, 26; and Deirdre Donahue, "Author Terry McMillan's Fresh Voice," *USA Today*, July 7, 1992, pp. D1–D2.

2. For an overview of the range of critical reactions to the novel and the film, see Jacqueline Bobo, "Sifting Through the Controversy: Reading *The Color Purple*," *Callaloo* 12, no. 2 (Spring 1989): 332–42.

3. For articles by black women in support of Alice Walker and the film, see Mary Helen Washington, *Invented Lives: Narratives of Black Women, 1860–1960* (New York: Anchor Press/Doubleday, 1987); two articles by Dorothy Gilliam, "*The Color Purple* Not as Simple as Black and White," *Washington Post*, December 23, 1985, p. B3, and "After the 'Purple' Shutout," *Washington Post*, March 27, 1986, p. B3; and Jill Nelson, "Spielberg's *Purple* Is Still Black," *Guardian*, January 29, 1986, pp. 1, 17.

4. John Fiske, *Understanding Popular Culture* (Boston: Unwin Hyman, 1989), p. 159.

5. Background information about *Daughters of the Dust* comes from several sources: Yvonne Welbon, "A Case Study of the Making and Marketing

of *Daughters of the Dust*," in Jacqueline Bobo, ed., *Channels of Resistance: Black Women Film and Video Artists* (forthcoming); Julie Dash, *Daughters of the Dust: The Making of an African-American Woman's Film* (New York: New Press, 1992); and an interview with the author on March 3, 1992.

6. *Daughters of the Dust*," *Variety*, February 11, 1991, p. 112.

7. Background information on the work of KJM3 is given in Jesse Algeron Rhines, "Distributing Difference," *Afterimage* 21, no. 1 (Summer 1993): 2.

8. Information about the composition of the audience is given in Rebecca Godfrey, "Straight Outta Sea Island," *Off Hollywood Report* 7, no. 1 (Spring 1992): 17. Cited in Welbon, "A Case Study."

9. Phoebe Hoban, "Phenomena: A Building Dust Storm," *New York Magazine*, March 30, 1992, p. 27.

10. See, e.g., Deirdre Donahue, "Author Terry McMillan's Fresh Voice," *USA Today*, July 7, 1992, pp. D1–D2; and Laura B. Randolph, "Black America's Hottest Novelist: Terry McMillan Exhales and Inhales in a Revealing Interview," *Ebony* (May 1993): 23–28.

11. Comment made by Malaika Adero, an associate editor at Simon and Schuster, in an article by Will Nixon, "Better Times for Black Writers?" *Publishers Weekly*, February 17, 1989, p. 37.

12. Quoted in ibid., pp. 37–38.

13. Daniel Max, "McMillan's Millions," p. 20.

14. Janice Radway, "Interpretive Communities and Variable Literacies: The Functions of Romance Reading," *Daedalus* (Summer 1984): 49–73.

15. Charlotte Brunsdon, "Text and Audience," in Ellen Seiter et al., eds., *Remote Control: Television, Audiences, and Cultural Power* (London: Routledge, 1989), pp. 116–29.

16. Brunsdon, "Text and Audience," p. 122.

17. Annette Kuhn, "Women's Genres," *Screen* 25, no. 1 (January–February 1984): 18–28.

18. Rosalind Brunt, "Engaging with the Popular: Audiences for Mass Culture and What to Say about Them," in Lawrence Grossberg et al., eds., *Cultural Studies* (London: Routledge, 1992), pp. 69–80.

19. Darlene C. Hine, "Female Slave Resistance: The Economics of Sex," *Western Journal of Black Studies* 3 (1979): 123–27.

20. Toni Morrison, *Beloved* (New York: New American Library, 1988), p. 251.

21. Hine, "Female Slave Resistance," p. 126.

22. Ibid., p. 127.

23. Patricia Hill Collins, *Black Feminist Thought: Knowledge, Consciousness, and the Politics of Empowerment* (London: HarperCollins Academic, 1990), p. 161.

1. Black Women as Interpretive Community

1. Edward Mapp, "Black Women in Films: A Mixed Bag of Tricks," in Lindsay Patterson, ed., *Black Films and Filmmakers: A Comprehensive Anthology from Stereotype to Superhero* (New York: Dodd, Mead, 1975), pp. 196–205.

2. Lorraine Hansberry, "This Complex of Womanhood," *Ebony* (August 1960): 40.

3. Political theorist Cornel West makes an important distinction between the characterization of black people as "victims" and the process of their "victimization." As West declares: "Although black people have never been simply victims, wallowing in self-pity and begging for white giveaways, they have been—and are—*victimized.*" See Cornel West, "Nihilism in Black America," *Dissent* 38, no. 2 (Spring 1991): 221–26, reprinted in Gina Dent, ed., *Black Popular Culture* (Seattle: Bay Press, 1992), p. 37–47.

4. Pearl Bowser, "Sexual Imagery and the Black Woman in American Cinema," in Gladstone L. Yearwood, ed., *Black Cinema Aesthetics: Issues in Independent Black Filmmaking* (Athens: Ohio University Center for Afro-American Studies, 1982), pp. 42–51.

5. Felly Nkweto Simmonds, "*She's Gotta Have It*: The Representation of Black Female Sexuality on Film," *Feminist Review* 29 (Spring 1988): 10–29.

6. Ibid., p. 14.

7. Jacquie Jones, "The New Ghetto Aesthetic," *Wide Angle* 13, nos. 3 and 4 (July–October 1991): 32–43.

8. Ibid., p. 39.

9. See, e.g., Paula Giddings, *When and Where I Enter: The Impact of Black Women on Race and Sex in America* (New York: Morrow, 1984; reprint, New York: Bantam Books, 1985); Gloria T. Hull et al., *All the Women Are White, All the Blacks Are Men, but Some of Us Are Brave* (New York: Feminist Press, 1982); and Patricia Hill Collins, *Black Feminist Thought: Knowledge, Consciousness, and the Politics of Empowerment* (London: HarperCollins Academic, 1990).

10. Angela Davis makes the case that black women developed the practice of rebellion during enslavement and that the foundation for resistance was laid by "subjecting women to the most ruthless exploitation conceivable." See her arguments in *Women, Race, and Class* (New York: Vintage, 1983), p. 23.

11. Quoted in Philip Foner, *Women and the American Labor Movement* (New York: Free Press, 1980), p. 441.

12. Ibid., p. 440.

13. *I Am Somebody*, dir. Madeline Anderson (1969).

14. Foner, *Women and the American Labor Movement*, p. 443.

15. Lawrence Grossberg, ed., "On Postmodernism and Articulation: An Interview with Stuart Hall," *Journal of Communication Inquiry* 10, no. 2 (Summer 1986): 54.

16. Ibid.

17. Ibid., pp. 54–55.

18. Lorraine Hansberry, "The Negro in American Culture." First presented as a radio program on listener-sponsored WBAI-FM, New York, January 1961. Reprinted in C. W. E. Bigsby, ed., *The Black American Writer* (Deland, Fla.: Everett/Edward, 1969), pp. 79–108.

19. Lorraine Hansberry, "Women Voice Demands in Capitol Sojourn," *Freedom* (October 1951): 6.

20. Thomas was confirmed by the Senate Judiciary Committee and later by a 52-to-48 vote in the Senate.

21. African-American Women in Defense of Ourselves, *New York Times*, November 17, 1991, p. 19.

22. Angela Davis, "JoAnne Little: The Dialectics of Rape," *Ms.* 3, no. 12 (June 1975): 74–77, 106–8.

23. Ibid., p. 106.

24. Ibid.

25. Hazel Carby, *Reconstructing Womanhood: The Emergence of the Afro-American Woman Novelist* (New York: Oxford University Press, 1987), p. 39.

26. Angela Davis, "The Black Woman's Role in the Community of Slaves," *Black Scholar* (December 1971): 6.

27. James Snead, "Recoding Blackness: The Visual Rhetoric of Black Independent Film," *Circular for the New American Filmmakers Series*, no. 23 (New York: Whitney Museum of American Art, 1985), pp. 1–2.

28. For a fuller comparison of the two films see the article by Jeremy G. Butler, "*Imitation of Life* (1934 and 1959): Style and the Domestic Melodrama," *Jump Cut* 32 (April 1986): 25–28.

29. Personal interview with the author on March 3, 1992, in Los Angeles.

30. Martina Attille and Maureen Blackwood, "Black Women and Representation," in Charlotte Brunsdon, ed., *Films for Women* (London: British Film Institute, 1986), pp. 202–8.

31. Kobena Mercer, "Diaspora Culture and the Dialogic Imagination: The Aesthetics of Black Independent Film in Britain," in Mybe B. Cham and Claire Andrade-Watkins, eds., *Blackframes: Critical Perspectives on Black Independent Cinema* (Cambridge: MIT Press, 1988), pp. 50–61; and "Recoding Narratives of Race and Nation," *Independent* (January–February 1989): 19–26.

32. Barbara Christian, "But What Do We Think We're Doing Anyway: The State of Black Feminist Criticism(s); or, My Version of a Little Bit of History," in Cheryl A. Wall, ed., *Changing Our Own Words: Essays on Criticism, Theory, and Writing by Black Women* (New Brunswick, N.J.: Rutgers University Press, 1989), pp. 58–74.

33. Ien Ang, "Wanted Audiences: On the Politics of Empirical Audience Studies," in Ellen Seiter et al., eds., *Remote Control: Television, Audiences, and Cultural Power* (London: Routledge, 1989), pp. 96–115.

34. Annette Kuhn, " 'The Married Love' Affair," *Screen* 27, no. 2 (March–April 1986): 5–21.

35. Ibid., p. 5.

36. See, e.g., a review by Stanley Kauffmann that appeared early in the film's run, "Stanley Kauffmann on Films: Two Women," *New Republic*, February 10, 1992, pp. 26–27.

37. Armond White, "Daughters Bites the Dust," *New York City-Sun*, January 22–28, 1992, pp. 15, 20.

38. Remarks made on episode of *Tony Brown's Journal* entitled "Purple Rage," *PBS*, April 6, 1986.

39. White, "Daughters Bites the Dust," p. 20.

40. At the time of this interview (1992), most of the black women who appeared in *The Color Purple* were well known. In the mid-1980s, when the film was made, only Oprah Winfrey was widely recognized. Whoopi Goldberg was a comic and nightclub performer who went on to star in other films after her performance in *The Color Purple*.

41. Personal interview on March 3, 1992, in Los Angeles.

42. To line out a hymn means that one person will spontaneously start singing a song without score, and others will follow that person's lead. The practice developed during enslavement, when songbooks were scarce—as was literacy, which was forbidden—and one person would teach others the words to a song.

43. Personal interview on March 3, 1992, in Los Angeles.

44. Toni Morrison, "Unspeakable Things Unspoken: The Afro-American Presence in American Literature," *Michigan Quarterly Review* 28 (Winter 1989): 1–34 (publication of the Tanner Lecture on Human Values at the University of Michigan, October 7, 1988).

2. Text and Subtext: *The Color Purple*

1. See *New York Times Book Review*, May 15, 1983, p. 38; and Walter Beacham, ed., *Beacham's Popular Fiction, 1950–Present* (Washington, D.C.: Beacham Publishing, 1986), p. 1441.

2. Nina Darnton, "*Color Purple* to Re-Open Nationwide," *New York Times*, January 9, 1987, p. C6.

3. *USA Today*, February 21, 1990, p. D3.

4. Karima A. Haynes, "Videoblack," *Ebony* (April 1992): 82.

5. I use the phrase "within the veil" to refer to black people speaking with one another intracommunity. Its use here is taken from two sources: the first is W. E. B. DuBois, *The Souls of Black Folk* (1903): "The Negro is a sort of seventh son, born with a veil, and gifted with second-sight in this American world,—a world which yields him no true self-consciousness, but only lets him see himself through the revelation of the other world."

The second reference is Lorraine Hansberry, who studied pan-Africanism with DuBois. In a CBS television interview conducted by Mike Wallace on May 8, 1959, Hansberry responded pointedly to Wallace's misplaced statement about the black middle class and their aspirations toward white ideals. Wallace based his comment on the work of black sociologist E. Franklin Frazier, who wrote of black self-hate. Hansberry responded: "Dr. Frazier is, of course, speaking from within the veil, and he is speaking with an intimacy [of black life] you might not as readily understand."

6. Alice Walker, *The Color Purple* (San Diego: Harcourt, Brace, Jovanovich, 1982), p. 12.

7. Margaret Walker, *Jubilee* (Boston: Houghton Mifflin, 1966; reprint, New York: Bantam, 1985), p. 9.

8. Paula Giddings, *When and Where I Enter: The Impact of Black Women on Race and Sex in America* (New York: Bantam, 1984), pp. 83–94.

9. Walker, *The Color Purple*, p. 69.

10. Barbara Christian, "From the Inside Out: Afro-American Women's Literary Tradition and the State," *Center for Humanistic Studies Occasional Papers*, no. 19 (Minneapolis: University of Minnesota, 1987), p. 17.

11. Audre Lorde, "The Uses of the Erotic: The Erotic as Power," in Lorde, *Sister Outsider* (Trumansburg, N.Y.: Crossing Press, 1984), pp. 53–59.

12. Christian, "From the Inside Out," p. 17.

13. Lorde, "The Uses of the Erotic," p. 54.

14. Cited in J. Hoberman, "Color Me Purple," *Village Voice*, December 24, 1985, p. 76.

15. Marti Wilson, "A Disappointment, but We Still Have the Book," *Black Film Review* 2, no. 2 (Spring 1986): 17.

16. Glenn Collins, "Spielberg Films 'The Color Purple,' " *New York Times*, December 15, 1985, section 2, p. 23.

17. BBC documentary, *Alice Walker and "The Color Purple,"* 1986.

18. Ibid.

19. David Breskin, "Steven Spielberg," *Rolling Stone*, October 24, 1985, p. 74.

20. BBC documentary, *Alice Walker and "The Color Purple,"* 1986.

21. Ibid.

22. Collins, "Spielberg Films 'The Color Purple.' "

23. Thomas Elsaessar, "Tales of Sound and Fury: Observations on the Family Melodrama," in Bill Nichols, ed., *Movies and Methods* (Berkeley and Los Angeles: University of California Press, 1985), 2:170.

24. Alternating patterns are basic to Hollywood production. With Spielberg's direction of *The Color Purple*, problems occur in the constant juxtaposition of the most powerful moments in Walker's novel with characterizations of black people that have previously been considered demeaning. The cut to Sofia and Harpo walking down the road, directly after the young Celie finds the piece of paper that Nettie leaves behind, is a case in point. The first image we see is that of the large derriere of a black woman, swinging from side to side. This image dominates the screen. Perhaps it is not intended to be derogatory, but there is a historical naïveté at work here that opens the director up to charges of culpable insensitivity.

25. M. H. Abrams et al., eds., *The Norton Anthology of English Literature*, 2 vols. (New York: Norton, 1968), 2:744.

26. Ellen Seiter, "The Promise of Melodrama: Recent Women's Films and Soap Opera" (Ph.D. diss., Northwestern University, 1981), p. 9.

27. David Morley, "Texts, Readers, Subjects," in Stuart Hall et al., eds., *Culture, Media, Language* (London: Hutchinson, 1980), p. 164.

28. Courtland Milloy, "On Seeing *The Color Purple*," *Washington Post*, February 18, 1986, p. C3.

29. Deborah E. McDowell, " 'The Changing Same': Generational Connections and Black Women Novelists," *New Literary History* 18, no. 2 (1987): 297.

30. Ibid., p. 296.

31. Rosalind Brunt, "Engaging with the Popular: Audiences for Mass Culture and What to Say about Them," in Lawrence Grossberg et al., eds., *Cultural Studies* (London: Routledge, 1992), p. 76.

3. Watching *The Color Purple*: Two Interviews

1. *Tony Brown's Journal*, PBS, April 6, 1986.

2. *The Phil Donahue Show*, April 25, 1986.

3. In an interview with Charlayne Hunter-Gault on the *MacNeil/Lehrer NewsHour*, PBS, March 31, 1988.

4. Explanation given by Daviau in the article by Al Harrell, "The Look of *The Color Purple*," *American Cinematographer* (February 1986): 50–56.

5. Christian's views were also expressed in two public lectures: "De-Visioning Spielberg and Walker: *The Color Purple*: The Novel and the Film" (Eugene, Ore.: Center for the Study of Women in Society, University of Oregon, May 1986); and "Black Women's Literature and the Canon," seminar, University of Oregon, December 7, 1987. See also Christian's extensive examination in the Monarch Notes study guide *Alice Walker's "The Color Purple"* (New York: Simon and Schuster, 1987). Another black female who wrote about black women's reactions to the film was Dorothy Gilliam, in "*The Color Purple* Not as Simple as Black and White," *Washington Post*, December 23, 1985, p. B3; and "After the 'Purple' Shutout," *Washington Post*, March 27, 1986, p. B3.

6. See, e.g., two early works written by black women that examined this issue: Zora Neale Hurston, *Their Eyes Were Watching God* (Philadelphia: J. B. Lippincott, 1937; reprint, New York: Negro Universities Press, 1969); and Gwendolyn Brooks, *Maud Martha* (New York: Harper, 1953). Toni Morrison takes up the subject again in her first novel, *The Bluest Eye* (New York: Holt, Rinehart, and Winston, 1970; reprint, New York: Simon and Schuster, 1972). Also, the topic is given provocative examination in a recently released independently produced film, *A Question of Color* (1992), by Kathe Sandler, a black female director.

7. Alice Walker, *The Color Purple* (San Diego: Harcourt, Brace, Jovanovich, 1982), p. 202.

8. Statement made in Lawrence Grossberg, ed., "On Postmodernism and Articulation: An Interview with Stuart Hall," *Journal of Communication Inquiry* 10, no. 2 (1986): 45–60.

9. Figures given in "The Black Church in America," *Progressions: A Lilly Endowment Occasional Report* 4, no. 1 (February 1992).

10. Cornel West, "Nihilism in Black America," *Dissent* (Spring 1991); reprinted in Gina Dent, ed., *Black Popular Culture* (Seattle: Bay Press, 1992), p. 40.

11. See her article "The Truth That Never Hurts: Black Lesbians in Fiction in the 1980s," in Joanne M. Braxton and Andrée Nicola McLaughlin, eds., *Wild Women in the Whirlwind: Afra-American Culture and the Contemporary Literary Renaissance* (New Brunswick, N.J.: Rutgers University Press, 1990), pp. 213–45.

12. Colloquial expression that means "general principles."

4. *Daughters of the Dust*

1. Jim Haskins, *James Van DerZee: The Picture Takin' Man* (Teaneck, N.J.: Africa World Press, 1991).

2. The interpretation of the passage "Thunder: Perfect Mind" in the Gnostic scriptures is given by Douglas M. Parrott and George W. MacRae. See their interpretation in James M. Robinson, ed., *The Nag Hammadi Library* (San Francisco: Harper and Row, 1988), pp. 295–96.

3. From an interview with black independent filmmaker Zeinabu irene Davis. See "Daughters of the Dust," *Black Film Review* 6, no. 1 (1990–91): 12–17, 20–21.

4. Personal interview on March 3, 1992, in Los Angeles.

5. Taken from interview with Houston A. Baker, Jr. See his article "Not Without My Daughters," *Transition: A International Review* 57 (1992): 164.

6. Quoted in Donald Bogle, *Toms, Coons, Mulattoes, Mammies, and Bucks* (New York: Continuum, 1989), p. 30.

7. Adrienne Lanier-Seward, "A Film Portrait of Black Ritual Expression: *The Blood of Jesus*," in Geneva Gay and Willie L. Baber, eds., *Expressively Black: The Cultural Basis of Ethnic Identity* (New York: Praeger, 1987), pp. 195–212.

8. Interview with bell hooks in the book by Dash, *Daughters of the Dust: The Making of an African-American Woman's Film* (New York: New Press, 1992), p. 36.

9. See their article "*Ganja and Hess*: Vampires, Sex, and Addictions," *Black American Literature Forum* 25, no. 2 (Summer 1991): 299–314.

10. Interview with bell hooks in Dash, *Daughters of the Dust*, p. 29.

11. Interview with Houston A. Baker, Jr., "Not Without My Daughters," p. 165.

12. Personal interview with author on March 3, 1992.

13. The actual words are used in the film with the permission of the author Paule Marshall, from her book *Praisesong for the Widow* (New York: Putnam, 1983).

14. Interview with bell hooks in Dash, *Daughters of the Dust*, p. 38.

15. Literary scholar Deborah McDowell notes black women's transference of their sexuality to their religion: "It has long been a stereotype that the church has provided black women a 'safe' and controlled release of unexpressed sexual desires." McDowell points to the work of Jewelle Gomez, who describes how black women have "hidden from their sexuality behind a church pew." See McDowell's endnote in her introduction to two novels by Nella Larsen, *Quicksand* (1928) and *Passing* (1929) (New Brunswick, N.J.: Rutgers University Press, 1986), p. xxxv.

16. Interview with bell hooks in Dash, *Daughters of the Dust*, p. 32.

17. Personal interview with the author on March 3, 1992.

18. Ibid.

19. Ibid.

5. Black Women Reading *Daughters of the Dust*

1. For information on the technical aspects of the making of *Daughters of the Dust* an excellent article in *Black Film Review* reprinted in *Wide Angle* is recommended. See the interview by Zeinabu irene Davis with Julie Dash in "*Daughters of the Dust*," *Black Film Review* 6, no. 1 (1990–91): 12–17, 20–21.

2. *Variety*, February 10, 1992, p. 8.

3. For a historical analysis of the impact of black film attendance see Jacqueline Bobo, " 'The Subject Is Money': Reconsidering the Black Film Audience as a Theoretical Paradigm," *Black American Literature Forum* 25, no. 2 (Summer 1991): 421–32.

4. Mary Carbine, " 'The Finest Outside the Loop': Motion Picture Exhibition in Chicago's Black Metropolis, 1905–1928," *Camera Obscura* 23 (May 1990): 8–41.

5. Ibid., p. 11.

6. Miller suggests that MGM was rescued from financial disaster by the success of its film *Shaft* (1971). See his article "From Sweetback to Celie: Blacks on Films into the '80s," in Mike Davis et al., eds., *The Year Left 2: An American Socialist Yearbook* (London: Verso, 1987), pp. 139–59. Film historian Douglas Gomery also provides an analysis of the history of black film attendance in his book *Shared Pleasures: A History of Movie Presentation in the United States* (Madison: University of Wisconsin Press, 1992).

7. Because of the proprietary nature of information concerning black film attendance, there are varying estimates of the size of the audience and the amount of money spent by black moviegoers. Several sources state that black people make up 25 percent of the film audience. See, for example, the following articles: John Leland, "New Jack Cinema Enters Screening," *Newsweek*, June 10, 1991, pp. 50–51; Joy Horowitz, "Black Actresses Are Still Waiting for Star Roles," *New York Times*, May 29, 1991, pp. C11 and C15; and James Greenberg, "In Hollywood, Black Is In," *New York Times*, March 4, 1990, Arts and Leisure section, pp. 1 and 22. A 1989 *Black Enterprise* article revealed that black moviegoers spent $1.11 billion of the $4.5 billion 1988 movie revenue (Pamela Johnson, "They've Gotta Have It" [July 1989], pp. 36–44.).

8. Miller, "From Sweetback to Celie," p. 150.

9. Ibid., p. 158.

10. Jacquie Jones, "The New Ghetto Aesthetic," *Wide Angle* 13, nos. 1 and 2 (July–October 1991): 32–43.

11. Ibid., p. 33.

12. See the article by Yvonne Welbon, "Calling the Shots: Black Women Directors Take the Helm," *Independent* (March 1992): 18–22.

13. See her comments in the interview with Greg Tate, "Of Homegirl Goddesses and Geechee Women: The Africentric Cinema of Julie Dash," *Village Voice*, June 1991 (special film issue), pp. 72, 78.

14. Statements made in an interview by bell hooks in Dash's book *Daughters of the Dust: The Making of an African-American Woman's Film* (New York: New Press, 1992), pp. 42, 50.

15. See Barbara Christian's analysis in "Nuance and the Novella: A Study of Gwendolyn Brooks's *Maud Martha*," in Maria K. Mootry and Gary Smith, eds., *A Life Distilled: Gwendolyn Brooks, Her Poetry and Fiction* (Urbana: University of Illinois Press, 1987), p. 245.

16. Ibid., p. 245.

17. Ibid.

18. John Fiske, *Understanding Popular Culture* (Boston: Unwin Hyman, 1989), p. 161.

Conclusion

1. Ten years after the 1954 U.S. Supreme Court ruling in *Brown vs. the Board of Education* that segregated schools were unconstitutional, the all-white school board in Boston continued to uphold the system of racially imbalanced schools. The board defied not only the constitution but a Massachusetts state law that outlawed the practice. In 1972 black parents in Boston filed a class-action suit in federal district court against the Boston school board. The court ruled in 1974 that the Boston school system was in fact operating two unequal school systems and ordered an immediate remedy of citywide busing of schoolchildren. This was to start at the beginning of the fall 1974 school year.

2. Telephone interview with the author on October 13, 1992.

3. Barbara Omolade, "It's a Family Affair: The Real Lives of Black Single Mothers," *Village Voice*, July 15, 1986, pp. 24, 26–29.

4. See her article "Black Ladies, Welfare Queens, and State Minstrels: Ideological War by Narrative Means," in Toni Morrison, ed., *Race-ing Justice, En-gendering Power: Essays on Anita Hill, Clarence Thomas, and the Construction of Social Reality* (New York: Pantheon, 1992), a collection of essays examining Anita Hill's testimony during the U.S. Senate Judiciary hearings on the appointment of Clarence Thomas to the U.S. Supreme Court, pp. 323–63.

5. Two excellent articles provide extensive details about Lani Guinier's nomination, the failure of the Clinton administration to provide adequate support, and Clinton's cowardice in withdrawing the nomination. See the article by Karen Branan, "Lani Guinier: The Anatomy of a Betrayal," *Ms.* (September–October 1993): 51–57; and the article by Guinier herself that

is excerpted from her forthcoming book, "Who's Afraid of Lani Guinier?" *New York Times Magazine*, February 27, 1994, pp. 38–44, 54–55, 66.

6. Cited in Karen Branan, "Lani Guinier," p. 57.

7. This phrase was repeated extensively in most of the media outlets. Guinier takes note of it in "Who's Afraid of Lani Guinier," p. 43.

8. Harriet E. Wilson, *Our Nig; or, Sketches from the Life of a Free Black, in a Two-Story White House, North. Showing That Slavery's Shadows Fall Even There* (Boston: author, 1859). See Gates's comments, in his introduction to the 1983 edition, on his efforts to authenticate the narrative (New York: Random House, 1983).

9. Mary Helen Washington, ed., *Invented Lives: Narratives of Black Women, 1860–1960* (New York: Anchor Press/Doubleday, 1987), p. 3.

10. See, e.g., Parkerson, "Did You Say the Mirror Talks?" in Lisa Albrecht and Rose M. Brewer, eds., *Bridges of Power: Women's Multicultural Alliance* (Santa Cruz: New Society Publishers, 1990), pp. 108–17; Smith, "Reconstituting the Image: The Emergent Black Woman Director," *Callaloo* 11, no. 4 (Fall 1988): 710–19; and Gibson-Hudson, "African-American Literary Criticism as a Model for the Analysis of Films by African-American Women," *Wide Angle* 13, nos. 3 and 4 (July–October 1991): 44–54, and "Aspects of Black Feminist Cultural Ideology in Films by Black Women Independent Artists," in Diane Carson et al., eds., *Multiple Voices in Feminist Film Criticism* (Minneapolis: University of Minnesota Press, 1994), pp. 365–79.

11. Collins, "Learning from the Outsider Within: The Sociological Significance of Black Feminist Thought," *Social Problems* 33, no. 6 (December 1986): S14–S32. Collins develops the idea of "standpoint" from the work of Nancy Hartsock on oppressed groups. See Hartsock, "The Feminist Standpoint: Developing the Ground for a Specifically Historical Materialism," in Sandra Harding and Merrill Hintikka, eds., *Discovering Reality* (Boston: Reidel, 1983), pp. 283–310.

12. Deborah K. King, "Multiple Jeopardy, Multiple Consciousness: The Context of a Black Feminist Ideology," *Signs: A Journal of Women in Culture and Society* 14, no. 1 (Autumn 1988): 42–72.

13. Collins, "Learning from the Outsider Within," pp. S16–S17.

Bibliography

Abrams, M. H. et al., eds. *The Norton Anthology of English Literature*. 2 vols. New York: Norton, 1968.

Anderson, James A. *Communication Research: Issues and Methods*. New York: McGraw Hill, 1987.

Andrade-Watkins, Claire. "La Force du Vodu." *Black Film Review* 6, no. 1 (1990–91): 18–20 (on Elsie Haas).

Ang, Ien. "Wanted Audiences: On the Politics of Empirical Audience Studies." In Ellen Seiter et al., eds., *Remote Control: Television, Audiences, and Cultural Power*, pp. 96–115. London: Routledge, 1989.

——. *Watching Dallas*. London: Methuen, 1985.

Ansen, David. "We Shall Overcome." *Newsweek*, December 30, 1985, pp. 59–60.

Attille, Martina and Maureen Blackwood. "Black Women and Representation." In Charlotte Brunsdon, ed., *Films for Women*, pp. 202–8. London: BFI, 1986.

Aufderheide, Pat. "The Color Lavender." *In These Times*, January 22–28, 1986, pp. 15–16.

Austin, Regina. "Sapphire Bound!" *Wisconsin Law Review* (1989): 539–78.

Baker Jr., Houston A. "Not Without My Daughters: Interview with Julie Dash." *Transition: An International Review* 57 (1992): 150–66.

Beal, Frances M. "The Purple Comes Through but Not the Black." *Frontline* (January 20, 1986): 16.

Belkin, Lisa. "Fame and Controversy for Danny Glover." *New York Times*, January 26, 1986, pp. 20–21.

Benson, Sheila. "*The Color Purple*." *Los Angeles Times*, December 18, 1985, pp. VI1, 4.

Blum, David. "Steven Spielberg and the Dread Hollywood Backlash." *New York Magazine*, March 24, 1986, p. 62.

Bobo, Jacqueline. "Black Women in Fiction and Nonfiction: Images of Power and Powerlessness." *Wide Angle* 13, nos. 3 and 4 (July–October 1991): 72–81.

——. "*The Color Purple*: Black Women as Cultural Readers." In E. Deidre Pribram, ed., *Female Spectators Looking at Film and Television*, pp. 90–109. London: Verso, 1988.

——. "*The Color Purple*: Black Women's Responses." *Jump Cut* 33 (February 1988): 43–51.

——. "The Politics of Interpretation: Black Critics, Filmmakers, Audiences." In Gina C. Dent, ed., *Black Popular Culture*, pp. 65–74. Seattle: Bay Press, 1992.

——. "Reading Through the Text: The Black Woman as Audience." In Manthia Diawara, ed., *Black American Cinema*, pp. 272–87. New York: Routledge, 1993.

——. "Sifting Through the Controversy: Reading *The Color Purple*. *Callaloo: A Journal of Afro-American and African Arts and Letters* 12, no. 2 (Spring 1989): 332–42.

-- and Ellen Seiter. "Black Feminism and Media Criticism: *The Women of "Brewster Place*." *Screen* 32, no. 3 (Autumn 1991): 286–302.

Bogle, Donald. *Blacks in American Films and Television*. New York: Garland, 1988.

——. *Toms, Coons, Mulattoes, Mammies, and Bucks: An Interpretive History of Blacks in American Films*. New York: Viking, 1973.

Bond, Jean Carey. "The Media Image of Black Women." *Freedomways* (1st quarter 1975): 34–37.

Bowser, Pearl. "Sexual Imagery and the Black Woman in American Cinema." In Gladstone L. Yearwood, ed., *Black Cinema Aesthetics: Issues in Independent Black Filmmaking*, pp. 42–51. Athens: Ohio University Center for Afro-American Studies, 1982.

Branch, Shelly. "A Geechee Girl Gets Ready for the Big Time." *Emerge* (October 1990): 93–94.

Brooks, Gwendolyn. *Maud Martha*. New York: Harper and Brothers, 1953.

Bruck, Peter and Wolfgang Karrer, eds. *The Afro-American Novel since 1960*. Amsterdam: B. R. Gruner, 1982.

Bruning, Fred. "When E.T. Goes to Georgia." *Maclean's*, March 24, 1986, p. 9.

Brunt, Rosalind. "Engaging with the Popular: Audiences for Mass Culture and What to Say About Them." In Lawrence Grossberg et al., eds., *Cultural Studies*, pp. 69–80. London: Routledge, 1992.

Butler, Cheryl B. "*The Color Purple* Controversy: Black Woman Spectatorship." *Wide Angle* 13, nos. 3 and 4 (July–October 1991): 62–69.

Cade (Bambara), Toni, ed. *The Black Woman: An Anthology*. New York: Signet, 1970.

Campbell, Loretta. "Reinventing Our Image: Eleven Black Women Filmmakers." *Heresies* 4, no. 4 (1983): 58–62.

Campenelli, Melissa. "The African-American Market: Community, Growth, and Change." *Sales and Marketing Management* (May 1991): 75–81.

Canby, Vincent. "From a Palette of Cliches Comes *The Color Purple*." *New York Times*, January 5, 1986, pp. 17, 30.

Carby, Hazel V. "It Jus Be's Dat Way Sometime: The Sexual Politics of Women's Blues." *Radical America* 20, no. 4 (1986): 9–22.

——. " 'On the Threshold of Women's Era': Lynching, Empire, and Sexuality in Black Feminist Theory." *Critical Inquiry* 12 (Autumn 1985): 262–77.

——. *Reconstructing Womanhood: The Emergence of the Afro-American Woman Novelist*. New York: Oxford University Press, 1987.

——. "White Woman Listen: Black Feminism and the Boundaries of Sisterhood." In Centre for Contemporary Cultural Studies, ed., *The Empire Strikes Back: Race and Racism in Seventies Britain*, pp. 212–35. London: Hutchinson, 1982.

Carlson, Peter. "As It Ponders *The Color Purple's* Soundtrack, Hollywood Hums 'I've Heard That Song Before.' " *People*, March 31, 1986, pp. 36–37.

Caughey, John L. "The Ethnography of Everyday Life: Theories and Methods for American Culture Studies." *American Quarterly* 34, no. 3 (1982): 222–43.

Cham, Mbye B. and Claire Andrade-Watkins, eds. *Blackframes: Critical Perspectives on Black Independent Cinema*. Cambridge: MIT Press, 1988.

Chambers, Veronica. "Finally, a Black Woman Behind the Camera." *Glamour* (March 1992): 111.

Chrisman, Robert and Robert L. Allen, eds. *Court of Appeal: The Black Community Speaks Out on the Racial and Sexual Politics of Clarence Thomas vs. Anita Hill*. New York: Ballantine Books, 1992.

Christian, Barbara. "Alice Walker." In Thadious Davis and Trudier Harris, eds., *Dictionary of Literary Biography: Afro-American Writers after 1955*, pp. 258–71. Detroit, Michigan: Gale Research Company, 1984.

——. *Black Feminist Criticism: Perspectives on Black Women Writers*. New York: Pergamon Press, 1985.

——. *Black Women Novelists: The Development of a Tradition, 1892–1976*. Westport, Conn.: Greenwood Press, 1980.

——. "But What Do We Think We're Doing Anyway: The State of Black Feminist Criticism(s); or, My Version of a Little Bit of History." In Cheryl A. Wall, ed., *Changing Our Own Words: Essays on Criticism, Theory, and Writing by Black Women*, pp. 58–74. New Brunswick, N.J.: Rutgers University Press, 1989.

——. "From the Inside Out: Afro-American Women's Literary Tradition and the State." *Center for Humanistic Studies Occasional Papers*, no. 19. Minneapolis: University of Minnesota, 1987.

——. "Gloria Naylor's Geography: Community, Class, and Patriarchy in *The Women of Brewster Place* and *Linden Hills*." In Henry Louis Gates, Jr., ed., *Reading Black, Reading Feminist*, pp. 348–73. New York: Penguin, 1990.

——. *Monarch Notes: Alice Walker's "The Color Purple" and Other Works*. New York: Simon and Schuster, 1987.

——. "Nuance and the Novella: A Study of Gwendolyn Brooks's *Maud Martha*." In Maria K. Mootry and Gary Smith, eds., *A Life Distilled: Gwendolyn Brooks, Her Poetry and Fiction*, pp. 239–53. Urbana: University of Illinois Press, 1987.

——. "Paule Marshall." Thadious Davis and Trudier Harris, eds., *Dictionary of Literary Biography: Afro-American Writers after 1955*, pp. 161–70. Detroit, Michigan: Gale Research Company, 1984.

——. "The Race for Theory." *Feminist Studies* 14, no. 1 (Spring 1988): 67–79.

——. "Trajectories of Self-Definition: Placing Contemporary Afro-American Women's Fiction." In Marjorie Pryse and Hortense J. Spillers, eds., *Conjuring: Black Women, Fiction, and Literary Tradition*, pp. 233–48. Bloomington: Indiana University Press, 1985.

Chua, Lawrence. "Two Women Filmmakers Tell Tales of the South." *Elle* (March 1992): 114.

Collins, Patricia Hill. *Black Feminist Thought: Knowledge, Consciousness, and the Politics of Empowerment*. London: HarperCollins Academic, 1990.

——. "The Social Construction of Black Feminist Thought." *Signs* 14, no. 4 (1989): 1–30.

"*The Color Purple* Brings New Black Stars to Screen in Shocking Story." *Jet* (January 13, 1986): 58–62.

"*The Color Purple.*" *People*, January 6, 1986, p. 18.

Corliss, Richard. "The Three Faces of Steve." *Time*, December 23, 1985, p. 78.

Corsaro, Kim. "The Color Purple." *Coming Up* (January 1986): 30.

"Cosby Gets NAACP Award; Assails Drugs, South Africa, and *Color Purple* Critics." *Jet*, March 24, 1986, pp. 28–29.

Curry, Jack. " 'Purple' Shutout: Color It Complex." *USA Today*, March 26, 1986, p. 1.

Darling, Lynn. "*Daughters of the Dust.*" *New York Newsday*, January 13, 1992, pp. 46–47.

Darnton, Nina. "*Color Purple* to Re-Open Nationwide." *New York Times*, January 9, 1987, p. C6.

Dash, Julie. *Daughters of the Dust: The Making of an African-American Woman's Film*. New York: New Press, 1992.

"*Daughters of the Dust.*" *Variety* (February 11, 1991): 112.

Davis, Angela. *Angela Davis: An Autobiography*. New York: International Publishers, 1988.

——. "The Black Woman's Role in the Community of Slaves." *Black Scholar* (December 1971): 1–14.

——. "Black Women and Music: A Historical Legacy of Struggle." In Joanne M. Braxton and Andree Nicola McLaughlin, eds., *Wild Women in the Whirlwind: Afra-American Culture and the Contemporary Literary Renaissance*, pp. 3–21. New Brunswick, N.J.: Rutgers University Press, 1990.

——. "JoAnne Little: The Dialectics of Rape." *Ms.* 3, no. 12 (June 1975): 74–77, 106–8.

——. "Let Us All Rise Together: Radical Perspectives on Empowerment for Afro-American Women." In Angela Davis, *Women, Culture, and Politics*, pp. 3–15. New York: Vintage, 1989.

——. *Violence Against Women and the Ongoing Challenge to Racism*. Freedom Organizing Pamphlet Series, no. 5. Latham, N.Y.: Kitchen Table/Women of Color Press, 1987.

——. *Women, Culture, and Politics*. New York: Vintage, 1990.

——. *Women, Race, and Class*. New York: Vintage, 1983.

Davis, Zeinabu irene. "*Daughters of the Dust.*" *Black Film Review* 6, no. 1 (1990–91): 12–17, 20–21.

——. "The Future of Black Film: The Debate Continues." *Black Film Review* 5, no. 3 (1990): 6, 8, 26, 28.

Day, Barbara. "Black Woman Makes 'the kind of film I've always wanted to see.' " *Guardian*, January 22, 1992, pp. 20, 19 (on *Daughters of the Dust*).

Dee, Ruby. "Some Reflections on the Negro Actress: The Tattered Queens." *Negro Digest* (April 1966): 32–36.

Denby, David. "Purple People-Eater." *New York Magazine*, January 13, 1986, pp. 56–57.

Dent, Gina C. ed. *Black Popular Culture*. Seattle: Bay Press, 1992.

Diawara, Manthia, ed. *Black American Cinema*. New York: Routledge, 1993.

-- and Phyllis Klotman. "*Ganja and Hess*: Vampires, Sex, and Addictions." *Black American Literature Forum* 25, no. 2 (Summer 1991): 299–314.

"Do Black Feminist Writers Victimize Black Men?" On Bob Morris, dir., *Tony Brown's Journal*. Portland, Ore.: PBS, KOAC, November 2, 1986.

Donahue, Deirdre. "Author Terry McMillan's Fresh Voice." *USA Today*, July 7, 1992, pp. D1–D2.

DuBois, W. E. B. *The Souls of Black Folk*. Chicago: A. C. McClurg, 1903. Reprint, ed. Donald G. Gibson. New York: Viking Penguin, 1989.

Dworkin, Susan. "The Strange and Wonderful Story of the Making of *The Color Purple*." *Ms.* (December 1985): 66–72, 93–95.

Early, Gerald. "*The Color Purple* as Everybody's Protest Art." *Antioch Review* 44, no. 3 (1986): 261–75.

"The Eighties and Me." *Publishers Weekly*, January 5, 1990, p. 21.

Elsaesser, Thomas. "Tales of Sound and Fury: Observations on the Family Melodrama." In Bill Nichols, ed., *Movies and Methods*, 2:165–89. Berkeley and Los Angeles: University of California Press, 1985.

Evans, Marie, ed. *Black Women Writers (1950–1980): A Critical Evaluation*. New York: Anchor Press/Doubleday, 1984.

Farley, Christopher John. "New Push for Parity in Hollywood." *USA Today* (January 24, 1992): D1–D2.

Featherston, Elena. "The Making of *The Color Purple*." *San Francisco Focus* (December 1985): 92–97, 218.

Filemyr, Ann. "Zeinabu irene Davis: Filmmaker, Teacher with a Powerful Mission." *Angles* (Winter 1992): 6–9, 22.

Fiske, John. *Understanding Popular Culture*. Boston: Unwin Hyman, 1989.

Foner, Philip. *Women and the American Labor Movement*. New York: Free Press, 1980.

Franklin, Oliver. "An Interview: Kathleen Collins." In *Independent Black American Cinema* (program pamphlet), pp. 22–24. New York: Theater Program of Third World Newsreel, 1981.

Fusco, Coco. *Young, British, and Black: The Work of Sankofa and Black Audio Film Collective*. Buffalo, N.Y.: Hallwalls, 1988.

Gable, Mona. "Author Alice Walker Discusses *The Color Purple. . . .*" *Wall Street Journal*, December 19, 1985, p. 48.

Gaines, Jane. "White Privilege and Looking Relations: Race and Gender in Feminist Film Theory." *Screen* 29, no. 4 (Autumn 1988): 12–26.

Gamman, Lorraine and Margaret Marshment, eds. *The Female Gaze: Women as Viewers of Popular Culture*. Seattle: Real Comet Press, 1989.

Gant, Liz. "Ain't Beulah Dead Yet? Or, Images of the Black Woman in Film." *Essence* (May 1973): 61, 72–73, 75.

Gates, Henry Louis, Jr., ed. *Reading Black, Reading Feminist*. New York: Penguin, 1990.

--, ed. *The Schomburg Library of Nineteenth-Century Black Women Writers*. London: Oxford University Press, 1988.

Gibson-Hudson, Gloria J. "African-American Literary Criticism as a Model for the Analysis of Films by African-American Women." *Wide Angle* 13, nos. 3 and 4 (July–October 1991): 44–54.

——. "Aspects of Black Feminist Ideology in Films by Black Women Artists." In Janice Welsch, Diane Carson, and Linda Dittmar, eds., *Multiple Voices in Feminist Film Criticism*, pp. 365–79. Minneapolis: University of Minnesota Press, 1994.

——. Biographical entries s.v. "Madeline Anderson," "Anita Bush," "Ayoka Chenzira," "Julie Dash," "Michelle Parkerson," and "Madame Sul-Te-Wan." In Dorothy Salem, ed., *African-American Women: A Biographical Dictionary*. New York: Garland, forthcoming.

——. "A Different Image: Integrating the Image of Black Women into Film Pedagogy." In Lester Friedman and Diane Carson, eds., *Multicultural Media in the Classroom: Strategies and Speculations*. Urbana: University of Illinois Press, forthcoming.

——. "The Films of African-American Women: A Select Filmography." *Black Film Review* 6, no. 4 (Summer 1991): 32–33.

——. "Moving Pictures to Move People: Michelle Parkerson Is the Eye of the Storm." *Black Film Review* 3, no. 3 (Summer 1987): 16–17.

——. "Through Women's Eyes: The Films of Women in Africa and the African Diaspora." *Western Journal of Black Studies* 15, no. 2 (1991): 79–86.

Giddings, Paula. *When and Where I Enter: The Impact of Black Women on Race and Sex in America*. New York: Morrow, 1984. Reprint. New York: Bantam, 1985.

Gilliam, Dorothy. "After the 'Purple' Shutout." *Washington Post*, March 27, 1986, p. B3.

——. "*The Color Purple* Not as Simple as Black and White." *Washington Post*, December 23, 1985, p. B3.

Glicksman, Marlaine. "Lee Way" (interview with Spike Lee). *Film Comment* (October 1986): 46–49.

Goldstein, William. "Alice Walker on the Set of *The Color Purple*." *Publishers Weekly*, September 6, 1985, pp. 46–48.

Gossage, Leslie. "Black Women Independent Filmmakers: Changing Images of Black Women." *Iris: A Journal About Women* (Spring–Summer 1987): 4–11.

Greenberg, James. "In Hollywood, Black Is In." *New York Times*, March 4, 1990, pp. 1, 22.

Greene, Laura. "A Bad Black Image in Film." *Essence* (May 1973): 70.

Grossberg, Lawrence. "History, Politics, and Postmodernism: Stuart Hall and Cultural Studies." *Journal of Communication Inquiry* 10, no. 2 (1986): 61–75.

——. "On Postmodernism and Articulation: An Interview with Stuart Hall." *Journal of Communication Inquiry* 10, no. 2 (1986): 45–60.

——. "Strategies of Marxist Cultural Interpretation." *Critical Studies in Mass Communication* 1, no. 4 (1984): 392–421.

-- et al., eds. *Cultural Studies*. London: Routledge, 1992.

Guy-Sheftal, Beverly. "Breaking the Silence: A Black Feminist Response to the Thomas/Hill Hearings (for Audre Lorde)." In Robert Chrisman and Robert L. Allen, eds., *Court of Appeal: The Black Community Speaks Out on the Racial and Sexual Politics of Thomas vs. Hill*, pp. 73–77. New York: Ballantine Books, 1992.

Gwaltney, John Langston. *Drylongso: A Self-Portrait of Black America*. New York: Random House, 1980.

Hall, Stuart. "Race, Articulation, and Societies Structured in Dominance." In UNESCO, ed., *Sociological Theories: Race and Colonialism*, pp. 305–45. Paris: UNESCO, 1980.

Hansberry, Lorraine. "Genet, Mailer, and the New Paternalists." *Village Voice*, June 1, 1961, pp. 10, 14–15.

——. "Me Tink Me Hear Sounds in de Night." *Theatre Arts* (October 1960): 9–10, 69–70.

——. "The Negro in American Culture." In In C. W. E. Bigsby, ed., *The Black American Writer*, pp. 79–108. Deland, Fla.: Everett/Edward, 1969.

——. "Negroes Cast in Same Old Roles in TV Shows." *Freedom* (June 1951): 7.

——. "The Negro Writer and His Roots: Toward a New Romanticism." *Black Scholar* (March–April 1981): 2–12.

——. "This Complex of Womanhood." *Ebony* (August 1960): 40.

——. "What Could Happen Didn't." *New York Herald-Tribune*, March 26, 1961, p. 8.

——. "Women Voice Demands in Capitol Sojourn." *Freedom* (October 1951): 6.

Harper, Frances Ellen Watkins. *Iola Leroy; or, Shadows Uplifted.* Philadelphia: Garrigues Brothers, 1892.

Harrell, Al. "The Look of *The Color Purple.*" *American Cinematographer* (February 1986): 50–56.

Harris, Kwasi. "New Images: An Interview with Julie Dash and Alile Sharon Larkin." *Independent* (December 1986): 16–20.

Hartman, S. V. and Farah Jasmine Griffin. "Are You as Colored as That Negro? The Politics of Being Seen in Julie Dash's *Illusions.*" *Black American Literature Forum* 25, no. 2 (Summer 1991): 361–73.

Haskins, Jim. *James Van DerZee: The Picture Takin' Man.* Teaneck, N.J.: Africa World Press, 1991.

Haynes, Karima A. "Videoblack." *Ebony* (April 1992): 82.

Hine, Darlene Clark. "Female Slave Resistance: The Economics of Sex." *Western Journal of Black Studies* 3 (1979): 123–27.

——. "To Be Gifted, Female, and Black." *Southwest Review* 67, no. 4 (Autumn 1982): 357–69.

Hoban, Phoebe. "Phenomena: A Building Dust Storm." *New York Magazine*, March 30, 1992, p. 27.

Hoberman, J. "Color Me Purple." *Village Voice*, December 24, 1985, p. 76.

Hobson, Dorothy. *Crossroads: Drama of a Soap Opera.* London: Metheun, 1982.

Holden, Stephen. " 'Daughters of the Dust': The Demise of a Tradition. *New York Times*, January 16, 1992, p. C19.

hooks, bell. "Black Women Filmmakers Break the Silence." *Black Film Review* 2, no. 3 (Summer 1986): 14–15.

——. "Dialogue Between bell hooks and Julie Dash." In Julie Dash, *Daughters of the Dust: The Making of an African-American Woman's Film*, pp. 27–67. New York: New Press, 1992.

——. *Talking Back: Thinking Feminist, Thinking Black.* Boston: South End Press, 1989.

——. *Yearning: Race, Gender and Cultural Politics.* Boston: South End Press, 1990.

Hopkins, Pauline Elizabeth. *Contending Forces: A Romance Illustrative of Negro Life North and South.* Boston: Colored Co-Operative Publishing, 1900.

Hull, Gloria T., Patricia Bell Scott, and Barbara Smith, eds. *All the Women Are White, All the Blacks Are Men, but Some of Us Are Brave.* Old Westbury, N.Y.: Feminist Press, 1982.

Hume, Scott. "Marketing to African-Americans: Barriers to Data Remain High." *Advertising Age*, July 1, 1991, p. 20.

Hurston, Zora Neale. *Their Eyes Were Watching God*. Philadelphia: J. B. Lippincott, 1937. Reprint. New York: Negro Universities Press, 1969.

Jackson, Elizabeth. "Perfect Image?" *Black Film Review* 6, no. 1 (1990–91): 22–24 (on Maureen Blackwood).

Jacobs, Harriet [Linda Brent]. *Incidents in the Life of a Slave Girl, Written by Herself*. Ed. L. Maria Child. Boston: author, 1861. Reprinted with an intro. by editor Jean Fagan Yellin. Cambridge: Harvard University Press, 1987.

Jaehne, Karen. "The Final Word." *Cineaste* 15, no. 1 (1986): 60.

Jewell, K. Sue. *From Mammies to Miss America and Beyond: Cultural Images and the Shaping of U.S. Social Policy*. New York: Routledge, 1993.

Johnson, Pamela. "They've Gotta Have It." *Black Enterprise* (July 1989): 36–44.

Jones, Jacquie. "The New Ghetto Aesthetic." *Wide Angle* 13, nos. 3 and 4 (July–October 1991): 32–43.

Jordan, June. *Civil Wars*. Boston: Beacon Press, 1981.

——. *On Call: Political Essays*. Boston: South End Press, 1985.

——. *Technical Difficulties: African-American Notes on the State of the Union*. New York: Pantheon, 1992.

Kael, Pauline. "Current Cinema: Sacred Monsters." *New Yorker*, December 30, 1985, pp. 68–70.

Kalbacher, Gene. "Quincy Jones: The Color Purple and Other Shades." *Jazziz* (February 1986): 8–11.

Kauffmann, Stanley. "Sign of the Times." *New Republic*, January 27, 1986, pp. 24–25.

——. "Stanley Kauffmann on Films: Two Women." *New Republic*, February 10, 1992, pp. 26–27.

Kelly, Ernece B. "Most Dangerous Film since *Birth of a Nation*." *Guardian*, February 19, 1986, p. 19.

Kempley, Rita. " 'Daughters of the Dust': Spirit of a Time Past." *Washington Post*, February 28, 1992, pp. C1, C3.

King, Deborah K. "Multiple Jeopardy, Multiple Consciousness: The Context of a Black Feminist Ideology." *Signs* 14, no. 1 (Autumn 1988): 42–72.

King, Mae. "The Politics of Sexual Stereotypes." *Black Scholar* 4, nos. 6 and 7 (1973): 12–23.

Klotman, Phyllis Rauch, ed. *Screenplays of the African-American Experience*. Bloomington: Indiana University Press, 1991 (contains overviews and complete scripts of *Losing Ground* by Kathleen Collins, *Illusions* by Julie Dash, and *A Different Image* by Alile Sharon Larkin).

Kopkind, Andrew. "*The Color Purple*." *Nation*, February 1, 1986, pp. 124–25.

Kuhn, Annette. " 'The Married Love' Affair." *Screen* 27, no. 2 (1986): 5–21.

——. "Women's Genres." *Screen* 25, no. 1 (January–February 1984): 18–28.

Lanier-Seward, Adrienne. "A Film Portrait of Black Ritual Expression: *The Blood of Jesus*. In Geneva Gay and Willie L. Baber, eds., *Expressively Black: The Cultural Basis of Ethnic Identity*, pp. 195–212. New York: Praeger, 1987.

Larkin, Alile Sharon. "Black Women Filmmakers Defining Ourselves: Feminism in Our Own Voice."In E. Deidre Pribram, ed., *Female Spectators Looking at Film and Television*, pp. 157–73. London: Verso, 1988.

Larsen, Nella. *Passing*. New York: Knopf, 1929. Reprinted with an intro. by Deborah E. McDowell. New Brunswick, N.J.: Rutgers University Press, 1986.

——. *Quicksand*. New York: Knopf, 1928. Reprinted with an intro. by Deborah E. McDowell. New Brunswick, N.J.: Rutgers University Press, 1986.

Lekatsas, Barbara. "Encounters: The Film Odyssey of Camille Billops." *Black American Literature Forum* 25, no. 2 (Summer 1991): 395–408.

Lindlof, Thomas R., ed. *Natural Audiences: Qualitative Research and Media Uses and Effects*. Norwood, N.J.: Ablex, 1987.

Lorde, Audre. "The Uses of the Erotic: The Erotic as Power." In Lorde, *Sister Outsider*, pp. 53–59. Trumansburg, N.Y.: Crossing Press, 1984.

Lubiano, Wahneema. "Black Ladies, Welfare Queens, and State Minstrels: Ideological War by Narrative Means." In Toni Morrison, ed., *Race-ing Justice, En-gendering Power: Essays on Anita Hill, Clarence Thomas, and the Construction of Social Reality*, pp. 323–63. New York: Pantheon, 1992.

——. "But Compared to What? Reading Realism, Representation, and Essentialism in *School Daze*, *Do the Right Thing*, and the Spike Lee Discourse." *Black American Literature Forum* 25, no. 2 (Summer 1991): 253–82.

Lufkin, Liz. "Danny Glover: Hot in Hollywood, at Home in the Haight." *San Francisco Focus* (December 1985): 98–100.

Lull, James. "Audiences, Texts, and Contexts." *Critical Studies in Mass Communication* 5 (1988): 239–43.

Mapp, Edward. "Black Women in Films: A Mixed Bag of Tricks." In Lindsay Patterson, ed., *Black Films and Filmmakers: A Comprehensive Anthology from Stereotype to Superhero*, pp. 196–205. New York: Dodd, Mead, 1975.

Marable, Manning. "Grounding with My Sisters: Patriarchy and the Exploitation of Black Women." In Manning Marable, *How Capitalism Underdeveloped Black America*, pp. 69–104. Boston: South End Press, 1983.

Marshall, Paule. *Brown Girl, Brownstones*. New York: Avon, 1959.

——. *The Chosen Place, the Timeless People*. New York: Harcourt, 1969.

——. *Praisesong for the Widow*. New York: Putnam's, 1983.

Martin, Sharon Stockard. "The Invisible Reflection: Images and Self-Images of Black Women on Stage and Screen." *Black Collegian* 9 (May–June 1979): 74–81.

Maslin, Janet. "Film: *The Color Purple*, from Steven Spielberg." *New York Times*, December 18, 1985, p. C18.

Max, Daniel. "McMillan's Millions." *New York Times Magazine*, August 9, 1992, pp. 20, 22, 24, 26.

——. "Will Hollywood Get Serious About Black Lit?" *Variety*, January 27, 1992, p. 68.

McDowell, Deborah E. " 'The Changing Same': Generational Connections and Black Women Novelists." *New Literary History* 18, no. 2 (1987): 281–302.

——. Introduction to Nella Larsen, *Passing* and *Quicksand*, pp. ix–xxxv. New Brunswick, N.J.: Rutgers University Press, 1986.

——. "New Directions for Black Feminist Criticism." In Elaine Showalter, ed., *The New Feminist Criticism: Essays on Women, Literature, and Theory*, pp. 186–99. New York: Pantheon, 1985.

McDowell, Edwin. "Black Writers Gain Audiences and Visibility in Publishing." *New York Times*, February 12, 1991, p. C11.

McMillan, Terry. *Disappearing Acts*. New York: Washington Square Press, 1989.

——. *Mama*. New York: Washington Square Press, 1987

——. *Waiting to Exhale*. New York: Simon and Schuster, 1992.

Mercer, Kobena. "Diaspora Culture and the Dialogic Imagination: The Aesthetics of Black Independent Film in Britain." In Mybe Cham and Claire Andrade-Watkins, eds., *Blackframes: Critical Perspectives on Black Independent Film*, pp. 50–61. Cambridge: MIT Press, 1988.

——. "Recoding Narratives of Race and Nation." *Independent* (January–February 1989): 19–26.

Milloy, Courtland. "On Seeing *The Color Purple*." *Washington Post*, February 18, 1986, p. C3.

——. "A 'Purple' Rage Over a Rip-Off." *Washington Post*, December 24, 1985, p. B3.

Mills, David. "A Dash of Difference." *Washington Post*, February 28, 1992, pp. C1, C3.

Moon, Spencer. "Behind the Scenes: A Pioneer in Public TV." *Black Film Review* 6, no. 4 (1991): 27–28 (on Madeline Anderson).

Morley, David. "Changing Paradigms in Audience Studies." In Ellen Seiter et al., *Remote Control: Television, Audiences, and Cultural Power*, pp. 16–43. New York: Routledge, 1989.

——. "The 'Nationwide' Audience: A Critical Postscript." *Screen Education* 39 (1981): 3–14.

——. *The "Nationwide" Audience: Structure and Decoding*. London: British Film Institute, 1980.

——. *Television, Audiences, and Cultural Studies*. London: Routledge, 1992.

——. "Texts, Readers, Subjects." In Stuart Hall, Dorothy Hobson, Andrew Lowe, and Paul Willis, eds., *Culture, Media, Language*, pp. 163–73. London: Hutchinson, 1980.

Morrison, Toni. *Beloved*. New York: Knopf, 1987.

——. *The Bluest Eye*. New York: Holt, Rinehart, and Winston, 1970. Reprint. New York: Simon and Schuster, 1972.

——. *Song of Solomon*. New York: New American Libary, 1977.

——. *Sula*. New York: Knopf, 1973. Reprint. New York: New American Library, 1982.

——. *Tar Baby*. New York: Knopf, 1981.

——. "Unspeakable Things Unspoken: The Afro-American Presence in American Literature." *Michigan Quarterly Review* 28 (Winter 1989): 1–34.

--, ed. *Race-ing Justice, En-gendering Power: Essays on Anita Hill, Clarence Thomas, and the Construction of Social Reality*. New York: Pantheon, 1992.

"Movie Maids: Eight New Hollywood Films Backtrack to Usual Stereotypes in Casting Negro Actors as Usual Maids and Menials." *Ebony* (August 1948): 56–59.

Muhammad, Abdul Wali. "Purple Poison Pulses Through Community." *Final Call* 27 January 1986: 4–5.

Muwakkil, Salim "Bad Image Blues." *In These Times*, April 9–15, 1986, pp. 24–23.

Naylor, Gloria. *The Women of Brewster Place*. New York: Viking, 1982.

Nelson, Jill. "Spielberg's *Purple* Is Still Black." *Guardian*, January 29, 1986, pp. 1, 17.

Nemiroff, Robert, ed. *A Raisin in the Sun: The Unfilmed Original Screenplay*. New York: Penguin Books, 1992.

Nicholson, David. "Alice Walker Has High Hopes for *Color Purple*." *Black Film Review* 2, no. 1 (1985): 1, 15–17.

——. "A Commitment to Writing: A Conversation with Kathleen Collins Prettyman." *Black Film Review* (Winter 1988–89): 6–15.

——. "Conflict and Complexity: Filmmaker Kathleen Collins." *Black Film Review* (Summer 1986): 16–17.

——. "From Coast to Coast *Purple* Aroused Passions." *Black Film Review* 2, no. 2 (1986): 18–19.

Nightingale, Virginia. "What's 'Ethnographic' About Ethnographic Audience Research?" *Australian Journal of Communication* 16 (1989): 50–63.

——. "What's Happening to Audience Research?" *Media Information Australian* 39 (February 1986): 18–22.

Nixon, Will. "Better Times for Black Writers?" *Publishers Weekly*, February 17, 1989, pp. 35–40.

Norment, Lynn. "*The Color Purple*: Controversial Prize-Winning Book Becomes Equally Controversial Movie." *Ebony* (February 1986): 146–55.

Okazawa-Rey, Margo. "Viewpoint: In Hollywood, Black Men Are In; Black Women Are Still Out." *Black Film Review* 6, no. 1 (1990–91): 25.

Parkerson, Michelle. "Did You Say the Mirror Talks?" In Lisa Albrecht and Rose M. Brewer, eds., *Bridges of Power: Women's Multicultural Alliances*, pp. 108–17. Santa Cruz: New Society Publishers, 1990.

——. "The Tragedy of Dorothy Dandridge." *Black Film Review* 4, no. 2 (Spring 1988): 10–11.

——. "Women Throughout the Disapora Tackle Their Firsts." *Black Film Review* 6, no. 1 (1990–91): 10–11.

Patterson, Lindsay, ed. *Black Films and Filmmakers: A Comprehensive Anthology from Stereotype to Superhero*. New York: Dodd, Mead, 1975.

Petry, Ann. *The Street*. Boston: Houghton Mifflin, 1946.

The Phil Donahue Show. Dir. David L. McGrail. Portland, Ore.: NBC, KGW, April 25, 1986.

Pinckney, Darryl. "Black Victims, Black Villains." *New York Review of Books*, January 19, 1987, pp. 17–20.

Proceedings of a Symposium on Black Images in Films, Stereotyping, and Self-Perception as Viewed by Black Actresses, Boston University, 1973. Boston: Afro-American Studies Program, Boston University, 1974.

"Purple Rage." On Bob Morris, dir., *Tony Brown's Journal*. Portland, Ore.: KOAC, April 6, 1986.

Radway, Janice A. "Identifying Ideological Seams: Mass Culture, Analytical Method, and Political Practice." *Communication* 9 (1986): 93–123.

——. "Interpretive Communities and Variable Literacies: The Functions of Romance Reading." *Daedalus* (Summer 1984): 49–73.

——. *Reading the Romance: Women, Patriarchy, and Popular Literature.* Chapel Hill: University of North Carolina Press, 1984.

Rahman, Aishah. "First Light of a New Day." *In These Times*, March 28–April 3, 1984, pp. 8–9.

——. "To Be Black, Female, and a Playwright." *Freedomways* 19, no. 4 (4th quarter 1979): 256–60.

Randolph, Laura B. "Black America's Hottest Novelist: Terry McMillan Exhales and Inhales in a Revealing Interview." *Ebony* (May 1993): 23–28.

Raspberry, William. "An Absence of Context." *Washington Post*, March 5, 1986, p. A19.

Reed, Ishmael. "Steven Spielberg Plays Howard Beach." *Black American Literature Forum* 21, nos. 1–2 (1987): 7–16.

Reid, Calvin. "Two Black Authors, Two Different Stories." *Publishers Weekly*, July 18, 1992, p. 9.

Rich, B. Ruby. "In the Eyes of the Beholder." *Village Voice*, January 28, 1992, pp. 60, 65 (on *Daughters of the Dust*).

Robertson, Nan. "Actresses' Varied Roads to 'The Color Purple.' " *New York Times*, February 13, 1986, p. 22.

Robinson, James M., ed. *The Nag Hammadi Library*. San Francisco: Harper and Row, 1988.

Rule, Sheila. "Director Defies Odds with First Feature, *Daughters of the Dust*." *New York Times*, February 12, 1992, pp. C15, C17.

Salaam, Kalamu ya. "What Use Is Reading?: Re-Reading Lorraine Hansberry." *Black Collegian* (March–April 1984): 45–48.

Salamon, Julie. ". . . As Spielberg's Film Version Is Released." *Wall Street Journal*, December 19, 1985, p. 48.

Seiter, Ellen. "Making Distinctions in TV Audience Research: Case Study of a Troubling Interview." *Cultural Studies* 4, no. 1 (1990): 61–84.

——. "The Promise of Melodrama: Recent Women's Films and Soap Opera." Ph.D. diss., Northwestern University, 1981.

-- et al., eds. *Remote Control: Television, Audiences, and Cultural Power*. New York: Routledge, 1989.

Seitz, Michael H. "Pop Purple." *Progressive* (February 1986): 40.

Shange, Ntozake. *for colored girls who have considered suicide/when the rainbow is enuf*. New York: Macmillan, 1977.

Shipp, E. R. "Blacks in Heated Debate over *The Color Purple*." *New York Times*, January 27, 1986, p. A13.

Simmonds, Felly Nkweto. "*She's Gotta Have It*: The Representation of Black Female Sexuality on Film." *Feminist Review* 29 (Spring 1988): 10–29.

Simon, John. "Black and White in Purple." *National Review*, February 14, 1986, pp. 56–57.

Sinclair, Abiola. "*Daughters of the Dust*: Hauntingly Beautiful, Powerful." *New York Amsterdam News*, January 18, 1992, p. 22.

Smith, Barbara. "*Color Purple* Distorts Class, Lesbian Issues." *Guardian*, February 19, 1986, p. 19.

——. "Toward a Black Feminist Criticism." In Elaine Showalter, ed., *The New Feminist Criticism: Essays on Women, Literature, and Theory*, pp. 168–85. New York: Pantheon, 1985.

——. "The Truth That Never Hurts: Black Lesbians in Fiction in the 1980s." In Joanne M. Braxton and Andree Nicola McLaughlin, eds., *Wild Women in the Whirlwind: Afra-American Culture and the Contemporary Literary Renaissance*, pp. 213–45. New Brunswick, N.J.: Rutgers University Press, 1990.

--, ed. *Home Girls: A Black Feminist Anthology*. New York: Kitchen Table/Women of Color Press, 1983.

Smith, Danyel. "Through the Looking Glass." *Bay Guardian*, April 1, 1992, p. 25.

Smith, Patricia. "Recasting the Stereotypes." *San Jose Mercury News*, September 9, 1991, p. 7B (on numerous black female filmmakers).

Smith, Valerie. "Black Feminist Theory and the Representation of the 'Other.' " In Cheryl A. Wall, ed., *Changing Our Own Words: Essays on Criticism, Theory, and Writing by Black Women*, pp. 38–57. New Brunswick, N.J.: Rutgers University Press, 1989.

——. "Gender and Afro-Americanist Literary Theory and Criticism." In Elaine Showalter, ed., *Speaking of Gender*, pp. 56–70. New York: Routledge, 1989.

——. "Reconstituting the Image: The Emergent Black Woman Director." *Callaloo: A Journal of Afro-American and African Arts and Letters* 11, no. 4 (Fall 1988): 710–19.

Snead, James. "Recoding Blackness: The Visual Rhetoric of Black Independent Film."In *Circular for the New American Filmmakers Series*, no. 23, pp. 1–2. New York: Whitney Museum of American Art, 1985.

Spillers, Hortense J. "Cross-Currents, Discontinuites: Black Women's Fiction." In Marjorie Pryse and Hortense J. Spillers, eds., *Conjuring: Black Women, Fiction, and Literary Tradition*, pp. 249–61. Bloomington: Indiana University Press, 1985.

Springer, Claudia. "Black Women Filmmakers." *Jump Cut* 29 (1984): 34–37.

Stark, John. "Seeing Red over *Purple*." *People*, March 10, 1986, pp. 102–6.

Stone, Judy. "A Dash of Black Life off Carolina Coast." *San Francisco Chronicle*, March 29, 1992, p. 27.

——. "Keeping 'Purple's' Spirit." *San Francisco Chronicle*, December 18, 1985, p. 67.

Tate, Claudia, ed. *Black Women Writers at Work*. New York: Continuum, 1983.

Tate, Greg. "Creative Sisterhood." *Village Voice*, June 1991 (special film issue), pp. 73, 76, 78 (on numerous black female filmmakers).

——. "Of Homegirl Goddesses and Geechee Women." *Village Voice*, June 1991 (special film issue).

Taubin, Amy. "Art and Industry." *Village Voice*, November 26, 1991, p. 66.

Taylor, Clyde. "Doing the Right Thing." *Art Forum International* (October 1989): 20–22.

——. "The Future of Black Film: The Debate Continues." *Black Film Review* 5, no. 3 (1990): 7, 9, 27–28.

——. "The Paradox of Black Independent Film." *Black Film Review* 4, no. 4 (Fall 1988): 2–3, 17–19.

——. "Shooting the Black Woman." *Black Collegian* 9 (May–June 1979): 94–96.

——. "Spike Lee and Black Women." *Nation*, June 4, 1988, pp. 800–803.

——. " 'Storming the Gates of Freedom': Three Films on Black Women." *Black Collegian* 12 (April–May 1982): 26.

Thomas, Deborah. "Julie Dash." *Essence* (February 1992): 32.

--, and Catherine Saalfield. "Geechee Girl Goes Home: Julie Dash on *Daughters of the Dust*." *Independent* (July 1991): 25–27.

Thomas, Kevin. "Salute Set for Black Women in Film." *Los Angeles Times*, January 29, 1982, part 6, p. 15.

Trescott, Jacqueline. "The Stories That Cry to be Read." *Washington Post*, July 2, 1992, pp. C1, C2.

Turan, Kenneth. "Director's Keen Vision, Light Touch Capture Gullah Culture." *San Jose Mercury News*, May 21, 1992, p. 3C.

——. "Movies." *California Magazine*, February 11, 1986, p. 42.

Turner, George. "Spielberg Makes All Too Human Story." *American Cinematographer* (February 1986): 58–64.

Walker, Alice. *The Color Purple*. San Diego: Harcourt, Brace, Jovanich, 1982.

——. "Finding Celie's Voice." *Ms.* (December 1985): 71–72, 96.

——. *In Search of Our Mothers' Gardens*. New York: Harcourt, Brace, Jovanich, 1983.

——. *Living by the Word: Selected Writings, 1973–1987*. San Diego: Harcourt, Brace, Jovanich, 1988.

Walker, Margaret. *Jubilee*. Boston: Houghton Mifflin, 1966. Reprint. New York: Bantam, 1985.

Wallace, Michele. *Black Macho and the Myth of the Superwoman*. New York: Verso, 1990.

Wallace, Michele. "Blues for Mr. Spielberg." *Village Voice*, March 18, 1986, pp. 21–27.

——. *Invisibility Blues: From Pop to Theory*. New York: Verso, 1990.

——. "Negative Images: Towards a Black Feminist Cultural Criticism." In Lawrence Grossberg, Cary Nelson, and Paula Treichler, eds., *Cultural Studies*, pp. 654–71. New York: Routledge, 1992.

Washington, Mary Helen. *Black-Eyed Susans: Classic Stories by and About Black Women*. New York: Anchor Press/Doubleday, 1975.

——. "Black Women Image-Makers." *Black World* 23 (August 1974): 2–15.

——. *Invented Lives: Narratives of Black Women, 1860–1960*. New York: Anchor Press/Doubleday, 1987.

——. *Midnight Birds: Stories by Contemporary Black Women Writers*. New York: Anchor Press/Doubleday, 1980.

——. Review of Barbara Christian's *Black Women Novelists*. *Signs: Journal of Women in Culture in Society* 8, no. 1 (August 1982): 177–82.

——. "These Self-Invented Women: A Theoretical Framework for a Literary History of Black Women." *Radical Teacher* 17 (1980): 3–7.

Watkins, Mel. "Sexism, Racism, and Black Women Writers." *New York Times Book Review*, June 15, 1986, pp. 1, 35–37.

Welbon, Yvonne. "Calling the Shots: Black Women Directors Take the Helm." *Independent* (March 1992): 18–22.

Wesley, Richard. " 'The Color Purple' Debate: Reading Between the Lines." *Ms.* (September 1986): 62, 90–92.

West, Dorothy. *The Living Is Easy*. Cambridge: Riverside Press, 1948. Reprint. New York: Arno Press, 1969.

White, Armond. "Daughters Bites the Dust." *New York City-Sun*, January 22–28, 1992, pp. 15, 20.

Wilkerson, Margaret. "Excavating Our History: The Importance of Biographies of Women of Color." *Black American Literature Forum* 24, no. 1 (Spring 1990): 73–84.

Williams, Sherley Anne. "Some Implications of Womanist Theory." In Henry Louis Gates, Jr., ed., *Reading Black, Reading Feminist*, pp. 68–75. New York: Penguin, 1990.

Willimon, William H. "Seeing Red over *The Color Purple*." *Christian Century*, April 2, 1986, p. 319.

Willis, Paul. "Notes on Method." In Stuart Hall, Dorothy Hobson, Andrew Lowe, and Paul Willis, eds., *Culture, Media, Language*, pp. 88–95. London: Hutchinson, 1980.

Wilson, Harriet E. *Our Nig; or, Sketches from the Life of a Free Black, in a Two-Story White House, North. Showing That Slavery's Shadows Fall Even There*. Boston: author, 1859. Reprinted with an intro. by editor Henry Louis Gates, Jr. New York: Random House, 1983.

Wilson, Marti. "A Disappointment, but We Still Have the Book." *Black Film Review* 2, no. 2 (Spring 1986): 17.

Yearwood, Gladstone L. *Black Cinema Aesthetics: Issues in Independent Black Filmmaking*. Athens: Ohio University Center for Afro-American Studies, 1982.

Index